# A Field Guide To
# The Las Vegas
# Natural History Museum
### By
### Mike Hughes

## C2C Publications

Photographs
By
**Kayla Hughes and Mike Hughes**

Other Books by Mike Hughes:

**The Northwest Dive Guide**          Travel Guide
Harbour Publishing Copyright 2009

**The North American Dive Guide**          Travel Guide
Copyright 2012

**Best of Intentions**          Spy-Thriller Fiction
Copyright 2012

**To Kill A Diver**    A murder mystery.    Fiction
Copyright 1998 printed 2013

**Whoops Airlines Enhanced**          Airline Cartoons
Copyright 1998 Printed 2013

**Whoops More Fowl Weather Enhanced**  Airline Cartoons
Copyright 1999 Printed 2014

**Whoops Diver's Guide Enhanced**          Scuba Cartoons
Copyright 1999 Printed 2014

**Aliens At Expom**          Science Fiction
Copyright 1986 Printed 2015

**Twas The Dive Before Christmas**          A Christmas Story
Copyright 2015 Printed 2015

**Mnemonic Devices** — catchy fun ways
to help us remember

please excuse my dear Aunt
Sally = order of operations

my very educated mother just
served us nachos = planets

Kings Play Chess On Fine
Grained Sand

Kingdom, phylum, class,
order, family, genus, species

This Book is dedicated to

Marilyn Gillespie

## Introduction

This book is intended to be used as a self walk through guide to the Las Vegas Natural History Museum. Most of the animals in this book are in alphabetical order. However, the International room is compiled as if you were walking through and starting with the monkey family then continuing around the room until you finish up with antelope family section. This way you can minimize the page turning to locate the next animal. The bird exhibit has been temporarily removed, but the birds are left in the book in case they are placed elsewhere. The museum is dynamic and changes occur all the time. Some donations of animals require the temporary replacement of other species, and rotating fall exhibits may also change the order or placement of animals on display.

As a marine biologist and tour guide, I have tried to make the information as accurate as possible. However, with this being said, all errors are strictly the work of the author and not the fault of the museum, as I compiled this book on my own. On certain pages where highlight space is limited, I use acronyms such as 10Mya to represent 10 million years ago. Certain animals in the Egypt Room were not mentioned as they are also found in the Africa Exhibit and/or in the International Room. The facial images of early hominids were taken at the Smithsonian Institute at the National Museum of Natural History in Washington DC and placed at the end of individual descriptions to lend a better visual image of certain species of early man.

It is my hope that the proceeds of this book will help fund current activities as well as future museum expansion projects. Not everyone has to write a book to help out the museum. You can also help out by becoming a museum volunteer or an annual member of the museum. Monetary donations are always graciously accepted.

# <u>Africa</u>

# African Lion

| Kingdom: <u>Animalia</u><br>Phylum: <u>Chordata</u><br>Class: <u>Mammalia</u><br>Order: <u>Carnivora</u><br>Family: <u>Felidae</u><br>Genus: *Panthera*<br>Species: *Leo*<br>**Binomial Name:**<br>***Panthera leo*** | |

## Wow Facts

- African lions live in plains or savanna habitats.
- The Jaguar and Tiger are their closest relatives, and lions evolved in Africa around one million years ago.
- Larger species of cave lions appeared 500,000 years ago, but died out around 10,000 years ago.
- In the late Pleistocene, some 10,000 years ago, humans were the only large land mammals more widespread than lions.
- Lions are the only cats that live in groups, which are called **prides**.
- Lions may scavenge up to 50 percent of their food.
- Lions are primarily nocturnal hunters and can sleep some 20 hours a day.
- Female lions are the pride's primary hunters. These **carnivores** often work together to prey upon antelopes, zebras, wildebeest, and other large animals of the open grasslands, but typically an individual lioness does the actual killing.
- A male lion can kill a hyena with one well-placed bite.
- Males are known to kill cubs in newly acquired prides in order to speed up the process of adult females being able to bear the new male's own offspring. Females are known to defend their pride from the advances of unfamiliar male lions to protect their existing young.
- Lions can live up to 14 years in the wild and more than 20 years in captivity.

# Anubis Baboons

Kingdom: Animalia
Phylum: Chordata
Class: Mammalia
Order: Primates
Family: Cercopithecidae
Genus: *Papio*
Species: *anubis*
**Binomial Name:**
***Papio Anubis***

## Wow Facts

- Anubis baboons or Olive baboons are found in savannah, grassland, and rainforest habitats.
- They have an elongated face that makes them resemble the Egyptian god Anubis.
- Males have long canine teeth and a mane of long hair.
- These **omnivores** eat seeds, flowers, fruits, grass, rhizomes, roots, tubers, tree gums, insects, eggs, rodents, hares, foxes, antelopes, sheep, goats, other primates, and small vertebrates.
- They have a cheek pouch to store food.
- Baboons use many vocalizations, and similar to humans, their facial expressions communicate volumes of information.
- Members of a **troop** do everything together including travel, eat, fight/defend, and they even sleep together. An average troop may consist of 15 to 150 individuals.
- As far as monkeys go, they are one of the largest.
- Average lifespan is 25 years in captivity
- Predators include: Leopards and chimpanzees.

# Bat-eared Fox

Kingdom: Animalia
Phylum: Chordata
Class: Mammalia
Order: Carnivora
Family: Canidae
Genus: *Otocyon*
Species: *megalotis*
**Binomial name:**
*Otocyon megalotis*

## Wow Facts

- Bat-eared foxes are found in arid grasslands and savannas, preferring areas where the grass is short.
- They first appeared 800,000 years ago during the middle Pleistocene.
- They dig dens to raise young and for shelter in extreme heat.
- The bat-eared fox is a **carnivore,** or more precisely an **insectivore**, and 80-90 percent of their diet is harvester termites. They also eat ants, beetles, crickets, grasshoppers, other insects, arthropods, fungi, birds, small mammals, and reptiles.
- In places such as the Serengeti, they are nocturnal 85 percent of the time, but in South Africa, they are diurnal during the winter.
- The bat-eared fox's name comes from their enormous ears, which are large in proportion to its head like those of many bats.

# Bontebok

Kingdom: Animalia
Phylum: Chordata
Class: Mammalia
Order: Artiodactyla
Family: Bovidae
Genus: *Damaliscus*
Species: *pygargus*

Binomial name:
***Damaliscus***
***pygargus***

## Wow Facts

- Bonteboks are found in South Africa and Lesotho.
- Bonteboks are **herbivores,** and live in grasslands and sparsely timbered regions.
- They eat plants, grass, leaves, and wild grass.
- Their horns are lyre-shaped and ringed along their entire length.
- There is a wide white strip is on their elongated nose with a white patch on their tail too.
- Bonteboks live in **herds** of up to 40 individuals.

# Cheetah

Kingdom: Animalia
Phylum: Chordata
Class: Mammalia
Order: Carnivora
Family: Felidae
Genus: *Acinonyx*
Species: *jubatus*
Binomial name:
***Acinonyx jubatus***

## Wow Facts

- Cheetahs are **carnivores** and eat animals such as hares, impalas, wildebeest calves, gazelles, and the young of warthogs, kudu, hartebeest, oryx, roan, and sable. They prefer to hunt in the early morning and late afternoon (diurnal).
- Cheetahs favor areas with tall grass and shrubs that have various elevated points from which to overview the area for prey.
- They have semi retractable claws like the fishing cat, the flat-headed cat, and the iriomote cat.
- Their nearest relatives are the puma and jaguarundi, and they evolved in Africa some 26-7.5 million years ago.
- Fastest mammal on land, the cheetah can reach speeds of just over 113km/h (70mph) over short distances, but during most hunts they reach speeds of 48-56km/h (30-35 mph), as most hunts require extreme maneuverability besides pure straight sprints.
- They are highly specialized with reduced weight, enlarged heart, large lungs, large nostrils, and an extremely flexible spine; they are the Ferrari of the cat world.
- They use their long (six ringed) end tail as a rudder as they cross distances of over 6m (20ft) when they leap.
- Cheetahs trip their prey and use their light jaw muscles and tiny teeth to suffocate their prey.

- A cheetah has a 50 percent chance of losing its food to other predators, so they have to eat fast.
- They are usually solitary animals and the females raise the young and hunt alone. Sometimes two or three solitary males will join forces and hunt as a pack and guard a single territorial range.
- Cheetahs vocalize with churring, growling, yowling, and purring sounds, but cannot roar. Bird chirping sounds by cubs can be heard by their mothers, but are ignored by predators such as lions.
- In ancient Egypt, cheetahs were kept as pets, but unless you are a king with thousands of servants and trained animal guards, don't try this at home.
- White cheetahs are rare, and usually have blue-gray (chinchilla) spots.
- Life span in the wild can be up to 14 years, with an average at 7 years and 20 years in captivity. Young cheetah mortality is 50 –75 percent, and in the Serengeti 90 percent.

# Gemsbok

Kingdom: <u>Animalia</u>
Phylum: <u>Chordata</u>
Class: <u>Mammalia</u>
Order: <u>Artiodactyla</u>
Family: *Bovidae*
Genus: *Oryx*
Species: *gazella*

**Binomial name:**
***Oryx gazelle***

## Wow Facts

- They prefer dry savannah, woodlands, rocky areas, dunes, and areas such as the Kalahari Desert, and physiologically don't depend on drinking water sources.
- Gemsboks are the largest Oryx species and have thick muscular necks.
- The gemsbok is an **herbivore** and primarily eats seeds, pods, fruits, and grass.
- The most distinctive features of this heavily built antelope are its long, rapier-shaped horns, striking black and white facial markings, and white socks with a black patch on the front legs.
- An occasional golden colored Oryx is a gemsbok with muted black body colors.
- They live in herds of 10 to 40 individuals and have one dominant male. In rainy seasons and during migrations, herds can range up to 200 individuals.
- From 1969 to 1977, 93 Gemsboks were released in New Mexico deserts and there are now over 3000 individuals.
- The average lifespan is 18 years in the wild, and 20 years in captivity.

# Hippopotamus

| |
|---|
| Kingdom: Animalia |
| Phylum: Chordata |
| Class: Mammalia |
| Order: Artiodactyla |
| Family: Hippopotamidae |
| Genus: *Hippopotamus* |
| Species: *amphibius* |

Binomial name:
**Hippopotamus**
**amphibius**

## Wow Facts

- They remain mostly hidden by water during the day, but not too deep, as they can't float and they are not great swimmers. They can however, run underwater at up to 8km/h (5mph).
- Their name means "river horse".
- Adults can hold their breath for 3-5 minutes.
- At dusk these mostly **herbivores** leave the water and walk up to 9.7km (6 miles) to find grass to graze on. An adult can eat 68kg (150 lb) of grass in 4-5 hours.
- Some 60 million years ago they split off from the ancestors of other artiodactyls that later evolved into camels, deer, pigs, and cattle.
- Some 54-52 million years ago, their common ancestor spit into whales and ancient lineages of hippopotamus.
- The family Hippopotamidae evolved in Africa 16-8 million years ago. Different species lived around different regions of Europe and Africa. The last species other than pygmy hippos died out just 1,000 years ago.
- Their skin secretes a natural red colored suntan substance often called "blood sweat".
- They have self sharpening teeth and their incisors can reach 40cm (1.3ft) in length.
- With one male in charge, they live in **schools** of up to 100 members. A group is also called pod, herd,

dale, and bloat.

- Similar to whales and dolphins, babies are born underwater and must swim to the surface for their first breath of air.
- They are the most dangerous animal in Africa, and they are responsible for killing up to 45 people in a single year. They may attack, whether you are swimming, sitting on a boat, or walking near a grass field. On land, they can gallop up to 30km/h (19mph).
- While marking their territory, they spin their tail to spread their excrement even more.
- Hippos can live 40-50 years in the wild and so far, up to 61 years in captivity.
- A red hippo represented the ancient Egyptian god "Set" and Set's consort "Taweret"; they were half hippo.
- Modern hippos in human lore include the ballerina hippos in Disney's *Fantasia*, Tasha in *Backyardigans*, and Moto-Moto in *Madagascar*.

# Klipspringer

Kingdom: Animalia
Phylum: Chordata
Class: Mammalia
Order: Artiodactyla
Family: Bovidae
Genus: *Oreotragus*
Species: *otragus*

Binomial name:
***Oreatragus***
***oreotragus***

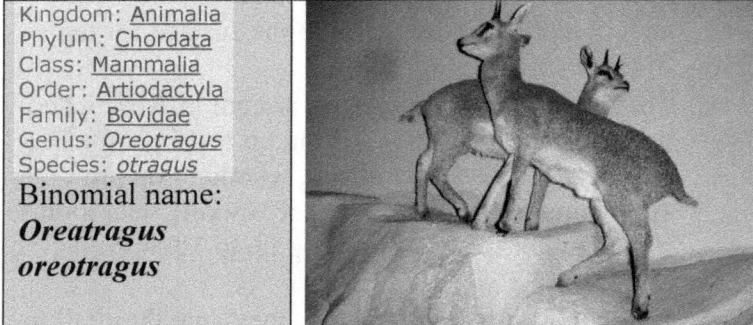

## Wow Facts

- The klipspringer is an **herbivore** that eats, shoots, and leaves.* They also eat fruits, berries, and succulents, and derive most of their water from the food they eat.
- They are found in South Africa up to the highlands of Ethiopia.
- Klipspringers prefer, rocky terrain, cliffs, steep mountains, and difficult to access river gorges.
- It is said that when standing on the tips of their hooves, they may take up no more flat surface area than a silver dollar coin, allowing them to climb and thrive where few other creatures can reach.
- Their loosely connected hollow hair stands straight up when they want to cool off. Their hair is unique among bovids, but found on pronghorns and on white tailed deer.
- Klipspringers are monogamous animals that are nearly always seen in pairs; usually with one offspring.
- Males are territorial and mark their area with dung.
- They mate for life and while one is eating, the other stands as a lookout for predators such as eagles, leopards, caracals, and humans.
- Maximum lifespan 14 years.

# Lechwe

Kingdom: <u>Animalia</u>
Phylum: <u>Chordata</u>
Class: <u>Mammalia</u>
Order: <u>Artiodactyla</u>
Family: <u>*Bovidae*</u>
Genus: <u>*Kobus*</u>
Species: <u>*leche*</u>
Binomial name:
***Kobus leche***

## Wow Facts

- These antelopes inhabit marshlands, wetlands, deltas, swamps, flooded plains, and reed beds of south central Africa: Angola, Botswana, Democratic Republic of the Congo, Namibia, and Zimbabwe.
- Height is 85-105cm (2.8-3.45ft) at the shoulders. Weight 60-130kg (130-290 lb). Males are larger than females.
- Their coat is golden brown. They have a white underbelly and a white ring around their eyes and black on front legs. Males are larger and have spiraled lyre shaped horns that first go back then curve up; 45-90cm (18-35 inch) long.
- Their hind legs are larger than their front legs. Their coat is greasy and water repellant. Their wide spread hooves help them run fast in mud and water, but slow on land. They are good swimmers too.
- These diurnal (morning and afternoon) active herbivores eat aquatic plants, water grasses, dry grasses, shrubs, and sedges. They rest on land during the heat of the day.
- They may be found in herds of 10-30 individuals or in herds of over a thousand. There are four sub species.
- Predators include: trophy hunters, crocodiles, pythons, lions, leopards, hyenas, and wild dogs.
- Males form breeding arenas (leks) where females may stop by to pick a mate.

# Leopard

| |
|---|
| Kingdom: <u>Animalia</u> |
| Phylum: <u>Chordata</u> |
| Class: <u>Mammalia</u> |
| Order: <u>Carnivora</u> |
| Family: <u>Felidae</u> |
| Genus: *Panthera* |
| Species: *pardus* |
| **Binomial name:** |
| ***Panthera pardus*** |

## Wow Facts

- They are found in woodlands, grasslands, savannas, and forests from Sub-Saharan Africa, Southeast Asia, and the Middle East to Siberia. During the Pliocene epoch (5.33-2.58 Mya) they lived in Italy.
- Leopards are **carnivores** and ambush birds, mammals, reptiles, and fish.
- They have a tawny or light yellow coat in warm dry habitats to a reddish-orange coat in dense forests and are covered with dark, irregular small circles called "rosettes."
- The leopard has a stocky muscular build with an elongated body, short legs, and a head made wider by powerful jaw muscles.
- Their scapula (shoulder blades) have specialized attachment sites for climbing muscles.
- To help move in the jungle or forests their ears are small and round and their whiskers on their upper lip, and protruding out of their eyebrows are long like those of a house cat, making them able to sense if the underbrush passing by their face is wide enough to accommodate the entire width of their body.
- They are usually nocturnal, but they may hunt on cloudy days as long as there are no human settlements nearby.
- They mark their territory with urine, feces, and claw marks.
- Although mostly solitary, they may communicate with one another by growling, roaring, and by spitting when

aggravated, and purring when content.

- There are eight subspecies of *Panthera pardus*. In Sri Lanka where there are no lions or tigers, leopards grow larger than anywhere else in the world.
- They can run up to 58km/h (36mph).
- They have been eliminated or exterminated from Hong Kong, Singapore, Kuwait, Syria, Libya, Tunisia, and perhaps Morocco.
- Males are 30% larger than females. Body size and color patterns of leopards vary geographically and most likely reflect adaptations to particular habitats.
- Leopards are one of the five big cats in the genus Panthera.
- Leopards look like a smaller version of the Jaguar and both Jaguars and Leopards may give birth to "melanistic", all black offspring, that are incorrectly, but colloquially termed Black Panthers. Melanism is a selective advantage for nocturnal ambush predators.
- A curiously rare genetic condition can overproduce red pigment or under produce dark pigment leaving the leopard strawberry colored or looking like a Pink Panther.
- Leopards may have emerged from the *Panthera* genus after snow leopards and tigers, but before lions and jaguars.
- DNA studies reveal that leopards are closely related to lions, but mitochondrial DNA studies show that they are closely related to snow leopards.
- Early extinct leopard species fossils from the Pleistocene and are 2-3.5 million years old. Modern leopards evolved in Africa 470,000-825,000 years ago.
- Because of their stealth, people are often unaware how close these big cats may live next to human communities.
- They can live 24 years in captivity and 12-17 years in the wild.
- Bagheera was a black leopard in Rudyard kipling's The Jungle Book.

# Nile Crocodile

| Kingdom: Animalia |
| --- |
| Phylum: Chordata |
| Class: Reptilia |
| Order: Crocodilia |
| Family: Crocodylidae |
| Genus: *Crocodylus* |
| Species: *niloticus* |
| **Binomial name:** |
| ***Crocodylus niloticus*** |

## Wow Facts

- Nile crocodile are only slightly smaller in size than saltwater crocodiles. They inhabit waterways up through Israel and over to Syria, along Mediterranean coastlines, the Red sea, lakes, rivers, marshlands, and the Nile delta. They have crossed the Indian Ocean as far away as Madagascar and the Comoros islands, where they live in caves: they became extinct in the Seychelles in 1820. They are an invasive species in Florida.

- Males may get as large as 6.1m (20ft) long and weigh 1,090kg (2,400 lb). Females are 30% smaller.

- These **carnivores** eat birds, reptiles, mammals, and fish; young eat bugs and insects. They are ambush predators.

- Unlike chimpanzees and gorillas that don't like to cross waterways, people don't fear crocodiles as much as they fear lions, but Nile crocodiles each year attack eight times as many humans as do lions. They don't always hide beneath the surface of water to ambush prey, but are known to hide along forest pathways, trails, and roadsides some 50m (170ft) from water.

- In Greek, kroko means "pebble", and dielos means "worm or man". *Niloticus* means from the Nile.

- They are closer related to American crocodiles than they are to West African crocodiles.

- They have ossified scutes on their back similar to prehistoric ankylosaurs. They have green eyes, nictitating membranes for eye protection, lachrymal glands to make tears to wash their eyes, and salt glands to remove excess salt. They have a four chambered heart similar to birds.

- They also have high concentrations of lactic acid in their blood which allows them to remain motionless for long periods of time, but excessive exercise can make the lactic acid levels spike so high that it could cause failure of internal organs.
- They have 64-68 teeth and that is 12 less teeth than alligators. They also have a bite force of 22,000 newtons, but not enough muscle power to open their mouth if merely duct tapped closed.
- They are usually seen basking on the banks of the river with their mouth open to help thermo regulate.
- They are sexually mature at 12-16 years of age. Females may lay over 20 some eggs in a hole they dug and guard the buried eggs until they start to chirp three months after incubation. The hatchlings can be 28cm (11 inches) long.
- Mongoose, wild pigs, and baboons eat the eggs, eagles and honey badgers eat the young. Pythons and other crocodiles eat the juveniles or smaller adults. Humans kill adults for meat and leather.
- Without crocodiles, lungfish and barbel catfish would eat all the smaller fish such as tilapia, which is a major food source for local communities.
- Life span is 50-60 years.

# Nyala

| |
|---|
| Kingdom: <u>Animalia</u><br>Phylum: <u>Chordata</u><br>Class: <u>Mammalia</u><br>Order: <u>Artiodactyla</u><br>Family: <u>Bovidae</u><br>Genus: <u>*Tragelaphus*</u><br>Species: <u>*angasii*</u><br>**Binomial name:**<br>***Tragelaphus angasii*** |

## Wow Facts

- Nyala are found in southeastern Africa near thickets in dry savanna woodlands, and prefer close proximity to high quality grassland and fresh water, but they can survive in areas where water is only available seasonally.
- They spend the hottest part of the day in shaded areas and feed during the evening and early morning.
- They have an alarm call that is a "dog-like" bark and they react to impala, baboon, and kudu calls.
- They graze and browse on leaves, twigs, flowers, fruits, and grass of many different species of plants.
- In the rainy season they feed on fresh green grass.
- Nyala are medium sized in comparison to other antelopes. Males are larger and have spiral horns with one to two twists and are yellow tipped. Females and juveniles are usually a rusty red color, but adult males become slate gray or bluish colored. Both males and females have a dorsal crest or ridge of long hair that runs from the back of the head to the base of the tail, and males also have a fringe of long hair along the midline of their chest and belly.
- Nyala are gregarious, generally staying in groups of two to 30 individuals. Old males live alone.
- They can live for 19 years. First seen 5.8 Mya.
- Predators include: lions, leopards, and cape hunting dogs. Juveniles: Baboons and birds of prey. Adult males are in high demand by big game hunters.

# Spotted Hyena

| |
|---|
| Kingdom: Animalia |
| Phylum: Chordata |
| Class: Mammalia |
| Order: Carnivora |
| Family: Hyaenidae |
| Genus: *Crocuta* |
| Species: *crocuta* |
| Binomial name: |
| ***Crocuta crocuta*** |

## Wow Facts

- Spotted hyena's live in many types of open, dry habitats including semi-deserts, savannahs, acacia bush, but they are also found in woodlands, scrub forests, and mountainous forests.
- Some 10 million years ago, ancestors of spotted hyenas diverged from those of the striped and brown hyenas. For millions of years they were found in grasslands of Europe and Eurasia. 12,500 years ago they became extinct in Europe as grasslands turned to woodlands, and were most likely outcompeted by early man and modern pack wolves.
- Spotted hyenas are more related to cats than they are to dogs and they are also closely related to meerkats.
- Spotted hyenas are **carnivores** and these skilled predators can take down wildebeest, zebras, and antelope. They will also scavenge if an easy meal is available.
- Spotted hyenas can eat and digest skin, bone, and other animal waste. A single hyena can eat a gazelle fawn in two minutes. 35 hyenas can eat an adult zebra in 36 minutes.
- Their bite force compared to a leopard is 40 percent stronger and they can crush bones better than a grizzly bear.
- Typically they catch their prey by running over distances at speeds of up to 61km/h (38mph) until

their prey collapses from exhaustion.

- Studies show that spotted hyenas and primate intelligence levels underwent convergent evolution and hyenas outperform chimpanzees on cooperative problem solving tests.
- By certain displays and scent marking, they appear to plan the hunt of specific species in advance, and can be deceptive if needed.
- They can hear another predator eating 10km (6 miles) away.
- Spotted hyenas are quite vocal and make a wide variety of sounds, including the whoops, grunts, giggles, whines, squeals, or "laughs" that has long been associated with their name.
- They live in clans of 3 to 80 individuals. All females are dominant to all males and are usually larger in size. Females stay with their natal clan for life.
- If a pride of lions has no male present, hyenas will harass them or drive them out of the local territory. They will even harass male lions if their ratios are greater than 5 to 1.
- While they are portrayed in *The Lion King* as cowardly and ugly, in real life they are extremely bold and curious, and will enter human camps and villages during the night.
- The average lifespan in captivity is 12 and up to 25 years, and they change color as they get older.

# Thomson's Gazelle

| |
|---|
| Kingdom: Animalia |
| Phylum: Chordata |
| Class: Mammalia |
| Order: Artiodactyla |
| Family: Bovidae |
| Genus: *Eudorcas* |
| Species: ***thomsonii*** |
| Binomial name: |
| ***Eudorcas thomsonii*** |

## Wow Facts

- Thomson's gazelles live in **herds** in short grasslands, dry plains, and open savannas.
- They are found in eastern Africa, in Kenya, Tanzania, and southern Sudan.
- Thomson's gazelles are **herbivores** and graze mainly on short grasses in the wet season, and bushes, twigs, seeds and clovers in the dry season.
- They have a lateral black stripe and long pointed slightly curved horns.
- The Thomson's gazelle can reach speeds of 80-96 km/h (50-60 mph), but it is their ability to zigzag that allows them to escape most predators. They can also display bounding leaps.
- Females can give birth twice a year and will head butt a male baboon to defend a fawn.
- They live 10-15 years in the wild.

# Vervet Monkeys

Kingdom: Animalia
Phylum: Chordata
Class: Mammalia
Order: Primates
Family: Cercopithecidae
Genus: *Chlorocebus*
Species: ***aethiops***
Binomial name:
***Chlorocebus aethiops***

## Wow Facts

- They are found in Senegal, Somalia, Ethiopia, and down to South Africa.
- They are typically found in wooded areas near water sources such as streams, rivers, and lakes. During the dry season they must drink water daily.
- These **omnivores** eat almost everything and anything including: leaves, young shoots, bark, flowers, fruit, bulb, roots, grass seeds, insects, grubs, eggs, baby birds, rodents, and hares.
- They are known to steal food from human settlements and don't mind raiding human crops.
- These old world monkeys travel together in groups of 10 to 70 members.
- They can be spiteful to one another, and exhibit human-like characteristics such as hypertension, anxiety, and alcohol abuse. Yes, they will steal alcohol too.
- Because of humans transporting them as pets, they are now found in many Caribbean nations such as Bermuda, Bahamas, Cuba, Jamaica, Haiti, St. Kitts and Nevis, and in warmer climate states such as Texas, Florida, Alabama, Louisiana, Arizona, and California.
- Predators include: leopards, snakes, raptors, and baboons.

# Warthog

| | |
|---|---|
| Kingdom: <u>Animalia</u><br>Phylum: <u>Chordata</u><br>Class: <u>Mammalia</u><br>Order: <u>Artiodactyla</u><br>Family: <u>Suidae</u><br>Genus: <u>*Phacochoerus*</u><br>Species: <u>*africanus*</u><br>Binomial name:<br>***Phacochoerus africanus*** |  |

## Wow Facts

- Warthogs are found in open and wooded savannas in sub-Saharan Africa.
- Warthogs are primarily **herbivores** and for the most part grazers, but also feed on roots, berries, fruit, bark of young trees, fungi, insects, eggs, and occasionally carrion.
- They have four wart-like protrusions on their head that are used as fat reserves and for defense when males fight.
- The two pair of tusks are used for digging, combat, and defense.
- The warthog has a good sense of smell and hearing, but poor vision.
- They live in family groups of females and young, called **soundings**. Males live alone or in bachelor groups.
- At night they take refuge in burrows.
- A sounding typically does not stray too far from their home range area and they may have several strategically placed burrows to choose from in order to escape predation.

# Waterbuck

Kingdom: <u>Animalia</u>
Phylum: <u>Chordata</u>
Class: <u>Mammalia</u>
Order: <u>Artiodactyla</u>
Family: <u>Bovidae</u>
Genus: *Kobus*
Species: *ellipsiprymnus*

Binomial name:
***Kobus ellipsiprymnus***

## Wow Facts

- Waterbuck prefer grassland habitats that are close to water such as lakes, rivers, and valleys.
- They live in herds of 6 to 30 members.
- Males have long spiral horns that curve back at the base and forward towards the ends.
- They have a white ring around their tail section and are one of the largest and heaviest species of antelope.
- Waterbuck are **herbivores** and they eat a variety of grasses, both medium and short in length, which makes up 75 to 95 percent of their diet.
- Despite its name, the waterbuck is not particularly fond of water, but will run into the water to escape predators.
- They secrete a musky odor substance to waterproof their body.
- They live 18 years in the wild and up to 30 years in captivity.

# White Rhinoceros

Kingdom: <u>Animalia</u>
Phylum: <u>Chordata</u>
Class: <u>Mammalia</u>
Order: <u>Perissodactyla</u>
Family: <u>Rhinocerotidae</u>
Genus: *Ceratotherium*
Species: *simum*

Binomial name:
***Ceratotherium***
***simum***

## Wow Facts

- Unfortunately, white rhinos are predominantly found in African game preserves and national parks. They prefer open areas with open woodlands and open grasslands near thick brush and water.
- White rhinos are **herbivores** and graze on grasses.
- White rhinos crop grass with their wide front lips. Black rhinos have narrower faces. The word "white" comes from the mispronounced Dutch word "wijd" meaning wide.
- They have longer heads than black rhinos, which also makes it easier to eat short grasses in dryer regions.
- They are thought to descend from the same ancestor *Ceratotherium praecox* some 7 million years ago.
- They have two horns that are made of solid keratin, and they have three toes on each foot.
- In captivity they can live up to 44 years of age.

# Zebra

| |
|---|
| Kingdom: <u>Animalia</u> |
| Phylum: <u>Chordata</u> |
| Class: <u>Mammalia</u> |
| Order: <u>Perissodactyla</u> |
| Family: <u>Equidae</u> |
| Genus: *Equus* |
| Species: *quagga* |
| Binomial name: |
| ***Equus quagga*** |

## Wow Facts

- The African plains zebra, formerly called *Equus burchelli,* roam the savannas of southeastern Africa. They prefer open grasslands, open woodlands, and open scrub environments.
- Zebras are **herbivores** that primarily graze on grass.
- Their white stripes are vertical and wider on their flanks and more narrow and horizontal on their legs.
- Each of the thousands of zebras that you may see on the savannah may look the same, but each individual zebra has a stripe pattern that is as unique as human fingerprints.
- **Harem** family groups consist of one male and up to six females, plus their young.
- Mountain zebras are smaller and have white underbellies and wide strips on their rump. Grevy's zebra is the largest species and looks more mule-like with numerous narrow stripes, and have a white belly.
- Zebras have black skin and black coat backgrounds with white stripes. Black and white stripes make them unattractive to flies that are attracted to polarized light.
- Zebras can walk, trot canter, and gallop, and zigzag when being pursued.
- There is evidence that they can see in color, and they have night vision, but not as good as most of their predators such as lions and hyenas. They also have good senses of hearing, smell, and taste.
- Lifespan: 9 years in the wild and 40 years in captivity.

# African Birds

# African Sacred Ibis

Kingdom: Animalia
Phylum: Chordata
Class: Aves
Order: Pelecaniformes
Family: Threskiornithidae
Genus: *Threskiornus*
Species: *aethiopicus*

Binomial name:
***Threskiornus aethiopicus***

- They are found almost everywhere in sub-Saharan Africa. They like to nest in tree colonies.
- Max length 68cm (27") long. They have a black rump, head, neck, legs, and fringe on wings, and a white body.
- They were introduced to England, France, Spain, Taiwan, and Florida.
- They eat fish, reptiles, small mammals, amphibians, insects, and invertebrates such as worms.

# Diederik Cuckoo

Kingdom: Animalia
Phylum: Chordata
Class: Aves
Order: Cuculiformes
Family: Cuculidae
Genus: *Chrysococcyx*
Species: *caprius*

Binomial name:
***Chrysococcyx caprius***

- They are found in sub-Saharan Africa. These copper-green and white birds prefer woodlands, savannas, and riversides where they eat insects and caterpillars.
- They are brood parasites and lay a single egg in the nest of weaver birds. The Cuckoo egg will hatch first and toss the weaver bird eggs out of the nest so that the weaver birds will expend all their energy raising the young cuckoo bird.
- Deed deed deed deed –er-ick is the call they make.

# Long-crested Eagle

Kingdom: Animalia
Phylum: Chordata
Class: Aves
Order: Accipitriformes
Family: Accipitridae
Genus: *Lophaetus*
Species: *occipitalis*

Binomial name:
***Lophaetus occipitals***

- They are found in sub-Saharan Africa. They like to sit and wait, perched in tall trees near forest edges, woodlands, rivers, grasslands marshlands, wetlands, and farmlands. They wait for food to present itself, then they swoop down.
- These **omnivores** eat small mammals such as rats, and mice, birds such as owls or smaller, frogs, fish, lizards, invertebrates, and even fruits.
- They are dark brown colored with tufts of feathers on their head.

# Woodland Kingfisher

Kingdom: Animalia
Phylum: Chordata
Class: Aves
Order: Coraciiformes
Family: Alcedinidae
Genus: *Halcyon*
Species: *senegalensis*

Binomial name:
***Halcyon senegalensis***

## Wow Facts

- They breed in equatorial or tropical Africa, but migrate north and south to woodlands far from water, where they eat insects.
- They are white with bright blue on their back and black on their shoulders. Their top bill is red and their lower bill black.
- They prefer to nest in old woodpecker nests. They are known to attack intruders; even humans.

# Prehistoric Life Gallery

# Acanthostega

Kingdom: <u>Animalia</u>
Phylum: <u>Chordata</u>
*Clade*: Tetrapopmorpha
Genus: <u>*Acanthostega*</u>
Species: <u>*gunnari*</u>
Binomial Name:
***Acanthostega gunnari***

## Wow Facts

- 365 Million Years Ago; in the Devonian period.
- The name means "Spiny roof".
- Habitat: rivers and swamps.
- 1m (3ft) long.
- This early tetrapod (four footed species) had eight digits on each front flipper like hand, but had no wrists for land movement; primitive feet with digits. It also had heavy underside scales to help with dragging the body on land or through shallow waters.
- Lungs were used to help them survive in low oxygenated waters, but the lungs were not supported by ribs for anything other than brief out of water excursions. They also had internal gills.
- Acanthostega had a complete jaw with teeth and could bite and hold on to prey.

# Allosaurus

Kingdom: Animalia
Phylum: Chordata
Order: Saurichia
Clade: Carnosauria
Family: Allosauridae
Genus: Allosaurus
Species: fragilis

Binomial Name:
*Allosaurus fragilis*

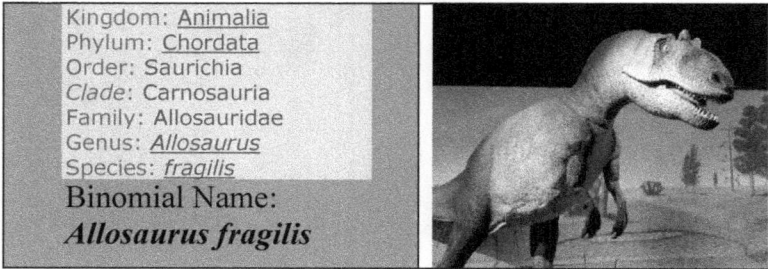

## Wow Facts

- 155-150 Million Years Ago; Late Jurassic.
- Greek for "different lizard"; pronounced al-oh-SORE-us.
- Habitat: Montana down to New Mexico and over to Arizona, Utah, Idaho, Colorado, Wyoming, and Texas. Outside North America: Portugal and perhaps Tanzania.
- This theropod was 8.5-12.2m (28-40ft) long. Top speed: 30-55 km/h (19-34mph).
- They had "Lacrimal" bone ridges over their eyes. Right in front of them they had narrow 20 degree binocular vision, but their necks were long and agile, which helped them track their prey as well as adjust their aim while taking bites.
- CT scans show that their brain was similar in shape to that of modern crocodiles. They had a furcula "wishbone".
- They had shorter legs than tyrannosaurids, but they had longer stronger arms equipped with three sharp claws. The legs were longer in juveniles than adults.
- They had a small head and small teeth and their bite force was similar to a Leopard (2,268 Newtons), but they could open their mouth 79 degrees wide, and similar to a great white shark they could take a huge amount flesh with each potential mortally wounding bite.
- Females had medullary bone tissue; now found only in female birds for supplying calcium to make eggs.
  - Their "holotype" tail vertebrae were once thought to be fossilized horse hoofs.

# Ammonoidea

Kingdom: Animalia
Phylum: Mollusca
Class: Cephalopoda
Subclass:
Ammonoidea

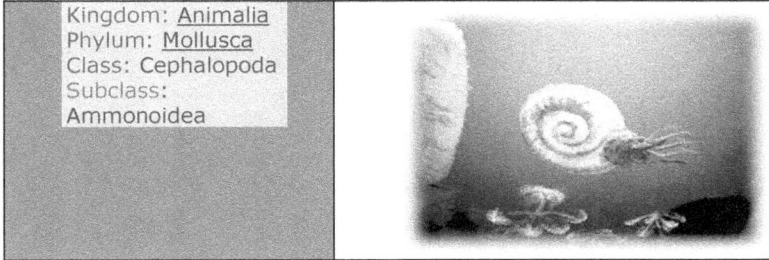

## Wow Facts

- 400-65 Million Years Ago; Devonian to Cretaceous.
- "Ammon form" The Egyptian god Ammon or Amun was pictured wearing horns similar to a ram's and thus this collection of mostly extinct species were named after Ammon.
- There are eight orders. Nautiloides are the only extant (living) species. Nautiloides produce eggs in small batches several times during their life span. Other extinct species may have released a single batch of eggs before the end of their life, similar to stream spawning salmon.
- The largest shell is 2m (6.5ft) wide and found in Germany, and   137cm (4,5ft) wide in North America. Females were larger than males to help with egg production.
- Species are separated by septa (partition walls), suture patterns (almost strait to leaf like patterns from the side view), and septal surfaces.
- The chambered part is called the phragmocone.
- Ammonoides had a (aptychus) horny plate or two calcitic plates to close over the opening of the exposed body chamber. Nautiloides use a leathery patch of skin to cover this opening.
- Ink is preserved in some fossils, and the mother of pearl coating is preserved in fossils buried in clay sediment.
- Soliclymenia species from the Devonian, 5cm (2 inch) long had a triangular shape.

# Ankylosaurus

| |
|---|
| Kingdom: Animalia<br>Phylum: Chordata<br>Order: Ornithischia<br>Family: Ankylosauridae<br>Tribe: Ankylosaurini<br>Genus: *Ankylosaurus*<br>Species: *magniventris*<br>Binomial Name:<br>*Ankylosaurus magniventris* |

## Wow Facts

- 68-66 Million Years Ago; Late Cretaceous.
- Pronounced ANK-ill-oh-SAUR-us. "Fused lizard "Named for fused bones which make the skeleton stronger.
- 6.25m (20.5ft) length. 1.7m (5.6ft) tall. 6 tonnes (13,000lb).
- Earlier species of ankylosaurids died out in North America, and 30 million years passed before new species of ankylosaurids entered and colonized North America.
- They had a well developed sense of smell.
- Their front beak tipped jaw, and back jaw leaf shaped teeth could cut through plants and leaves. They had no grinding teeth, so they must have had a strong digestive system for un-chewed food.
- Four horns pointing backwards protected the head and neck region. Plates of bones called osteoderms of different sizes were embedded in the skin and protected the entire body including their eyelids.
- They had a Club on end of their tail made out of two fused osteoderms on the end of their vertebrae.
- Gargoyleosaurus, one of the first and smallest ankylosaurs, had short spikes on its back and longer spikes on the sides of its body; 4m (13ft) long.

# Argentinosaurus

Kingdom: Animalia
Phylum: Chordata
Clade: Dinosauria
Order: Saurichia
Family: Antarctosauridae
Genus: Argentinosaurus
Species: huinculensis

Binomial Name:
**Argentinosaurus huinculensis**

## Wow Facts

- 94-77 Million Years Ago; Late Cretaceous Epoch.
- "Argentine lizard". From forests of Argentina.
- 30- 40 meters (98-130ft) long. 65-110 tons.
- One of the largest creatures to ever walk on Earth.
- Top speed 8km/h (5mph).
- They are thought to eat conifers and bushes and had gastroliths (stones) in stomach to help grind up food.
- Hundreds of adults gathered to nest and lay eggs, then walked away to keep from crushing the 22cm (8.7inch) eggs.
- Hatchlings grew 25,000 times their original size in less than 15 years to become adults.
- They are thought to live in herds.
- Long neck sauropods lived for a longer period of time in South America than in North America.

# Camarasaurus

Kingdom: Animalia
Phylum: Chordata
Order: Saurichia
*Clade*:
Camarasauromorpha
Family: Camarasauridae
Genus: *Camarasaurus*
Species: *lentus, grandis, & supremus*

Binomial Name:
Three Species

## Wow Facts

- 155-145 Million Years Ago; Late Jurassic.
- KAM-a-ra-SAUR-us. "Chambered Lizard". Named after hollow chambers in vertebrae.
- They lived on the plains of Alberta, Wyoming, Colorado, Utah, and New Mexico.
- The most common species was *C. lentus* at 15m (49ft) long. *C. supremus* was 23m (75ft) long.
- They had a large strong square box like skull with many finestrae (openings or holes) and a blunt snout.
- Front limbs were shorter than back limbs. They had five toes with a single claw on each front inner toe.
- They replaced their 19cm (7.5inch) chisel like teeth every 62 days. They are thought to masticate "chew" coarser conifer branches and ferns.
- Thought to move in herds or at least family groups.
- By 20 years old they were mature, and died by age 26.

# Coelacanths

| | |
|---|---|
| Kingdom: <u>Animalia</u><br>Phylum: <u>Chordata</u><br>Class: Sarcopterygii<br>Orders:<br>Coelacanthiformes<br>Family: Latimeriidae<br>Genus: *Latimeria*<br>Species: *menadoensis and chalumnae*<br>**Binomial Name:**<br>***Latimeria chalumnae*** |  |

## Wow Facts

- 409 Million Years Ago (Early Devonian Period) to present.
- Name means "hollow spine" and pronounced SEE-la-Kanth.
- These lobed fin fish (Sarcopterygii) were thought to have died off 65 million years ago, but two living species have been recently found. The light speckled and bluish colored specie, *Latimera chalumnae*, was caught by fishermen off the east coast of Africa in 1938. The speckled and brownish colored specie was discovered in a Menado fish market near Sulawesi, Indonesia in 1997. These two species are thought to have diverged 40 million years ago.
- They are primarily nocturnal drift hunters.
- They are usually caught as bycatch. They exude oils, urea, and esters that give their flesh an undesirable flavor.
- Although they diverged some 390 million years, they are still closer related to lung fish, reptiles, and mammals than they are to ray finned fish.
- They have an oil filled notochord, a small tube like heart, a brain filled with 98% fat, and a lateral sensory organ on their frontal head region.
- Females are larger than males and give live birth. They grow to 2m (6.5ft) long and 90kg (198lb).
- They can live for 60 years of more.

# Compsognathus

| | |
|---|---|
| Kingdom: <u>Animalia</u><br>Phylum: <u>Chordata</u><br>*Clade*: Dinosauria<br>Order: Saurichia<br>Family: Compsognathidae<br>Genus: <u>Compsognathus</u><br>Species: <u>longipes</u><br>**Binomial Name:**<br>***Compsognathus longipes*** |  |

## Wow Facts

- 150.8 Million Years Ago; Late Jurassic period.
- Greek name for "refined or pretty jaw"; pronounced comp-sog-NATH-us.
- About 1.3m (4.25 ft) long and half this length was made up by tail.
- Their fossils were first found in Germany and France.
- Their fossils are mixed with other marine fossils and they are presumed to have been the top predator on islands home to small lizards and mammals.
- They may have been covered by primitive feathers.
- The swallowed remains of the last meal, a whole lizard, was found in the stomach of one fossil.
- Recent findings have shown that they had three digits on their forelimbs. They balanced on their toes, used their tail for balance, they had long legs compared to their body size, and their light refined bone structure made them fast and accurate predators; similar convergent adaptations can be found in the fast running cheetah.
- They also had a comparatively long neck to move their head independently of their body movement and the neck and head could thus be used to probe dense bushes and branches for prey.
- Their large eyes tell us that they were extremely visually oriented predators and they may possibly have had better night vision to out compete other smaller eyed species.

# Crinoid

Kingdom: Animalia
Phylum: Echinodermata
Classes: Crinoidea, Eocrinoidea, Cystoidea

## Wow Facts

- 350 Million Years Ago; Devonian Period to present. There are over 600 extant (living) species.
- Name means "Lilly form."
- The largest fossil crinoid is 40m (130ft) in length.
- 1m (3.3ft) long stalked species are typically found in deeper water down to 6,000m (20,000ft). Free swimming species are the most common species.
- Stalked crinoids have five arm symmetry and the main body parts are the stem, calyx, and arms.
- The arms have feather like appendages called pinnules and tube feet. Oxygen is absorbed through the tube feet.
- They have a hydraulic pressure vascular system for operating tube feet and a separate haemal system for transporting nutrients and oxygen.
- They basically sit upside down with their mouth facing upwards and in center of the tegmen, "roof covering", and have an excrete pore at the edge of the tegmen.
- They filter feed by using sticky mucus that they move towards their mouth by using their tube feet as a conveyer belt system.
- Digestive and reproductive organs are located in the calyx.
- Fossil coprolites of placoderm fish and squid contain ossicles (bone like structures) of crinoids.

# Deinonychus

Kingdom: Animalia
Phylum: Chordata
Class: Dinosauria
Order: Saurischia
Family:
Dromaeosauridae
Genus: *Deinonychus*
Species: *antirrhopus*
Binomial Name:
***Deinonoychus***
***antirrhopus***

## Wow Facts

- 115-108 million years ago; early Cretaceous.
- Greek for "terrible claw; die-NAH-nih-cuss.
- 73kg (161lb)-100kg (220lb) and 3.4m (11ft) long.
- They lived in North American forests.
- They had a rigid pole counter balancing "antirrhopus" tail made by tendons overlapping several vertebras.
- They had 70 curved blade teeth with a bite force between 4,100-8,200 Newtons; so a greater bite force than a hyena.
- With a length of foot to tibia ratio of only .48 they were not as fast as an ostrich (.98).
- The three digit forelimbs are similar to archaeopteryx.
- The feet had a large sickle like claw on the second toe and fossilized foot tracks show that they kept the claw or talon up off the ground and walked on the third and forth toe.
- They may have used the large talon to attack or defend by stabbing, similar to modern cassowary birds.
- They may have hunted in packs like komodo dragons and just like komodo dragons; smaller ones may have been eaten.
- More primitive and older species in this dromeosaurid Family had feathers, so *deinonychus*

most likely had feathers too.
- First dinosaur thought to have used body heat "endothermic" to incubate eggs. Young had more curved claws to possibly spend more time in tree habitats.
-  Their looks and habits were used in the movie "Jurassic Park", but they were renamed "Velociraptors" to sound cooler.

# Dimetrodon

Kingdom: Animalia
Phylum: Chordata
Order: Synapsida
Clade: Camarasauromorpha
Family: Sphenacodontidae
Genus: Dimetrodons
Species: limbatys ,grandid, teutonis
Binomial Name: Some
12-15 total Species

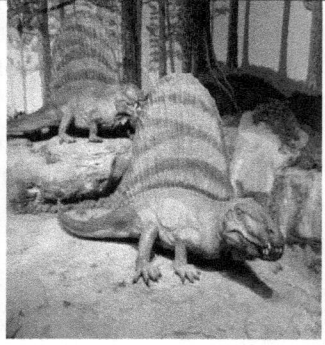

## Wow Facts

- 295-272 Million Years Ago; Early Permian.
- Greek for "two measures of teeth"; pronounced die-MET-roe-don.
- This extinct genus of synapsid lived in wetlands and swamps of North America and fossils are mostly from Texas and Oklahoma; later found in Germany, Utah, Arizona, Ohio, & New Mexico.
- 1.7-4.6m (5.6-15ft) long. 28-250kg (62-552lb). *D. Grandis* was the largest specie.
- Males are thought to be larger than females.
- This pelycosaur "sail reptile" went extinct 40 million years before the rise of dinosaurs and is closer related to mammals than reptiles.
- The sail made out of elongated neural spines was used for heat regulation and/or sexual display.
- Synapsida and Sauropsida clades split apart 310 million years ago.
- They had two sizes of tear drop shaped teeth, 80 teeth in total, arranged along their jaw line and included two large pair of canine teeth. Most species had serrated teeth.
- They were so successful that they became one of the most common fossils of the Permian period.

# Diplocaulus

| Kingdom: Animalia |
|---|
| Phylum: Chordata |
| Class: Amphibia |
| Order: Nectridea |
| Family: Diplocaulidae |
| Genus: Diplocaulus |
| Species: Five species |

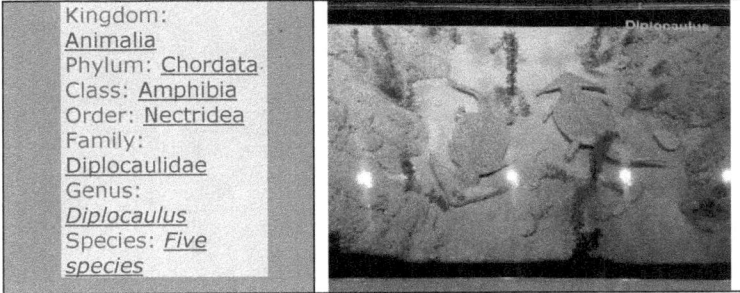

## Wow Facts

- 299-251 million years ago; early to late Permian.
- Greek for "double caul".
- 1m (3.3ft) long.
- Diplocaulus was the largest (lepospondyl) tetrapod amphibian.
- Found in morocco, and Texas.
- Their head was shaped like a boomerang and a flap of skin may have run the length of its body from the ends of the cauls down to the tail and would have therefore displayed convergent evolution traits similar to the genus of paradoxides trilobites which had semicircular heads with trailing spines and resembled the head of *Diplocaulus*.
- They may have had electro sensors along the length of their head to detect prey similar to today's scalloped shaped hammerhead sharks.
- They are thought to have moved up and down like a dolphin, whale, or Spanish dancer nudibranch.

# Dunkleosteus

| Kingdom: Animalia |
| Phylum: Chordata |
| Class: Placodermi |
| Order: Arthodira |
| Family: Dunkleosteidae |
| Genus: *Dunkleostus* |
| **Species:** *terrelli* |

**Binomial Name:**
***Dunkleosteus terrelli***

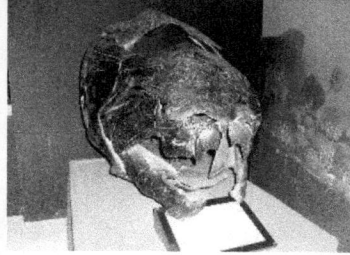

## Wow Facts

- 380-360 million years ago; late Devonian.
- Greek for "Dunkle's bone" in honor of David Dunkle the curator of vertebrate zoology at the Cleveland Museum of Natural History.
- Largest 10m (33ft) long and 3-4 tons. *D. terrelli* was the largest species.
- They have no teeth, but instead use sharp bony plates that could break though armor plates of smaller placoderms, ammonoids, and arthropods with at least 6000 Newtons of force. The *Megalodon* shark had a stronger bite force.
- Young *Dunkleoteus* perhaps ate softer prey.
- Dunkleosteus are found in shallow seas worldwide.
- There were at least ten different species of these armored fish and they survived for more than 70 million years.
- Fossils are found with boluses of fish bones, so perhaps they needed to periodically regurgitate bones as opposed to digesting them.
- While their 5cm (2 inch) thick heads fossilized quite well, the rest of their body composed of soft flesh did not, so we are left to speculate on what the larger species exactly looked like, so scientists use small well preserved placoderms to measure and infer what larger species must have looked like.

# Eryops

| |
|---|
| Kingdom: Animalia |
| Phylum: Chordata |
| Class: Amphibia |
| Order: Temnospondyli |
| Family: Eryopidae |
| Genus: *Eryops* |
| Species: *megacephalus* |

Binomial Name:
*Eryops megacephalus*

## Wow Facts

- 300-295 million years ago; early Permian.
- Greek for "long face"; pronounced EH-ree-ops.
- Swamps of North America (Texas & New Mexico) and Western Europe. Many well preserved fossils have been found in the Texas Red Beds.
- Averaged 1.5-2m (4.9-6.6ft) long. Biggest 3m (9.8ft) long.
- Weight 90kg (200lb).
- Wide stocky body with a flat skull and a crocodile like form.
- Ribs were short and used for body support. It is thought that Eryops gulped air into its mouth and then pushed the air back to its lungs.
- They swallowed food whole and had teeth on the roof of the mouth (palate) to help hold prey until it could be swallowed.
- Legs spread out from the sides of the body making it barely able to lift its body off the ground and also making it a slow walker on land.
- *Eryops* could have used the buoyancy effect to walk in water to hunt more efficiently; their tail was too narrow to be used effectively for swimming.

# Eurypterid

Kingdom: Animalia
Phylum: Arthropoda
Class: Merostomata
Order: Eurypterida
Family: Some 20 families
Genus: *Euryterus*
Species: *246-300 species*

## Wow Facts

- 470-248 million years ago; mid-Ordovician to late Permian.
- *Eury* means "Broad" and *pteron* means "wing".
- The largest, *Pterygotus*, was 3m (9.8ft) long.
- Also called sea scorpions although later species could walk on land to exploit ponds and lakes.
- Most are composed of 12 segments and the first two legs worked as paddle fins. They also had chelicerae; scorpion like pinching claws.
- They had six pair of book gills.
- They molted (ecdysis) at stages to escape the old outer hard shell covering, increase their size, and then secrete a new outer shell covering similar to scorpions, shrimps, lobsters, and crabs.
- They died out during the Permian-Triassic cataclysmic extinction event around 252 million years ago.
- They may be the ancestors of arachnids such as spiders, scorpions, and ticks.

# Eusthenopteron

Kingdom: Animalia
Phylum: Chordata
Class: Sarcopterygii
Order: Temnospondyli
Family: Tastichopteridae
Genus: *Eusthenopteron*
Species: *E .foordi & E. savesoderberghi*

## Wow Facts

- 385 million years ago; Late Devonian. Miguasha Quebec.
- Pronounced YOU-sthen-OP-teh-ron.
- Largest 1.8m (6ft) long and 22.7kg (50 lb). Smallest 29mm (1ft) long.
- It was a prehistoric sarcopterygian "lobefin" fish that lived in the northern hemisphere.
- It had early tetrapod traits such as internal nostrils, labryrinthodont (folded enamel) teeth, and a two part cranium.
- It had a humerus, ulna, and radius in each front lobed fin as well as a corresponding femur, tibia, and fibula in each pelvic fin.
- The long bones had growth plates and it may be the first specie to have bone marrow.
- It had a "three lobbed" caudal (tail) fin.
- Fossil reveal that it was covered by large scales.
- It is one of the historical links between fish and early tetrapods (four legged creatures).

# Hagfish

| | |
|---|---|
| Kingdom: Animalia<br>Phylum: Chordata<br>Class: Myxini<br>Former: Agnatha<br>Order: Mixiniformes<br>Family: Mixinidae<br>Genus: *Eptatretus*<br>Species: *stouti*<br><br>Binomial Name:<br>*Eptatretus stouti* |  |

## Wow Facts

- 300 million years ago to present, and unlike lampreys, only live in saltwater. They have internal gill pouches or can absorb oxygen directly through their skin.

- Largest species 127cm (4ft 2") long. Average 0.5m (19.7") long. Smallest species 4cm (1.6 inch) long.

- They have a skull, no vertebral column, no jaws, and a paddle tail. They may have 6-8 barbels around mouth. Two pair of comb-shaped teeth can pierce potential food sources and bring them inside the mouth.

- Two simple eye spots without lenses may be present to detect light, but not present in *Epatretus stouti*.

- They are also called "Slime eels" as they have some 100 glands on sides of their body to exude for protection some 20 liters (5 1/4 gallons) of fibrous slime. The slime can fill the gills of a fish and cause it to suffocate. The slime can also protect hagfish from a host fish's acidic stomach secretions as the hagfish eats the host fish from the inside out.

- They can tie themselves in an overhand knot as an evolutionary defense tactic or use as a traveling knot to remove slime from the length of their body.

- One of their favorite foods is polychaete worms, but shrimp, fish, and whale flesh are also eaten. They can go months without food.

- Koreans considered them a delicacy, and their skins are made into wallets and purses under the name "Eel Skin".

# Helicoprion

| | |
|---|---|
| Kingdom: Animalia<br>Phylum: Chordata<br>Class: Chondrichthyes<br>Subclass: Holocephali<br>Order: Eugeneodontida<br>Family: Heliocoprionidae<br>Genus: *Helicoprion*<br>Species: *bessonovi*<br>**Binomial Name:**<br>***Helicoprion***<br>***bessonovi*** |  |

## Wow Facts

- 290-250 million years ago; Early Permian to Early Triassic. Greek for "spiral saw"; pronounced HELL-ih-COPE-ree-on.

- Most species thought to be 3-4m (9.8-13ft) long largest species 7.5-24.6ft) long. The largest tooth whorl 60cm (24 inches).

- They survived the Permian-Triassic extinction where 95% of all species died off, then became extinct a mere million years later.

- For more than 100 years, the "tooth whorl" cluster of teeth was all we knew about this class of sharks and they were classified by teeth size, shape, width apart, and size of compound root.

- Some eight extinct species are described so far. The closest living relatives are the chimaeras "ratfish".

- At one point, it was anyone's guess where the tooth whorl fit in the shark's mouth or how they used the tooth whirl to hunt for prey. In 2013 a high resolution of a CT scanner of a related species of eugeneodont proved that the jaw saw or tooth whorl was housed or embedded inside the lower jaw bone. If the whorl of teeth protruded from the mouth is would have put considerable drag on the shark, so it is more likely that the whorl of teeth was hidden inside the closed mouth until deployed to hunt.

- As seen on documentary shows, Japanese fishermen deploy lures into the water and squid latch on immediately. Perhaps helicoprion sharks extended their whorl of teeth in the same manner as a lure. The squid latched on and were brought back into the mouth. The shark could swallow and re-deploy the tooth whorl/lure within seconds. Eating the soft tissue bodies of squids would also have helped retain teeth in good condition, as it is known that many earlier shark species did not replace their teeth as fast as modern sharks, and tooth damage, wear, and repair could have been more of an issue for earlier sharks.
- They lived in marine waters of Gondwana and Pangaea. Fossils are found from Canada to Mexico to China. In the United States: Idaho, Nevada, Wyoming, Texas, Utah, and California.
- *H. ferreiri* was found on China Mountain near Contact, Nevada.
- *H. Nevadensis* has been described from a single partial fossil.

# Herrerasaurus

Kingdom: Animalia
Phylum: Chordata
Class: Dinosauria
Order: Saurischia
Family: Herrerasauridae
Genus: *Herrerasaurus*
Species: *ischigualastensis*

Binomial Name:
***Herrerasaurus ischigualastensis***

## Wow Facts

- 235-221 million years ago; late Triassic.
- (Greek for "Herrera's lizard"); pronounced herr-RARE-oh-SORE-us.
- 3-6m (9.8-19.7ft) long. Weight 210-350 kg (460-770lb).
- It is thought to be an early theropod (wild beast foot) carnivore or one of the oldest saurischian dinosaurs, and displays many evolutionary convergent traits.
- It had a basic theropod skull up to 56cm (22 inches) in length and the lower jaw was movable. The pubis bone extends backwards similar to dromaeosaurids (feathered dinosaurs) such as *Deinonychus* and birds.
- Its hands had 5 digits; the first two fingers and the thumb had claws while 4th and 5th digits had small stubs.
- The feet had 5 toes but it walked on only the middle three that had full claws. Long legs made it a fast and agile top predator. The arms were medium length, but long compared to *T. rex*.
- Its fossils were first found in Argentina.
- Recovered coprolites (fossilized dung) reveal bits of digested bone.

# Horseshoe Crab

Kingdom: Animalia
Phylum: Arthopoda
Class: Merostomata
Order: Xiphosura
Family: Limulidae
Genus: *Limulus*
Species: *polyphemus*

Binomial Name:
***Limulus polyphemus***

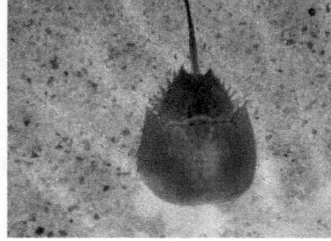

## Wow Facts

- 450 million years ago to present; late Ordovician.
- *L. polyphemus* lives in the Atlantic ocean along the east coast of North America and in the Gulf of Mexico Three other extant (living) species are found in Asia (Indo Pacific).
- Females are larger than males; up to 60cm (24inches).
- These living fossils are related to Arachnids such as scorpions, ticks, and spiders.
- Body segmented; head (prosoma), abdominal region (opisthosoma), and tail (telson).
- They swim upside down at a 30° angle and can use their telson to flip their body right side up if necessary.
- They have nine eyes. The two lateral eyes are compound eyes. The two median eyes can detect visible and ultraviolet light. Overall, horseshoe crabs have poor sight even though their cones and rods are 100 times larger than those found in humans.
- The five pair of legs that surround their mouth are used for walking, swimming, and the base of the legs are additionally used to tear and chew food. Like starfish, they can regenerate limbs. They also use a gizzard with sand granules to grind up food.
- They eat mollusks, annelids, other invertebrates, and fish.
- The first pair of legs on males are claspers used to hold on to females.

- Behind their legs are book gills.
- They become sexually mature in nine years. They spawn in late spring and females can lay thousands of eggs at one time or some 60-120,000 eggs over the spawning season, but like wild salmon, they only return home and spawn in sand in which they themselves were hatched.
- They live 20-40 years. As a single species, *Limulus polyphemus* has only been around 20 million years.
- The Red Knot, is a migratory bird that depends on horseshoe crab eggs for food. Atlantic Loggerhead turtles are also known to eat them. The eggs are eaten by humans in Asia.
- For some time they were exploited in the United States as an easy inexpensive source of fertilizer.
- One thing that has helped save them from recent extinction is that like cephalopod and gastropod mollusks, horseshoe crabs have blood made out of copper "hemocyanin", not iron "hemoglobin", and their clear colored blood turns blue when oxygenated. More importantly, their blood contains amebocytes (similar to white blood cells) that have granules with clotting factors that are used for testing bacterial endotoxins. Their blood is harvested and used to test for germs on the surfaces of space station and also used in medical research.
- As living vital blood donors, 3-30% of their blood is collected from each individual horseshoe crab; the amount of blood taken depends on factors such as the amount of stress occurred during handling and transportation in order to keep their deaths as low as possible. After their donation, their blood volume will return to normal in a week, and their blood cell count will recover within 2-3 months. Needless to say, each quart of their blood is now worth thousands of dollars and has helped save untold numbers of human lives.

# Ichthyosaur

Kingdom: Animalia
Phylum: Chordata
Class: Reptilia
Order: Ichthyosauria
Family: Ichthyosauridae
Genus: *Shonisaurus*
Species: *popularis*
Binomial Name:
***Shonisaurus***
***popularis***

## Wow Facts

- 248-90 million years ago; Mesozoic Era in all oceans.
- In Greek it means "fish lizard"; pronounced ICK-thee-oh-SORE-us. They were not part of the group called dinosaurs.
- The largest, *Shastasaurus,* was 23m (75ft) long.
- These ocean-going reptiles derived from a land dwelling egg laying tetrapod that went back into the oceans and similar to the four legged ancestors of mammalian whales, over time they became streamlined, front feet turned into fins, tails became fish like, and by the Triassic period, species even evolved dorsal fins. This convergent evolutionary analogous aquatic form can most visually be compared between ichthyosaurs and modern dolphins and whales. The elongation of their nose may have provided them with the same benefits and use as the modern swordfish, and they may have used their long rostrum to swing and stung fish or ammonoids before eating them.
- Until the Jurassic period, ichthyosaurs included over 50 species and were the top ocean predator. Mosasaurs and plesiosaurs eventually inherited the seas. By the late Cretaceous (95-90 million years ago) the last species went extinct; *Platypterygius hercynicus.*
- *Shonisaurus popularis*, the State fossil of Nevada, was 17m (56ft) long. They cruised the Western Interior Seaway 215 million years ago. 25 individuals died on

the seabed of what is now the state park in Berlin, Nevada.

- Coprolites (fossilized dung) show that they ate fish, cephalopods, and squids, and some may have been ram feeders for small fish; a feeding tactic used by some species baleen whales. Some species of Ichthyosaurs could eat fish or other species their own size.
- Their tails were mostly asymmetric "heterocercal" and the lower lobe was longer than the top lobe which is just opposite of some modern day sharks. They cruised at 2-5 km/h moving their tailfin side to side like sharks and fish. They used their pectoral fins as rudders similar to pink river dolphins. Their hand fins displayed five to ten digits (polydactyl) depending on the species.
- Ichthyosaurs breathed air through nostrils on the sides of their skull.
- They had the largest eye socket of all vertebrates and each large eye contained a scleral ring of bone. The large eye helped them to see better in dark waters, and the scleral ring enabled them to withstand water pressure at depth.
- These sea going reptiles typically had large conical teeth, but teeth size and type varied between species. From the oxygen ratios in the teeth we can determine that their body temp (35-39° C) was 20° greater than the surrounding water making them warm blooded.
- They also gave live birth to their young. The young were born tail first to keep from drowning during birth; similar to whales and dolphins today. Fossils of ichthyosaurs in various stages of birth have been excavated.

# Meganeura

| Kingdom: Animalia |
| --- |
| Phylum: Arthropoda |
| Class: Insecta |
| Superorder: Odonatoptera |
| Order: Meganisoptera |
| Family: Meganeuridae |
| Genus: *Meganeura* |
| Species: *At least three* |

## Wow Facts

- 305-299 million years ago; Late Carboniferous to Permian. Greek for "large nerved".
- *M. monyi* had wings 65cm (25.6 inch) long.
- Scientists once thought that meganuera were able to grow so big because the oxygen content during the Carboniferous made up some 32% of the air. This may have initially been the state in the Carboniferous, but during the early Permian the percent of oxygen in air had dropped to 23%: currently sea level air is made up of 21% oxygen, 79% nitrogen and tiny amounts of trace gasses. Even at 23% oxygen in the Permian, meganeura were still large.
- Meganeura had a breathing system that may have included a tracheal breathing system of diffusing oxygen through their body with the help of rapid cycles of tracheal compressions and expansions.
- It can be said that they were not true giants like the small reptiles that later evolved into 30m (100 plus feet) long sauropods, but to go from small dragon flies to 1m (3ft) wide four winged predators was quite a feat for a species of insects.
- They also lived in a time where aerial vertebrate predators had not evolved yet; meaning there no birds or winged reptiles to pluck them out of the sky.
- In the Permian predator reptiles became bigger, more diverse, and had bigger appetites. To Permian reptiles, meganuera would have seemed better than a meal specially flown in and delivered fresh.

# Parasaurolophus

Kingdom: Animalia
Phylum: Chordata
Clade: Dinosauria
Order: Ornithischia
Suborder: Ornithopoda
Family: Hadrosauridae
Genus: *Parasaurolophus*
Species: *walkeri*

Binomial Name:
***Parasaurolophus walkeri***

## Wow Facts

- 76.5-66 million years ago; Late Cretaceous.
- Greek for "near crested lizard"; pronounced pah-ra-sore-OLL-oh-fuss.
- Males were larger than females 9.5m (31ft) long. The skull was 1.6m (5ft 3 inches) long.
- This **herbivore** walked as a biped, but foraged for plants by moving on all for legs as a quadruped.
- Their large muscular upper forelimbs were thought to be used to push through heavily forested areas.
- They lived in forested areas along the western edge of The Western Interior Seaway from Alberta Canada down to New Mexico and Utah.
- Of the three known species *P. walkeri* had the largest crest. The crest was hollow and could make an extremely loud noise to communicate or warn others or used determine who was the dominant male. The crest was short in juveniles.
- Only a very few good specimens have been found making it very difficult to discern more about this unique family hadrosaurian dinosaurs.
- The three known species include: *P. walkeri, P. tubicen , and P. crytocristatus*.
- Parasaurolophus are hadrosaurids from the subfamily Lambeosaurinae.

# Pederpes

| | |
|---|---|
| Kingdom: <u>Animalia</u><br>Phylum: <u>Chordata</u><br>Superclass:<br>Tetrapoda<br>Family:<br>Whatcheeidae<br>Genus: *Pederpes*<br>Species: *finneyae*<br><br>Binomial<br>Name:<br><br>***Pederpes***<br>***finnyae*** |  |

## Wow Facts

- 348-347.6 million years ago; Early Carboniferous.
- Greek for "Peter's foot"; pronounced ped-URP-ease.
- 1 meter (3.28ft) long. 2.2-5.5kg (5-10lb).
- Earliest known carboniferous tetrapod to show feet facing forward for greater land maneuverability and speed.
- Either had five or six digits on hands; not sure due to the state of recovered partial skeletons.
- Fossils found from Scotland to Texas.
- Used muscle contractions to breath in air. Modern amphibians use their throat pouch to pump in air.
- Bones show signs that it may have had lateral lines for in water sensory perception.
- Ears appear better adapted for water use.
- They had elevated eye sockets; perhaps they ambushed prey near shore similar to crocodiles today.
- The discovery of *Pederpes* helped prove and fill in a middle transition slot for species of creatures on the road from an aquatic form to terrestrial tetrapods.

# Prehistoric Mammals

Kingdom:
**Animalia**
Phylum:
**Chordata**
Class: Mammalia

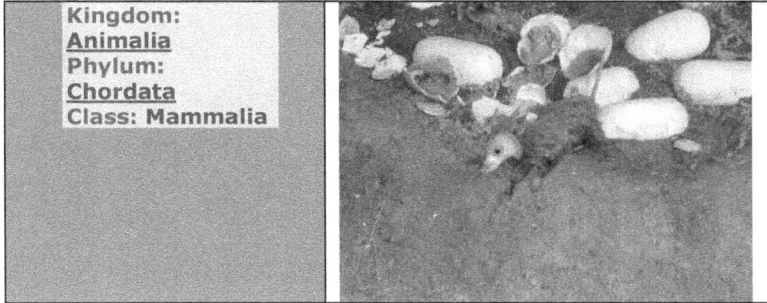

## Wow Facts

- 225 million years ago; Late Triassic. *Adelobasileus* was a mammal-like synapsid discovered in Texas. It was a transitional animal and ancestor for all modern mammals.

- 200 million years ago: Late Triassic. *Megazostrodon*: It had some mammal-like features as well as non-mammal-like features. It had four types of teeth: incisors, canines, premolars, and molars. It had a single bone in lower jaw; reptiles had seven bones in their lower jaw. The other former jaw bones moved to the middle ear to improve hearing. They also had a short rib cage and bigger lungs. They are thought to lay leathery eggs like reptiles and extinct monotremes.

- 83 million years ago: Late Cretaceous. ***Alphadon*** was thought to be a true marsupial similar to kangaroos and koalas today and it is shown in the display case competing for dinosaur eggs with Troodons. They are thought to look like an opossum, but they are described by the mere discovery of its teeth.

- Recently, a true mammal, *Eomaia*, was discovered in China with well preserved outlines of fur, long tail, and even ears. The hands and feet were well adapted for climbing. They were 20cm (8 inches) long. Thought to have emerged in the Early Cretaceous some 146 million years ago.

# Scapanorhynchus

Kingdom: Animalia
Phylum: Chordata
Class: Chondrichthyes
Subclass: Elasmobranchii
Genus: *Scapanorhynchus*
**At least four extinct species.**
*S. praeraphiodon, S. rapax,
S. raphiodon, S. texanus.*

## Wow Facts

- 84.9-66 million years ago; early Cretaceous.
- Pronounced "SKAP-an-o-rink-us"; means "spade snout".
- 65cm (2.1ft) to 3m (10ft) long; such as *S. texanus*.
- Teeth are up to 5cm (2 inches) long and they have striations on the front teeth that go down into the root.
- It is considered to be a prehistoric relative of the deep water goblin shark, *Mitsukurina owstoni*, but their fins and teeth are quite different.
- They had electro-receptor ampullae of Lorenzini in the elongated snout to detect prey in dark or low visibility marine waters.
- They had a long tail with a weaker lower lobe, so most likely they were not the fastest swimmers.
- Many of their fossils are found in shallow marine waters too, so they either remained in shallow waters full time or like ancient six gill sharks that still roam today's Puget Sound in Washington State; they surface at night; when they are known to feed closer to shore.

# Stethacanthus

Kingdom: Animalia
Phylum: Chordata
Class: Chondrichthyes
Subclass: Elasmobranchii
Order: Symmoriida
Family: Stethacanthidae
Genus: *Stethacanthus*
Species: *altonensis*

Binomial Name:
***Stethacanthus altonensis***

## Wow Facts

- 385-320 million years ago; Late Devonian to Early Carboniferous.
- In Greek it means "chest spine"; pronounced STEH-thah-CAN-thuss, and this refers to the anvil shaped brush on the dorsal fin of mature males. The brush is actually made of calcified cartilage strands. Males had a patch of raised spiked denticles on their forehead too.
- 1.5m (5ft) long.
- Behind each pectoral fin they had an elongated whip like structure.
- Some species had heterocercal tails (top lobe more muscular and longer), while others had homocercal tails (tailfin uniform).
- Approximately seven extinct species.
- Thought to be slow moving or bottom dwellers. Modern sharks of the same size such as bamboo sharks and silky hound sharks do not need to be constantly moving in order to get enough oxygenated water to exchange across their gills like larger sharks need to.
- Some species may have been migratory and left lots of teeth in breeding grounds.
- The Beardson shark fossil from Scotland is one of the best preserved cartilaginous fossils in the world.

# Tiktaalik

Kingdom: Animalia
Phylum: Chordata
Class: Sarcopterygii
Genus: *Tiktaalik*
Species: *roseae*

Binomial Name:
***Tiktaalik roseae***

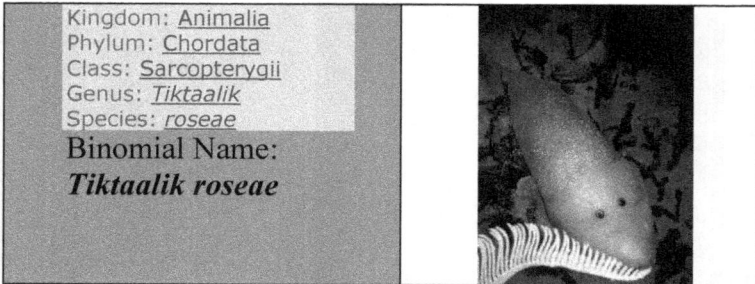

## Wow Facts

- 375 million years ago; Late Devonian in shallow seas.
- Inuktitut word of "burbot"; a freshwater cod fish.
- 91cm-2.74m (3-9ft) long and thin body.
- It was called a "fishapod" as it was part fish (gills, scales, & fins) and part tetrapod (lungs, rib bones, & neck with detached pectoral girdle).
- This sarcopterygian (lobe-finned fish) had a mobile neck with shoulders, elbows, wrist bones, and (finger-like) rays. It could walk on land similar to a modern mudskipper. Not the best type of locomotion, but enough to move from one pool of water to the next.
- It was also one of the first creatures to have a neck; giving it more mobility to hunt. With its small teeth it could hunt like a crocodile and look up towards the surface or peer out of the water to catch prey such as fish and insects.
- Its flat crocodile shaped head had spiracles above the eyes and it may have breathed using primitive lungs as well as gills.
- First discovered in river bed sediments on Ellesmer Island between Greenland and eastern North America. This area once had a warmer climate, as it was part of the Laurentia Continent that eventually drifted from the equator.

# Triceratops

| |
|---|
| Kingdom: <u>Animalia</u><br>Phylum: <u>Chordata</u><br>Orders: Ornithischia<br>Family: Ceratopsidae<br>Genus: *Triceratops*<br>Species: *horridus &<br>prorsus*<br>**Binomial Name:**<br>***T. horridus & T.<br>prorsus*** |

## Wow Facts

- 76.5-66 million years ago; Late Cretaceous in the woodlands of North America; Colorado, Wyoming, South Dakota, Montana, Saskatchewan, and Alberta.
- Greek for "three-horned face"; pronounced try-SEH-rah-tops.
- 7.9-9m (26-29.5ft) long. 2.9-3m (9.5-9.8ft) tall. Skull 2.5m (8.2ft) long and comprising up to one third of the total body length.
- Although there were many species in the ceratops family, there are currently only considered two species in the genus of triceratops.
- Their ancestors are found in Asia during the Late Jurassic period; *Yinlong*.
- They had a short horn on their nose above their nostrils and a horn above each eye, 1m (3.3ft) long. They had a large frill that could be used for species identification, for courtship, and for dominance, as with deer, elk, moose, mountain goats, big horn sheep, or for display purposes as with the rhinoceros beetle.
- The frill was composed of fibrolamellar bone that heals fast which could have come in handy especially after nonfatal confrontations with other males.
- These **herbivores** had batteries of some 432-800 teeth that were replaced throughout their life. Their mouth was also tipped with a beak similar to parrots

and octopus that could easily grasp and pluck ferns and fronds.
- Their front feet had three hooves and the back feet had four hooves.
- 47 complete skeletons have been found in the Hell Creek Formation near Fort Peck Lake, Montana.
- The Museum of the Rockies in Bozeman Montana has an extremely good collection of fossils which dramatically and clearly show facial horns begin to grow at an early age until adult hood. The Yoshi's Trike specimen has 115cm (3.77ft) long horns.
- A healthy bull triceratops was more than a match against a *Tyrannosaurus rex*.
- Triceratops became extinct during the Paleogene extinction event 66 million years ago.

# Trilobite

Kingdom:
Animalia
Phylum:
Arthropoda
Classes:
Trilobita

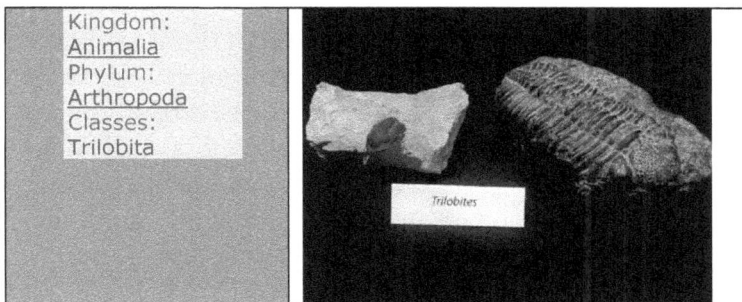

Trilobites

## Wow Facts

- 521-250 million years ago; Early Cambrian to late Permian.
- Name means "three lobes". They had three tegmata, (sections): a cephalon (head), thorax (body) and a pygidium (tail).
- *Isoteles rex* was the largest species at 72cm (2.4ft) long; the smallest species was 3mm (.12 inch) long.
- They had a toothless mouth and some were predators, scavengers, filter feeders, plankton feeders, and some may have had symbiotic relations with sulfur bacteria similar to deep benthic thermal vent sea crabs do today.
- Many had complex eyes consisting of one to thousands of lenses each made of pure calcite ($CaCO_3$); calcium carbonate is see through in it's pure form.
- They are thought to hatch from eggs and undergo several molting instars where initial new segments were added with each instar and later they molted (ecdysis) similar to lobsters as they grew and escaped from their old exoskeleton by breaking out through the back of the body where the head and thorax segments meet.
- Species specific exoskeletons can be used to determine different periods of time in layered deposits. Their ancient leg and burrow tracks are found on fossilized sea beds.

- Many trilobite fossils are found "enrolled" or rolled up like a pill bug.
- There were thousands of species of these marine creatures in at least nine different orders over some 271 million years. Some survived several mass extinctions, but only the Order Proetida clinging to the shallow shelves made it through the Devonian mass extinction to finally get wiped out during the Permian extinction when the seas became low.
- Early humans around the world drilled holes in trilobite heads and wore them as necklaces.

# Troodon

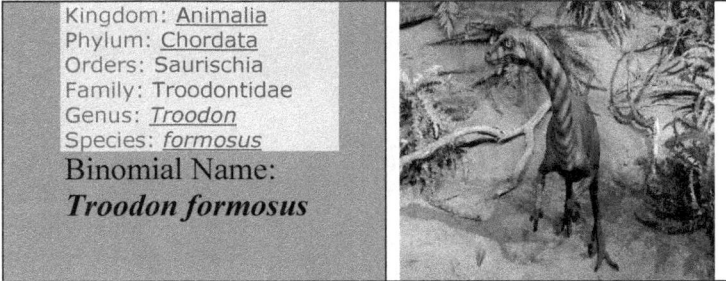

Kingdom: <u>Animalia</u>
Phylum: <u>Chordata</u>
Orders: Saurischia
Family: Troodontidae
Genus: *Troodon*
Species: *formosus*

Binomial Name:
***Troodon formosus***

## Wow Facts

- 77.5-66 million years ago; Late Cretaceous to the (KT) Cretaceous-Paleogene Extinction event. Fossils found from Alaska down to the plains of Montana, Wyoming, and over to Asia.
- .9m (3ft) tall and 2.4m (7.9ft) long. 50kg 110 lb.
- They have a sickle shaped claw on the second toe of each foot with three semi-manipulating digits on each hand.
- They had one of the largest brains per body size of any dinosaur and may have been as smart as primitive mammals, ostrich, or emu.
- These predators used their serrated teeth to slice through flesh.
- Their large binocular vision eyes may have been used to hunt at night.
- Because of the large number of their nests found, scientist believe that in nests, females laid 16-24 eggs; two at a time. Males brooded the eggs, similar to male ostriches from Africa, until they all hatched at about the same time; 45-65 total nesting days.
- Juveniles became adults within 3-5 years.
- There were at least two species and possibly more: *T. formosus* and *T. inequalis*.

# Tyrannosaurus

| |
|---|
| Kingdom: Animalia |
| Phylum: Chordata |
| Orders: Saurischia |
| Family: Tyrannosauridae |
| Genus: *Tyrannosaurus* |
| Species: *rex* |
| Binomial Name: ***Tyrannosaurus rex*** |

## Wow Facts

- 68-66 million years ago; Late Cretaceous. They lived on the Western Inland continent of Laromidia and their fossils are found in Canada down to New Mexico, Wyoming, and Texas. They inhabited various ecosystems from forests, coastal inlands, semiarid plains, to the gulf coast, and bayou. They became extinct during the Cretaceous - Paleogene extinction event; over 50 specimens found.
- Greek for "tyrant lizard king"; pronounced tih-RAN-oh-SORE-us REX.
- They were 12.3m (40ft) long, 4m (13ft) tall at the hips, and their skull was 1.5m (4.9ft) long or almost as big as a smart car. The largest skull found was 150cm (59 inches) long. Finestrae or holes in the large wide skull helped make it lighter and still retain structural integrity.
- They had one of the largest bite forces of any dinosaur. They had 58 teeth and the larger teeth were over 30cm (12 inches) long and they could open their jaw some 63° delivering one devastatingly large and powerful bite.
- Their arms were short 1m (3.3ft) long, but strong, and the

two clawed digits could have been used for at least holding on to captured prey until delivering a lethal bite or used for grasping while mating.

- Fossilized foot prints are 83cm (33inches) long and 71cm (28 inches) wide.
- Binocular vision is mostly found in predators, and *T.rex* eyes were better than a hawk with 55° binocular vision. They could see 13 times sharper than an eagle and 3.6 times better than a human. They could discern objects 6km (3.7miles) away compared to humans 1.6km (1mile) away.
- They had a high sense of smell and were tuned in to hearing low frequency sounds.
- Some scientist believe that they could run 40km/h (25mph) while others think that because of their possible weight of over 7 tons, that they could only run half that speed. Still other scientists believe that portions of muscles in the tail region could help make *T.rex* a relatively fast power walker. Even at half speed, a sick or wounded triceratops or hadrosaur would have had little chance of escape.
- *T.rex* had a large brain to body size similar to crocodiles and had one of the largest brains for a non-avian dinosaur. All this intelligence, eye sight acuity, developed hearing, and sense of sound would be evolutionary overkill for just a scavenger. *T.rex* could have been more like a current day hyena that recently has been found to act as predator first, but when times are tough or the meal easy, they can readily convert to being a scavenger.
- *T.rex* tooth marks have been found on Hadrosaurs and on Triceratops.
- They are thought by many scientists to be warm blooded.
- At least during the juvenile stages they are thought to have had some downy like feathers similar to a related species of Tyrannosauroid found in China; *Dilong paradoxus.*
- The oldest known, *T.rex* named Sue, lived until 28 years old.

# Zygorhiza

| | |
|---|---|
| Kingdom: <u>Animalia</u><br>Phylum: <u>Chordata</u><br>Class: <u>Mammalia</u><br>Order: Cetacea<br>Suborder: Archaeoceti<br>Family: Basilosauridae<br>Subfamily: Durodontinae<br>Genus: <u>*Zygorhiza*</u><br>Species: <u>*kochii*</u> |  |

**Binomial Name:**
***Zygorhiza kochii***

## Wow Facts

- 43-34 million years ago; Late Eocene.
- Greek for "yoke root"; pronounced ZIE-go-RYE-za.
- 5m (17ft) in length.
- Fossils have been found in Louisiana, Alabama, Mississippi, and New Zealand.
- They are the State fossil of Mississippi.
- They had rudimentary hind limbs and hinged elbows on the front flippers that may have been used to help haul them ashore and give birth.
- They had a long head on a short body.
- The skeleton in the Mississippi Museum of Natural Science is named "Ziggy".

# Egypt
# Room
# Live
# Animal

# Egyptian Fattail Scorpion

Kingdom: Animalia
Phylum: Arthropoda
Class: Arachnida
Order: Scorpiones
Family: Buthidae
Genus: *Androctonus*
Species: 18 total
**Binomial name:**

## Wow Facts

- They live in deserts, scrublands, tropical, subtropical regions with sand or stony soil.
- They are found in Armenia down to the Middle East, Northern Africa, over to parts of Asia, and down to India.
- They can live in burrows, under rocks, under wood debris, in homes, or live on steep slopes of sand dunes.
- These eight legged creatures are nocturnal and come out at night to feed, mate, and defend their territory. The eat spiders, lizards, insects, and other scorpions. They will try and kill and eat anything that moves and is smaller than they are.
- The Greek word "andras" means man, and "kteinen" means to kill. Fatttail or fat-tailed is derived from their fat metasoma or tail.
- They are one of the most potent and dangerous scorpions in the world and they cause paralysis and respiratory arrest. They kill several humans each year. Their venom is used in medical research to fight brain cancer.
- Females may have 30-45 scorplings on her back until their first molt.
- They average 10cm (4 inches) in length.
- Sand storms that can rip off paint don't bother them because of the dimple or dome shaped contour of their exoskeleton.
- *A. amoreuxi* and *A. australis* are both used in the exotic animal trade.

# Egypt Room Displayed Animals

# Dromedary Camel

| Kingdom: <u>Animalia</u><br>Phylum: <u>Chordata</u><br>Class: <u>Mammalia</u><br>Order: <u>Artiodactyla</u><br>Family: <u>Camelidae</u><br>Genus: <u>*Camelus*</u><br>Species: <u>*dromedarius*</u><br>**Binomial name:**<br>***Camelus dromedarius*** |  |

## Wow Facts

- The dromedary camel is also called the Arabian camel; they haven't lived in the wild for over 2,000 years. They were first domesticated some 4,000 years ago.
- They now live in arid regions of the Middle East, Africa, and the Sahara desert. They were exported around the world to such places as France, Spain, the United States, and Australia. Eighty percent of the world's dromedary camel population is in Africa, and Australia has the largest population of feral dromedary camels.
- Dromedary camels have one hump on their back. Bactrian camels, both domestic and wild, have two humps. The humps are fat deposits held together by fibrous tissues and the fat is used as stored energy. Also by locating fat deposits away from other parts of the body camels are able to reduce the amount of trapped heat inside their body.
- Dromedary camels are even toed ungulates with a long curved neck and a narrow chest. They have padded feet and long hair on their throat, shoulders, and hump year round. Bactrian camels have more (thicker) and longer hair that they shed after the end of each Gobi desert winter.
- They have double layered eye lashes, bushy eyebrows, small rounded ears, and lockable nostrils. They have a rete mirabile network used to stay cool, and they are the only mammal to have oval shaped

red blood cells. Their skin is black like zebras and polar bears, but their coat is typically colored brown to white. Their front feet are larger than the back feet and they move both legs on one side of their body at a time.

- Dromedary camels form herds of 20 individuals with one dominant male. Males are larger than females and are 2m (6.6ft) tall at the shoulder and 600kg (1300lb). Males hang their long pink soft palate out of their mouth and coated with foamy saliva to attract females.
- They can lose up to 30% of their total water content. They can drink brackish or salty water to stay alive. In hot weather they drink every 10-15 days and can drink 10-20L (2.2-4.4gal) per minute.
- They eat over 330 species of plants and will chew spiny plants with their mouth open. They chew at least 40-50 times and will ruminate after grazing some 8-12 hours, and if starving they will even eat fish and bones. When they get nervous, they tend to vomit.
- The lamini tribe which includes alpaca, guanaco, vicuňa, and llama spit from the camalini tribe 25 million years ago in the early Miocene.
- Dromedary and Bactrian camels split 8 million years ago, although there was cross breading for thousands of years as well as still to this very day. Hybrids may be stronger and larger than their parents, but second generation hybrids may be runts and bad tempered.
- The oldest and smallest extinct camel was *Protylopus* which lived in North America in the Eocene some 56 Mya. Extinct camels crossed the Bering Sea during the Pliocene to Pliestocene Epochs some 5-1.65 Mya. The oldest dromedary jaw fossil is from Saudi Arabia 8,200 BC.
- A Dromedary fetus still has two humps, but they merge in to one by the time they are born. So we

know dromedary camels originally descended from the Bactrian camel line.

- Domesticated Dromedary were brought into Egypt with the invasion of Cambyses in 525BC. Dromedary camels were the ships of the desert or the cargo truck of the day. Besides hauling cargo, humans use them for milk, meat, wool, riding, and racing. Some races include the Arabian Dilool, the Egyptian Hageen, and the Sahara Mehara.
- Life span is 40 years. Gestation is 15 months and they have one calf. They mature in 3-5 years.

# Glossy Ibis

Kingdom: <u>Animalia</u>
Phylum: <u>Chordata</u>
Class: <u>Aves</u>
Order: <u>Pelecaniformes</u>
Family: <u>Threskionithidae</u>
Genus: *<u>Plegadis</u>*
Species: *<u>falcinellus</u>*
**Binomial name:**
*Plegadis falcinellus*

## Wow Facts

- This nomadic bird is found worldwide and they prefer warmer climates.
- They feed in shallow waters of lakes stream, rivers, ponds, marshlands, lagoons, reservoirs, sewer ponds, and irrigation systems on farmlands.
- They prefer to hunt around bushes, reeds, and papyrus.
- They use their sickle shaped beak to feed on aquatic beetles, dragonflies, grasshoppers, crickets, flies, worms, leeches, snails, crabs, crayfish, frogs, lizards, and snakes.
- They are 48-66cm (19-26 inches) long.
- They prefer to flock in trees with other birds.
- They build nests 1-7m (3.3-23ft) above water and lay 3-4 eggs that incubate for 20-23 days.
- Breeders are reddish brown with light emerald green colored wings.
- Non-breeders and young are dull brown in color.
- They are threatened by loss of water habitats through wetland degradation, drainage, increased salinity of water and invasive species of plants.

# Indian Cobra

| | |
|---|---|
| Kingdom: <u>Animalia</u><br>Phylum: <u>Chordata</u><br>Class: <u>Reptilia</u><br>Order: <u>Squamata</u><br>Family: <u>Elapidae</u><br>Genus: *Naja*<br>Species: *naja*<br>**Binomial name:**<br>*Naja naja* | |

## Wow Facts

- These **carnivores** are found in the Kabul river valley in Afghanistan, India, Pakistan, Bangladesh, Nepal, and Sri Lanka.
- They are habitat generalists and live in forests, plains, wetlands, villages, and agricultural lands such as rice paddy fields and wheat fields. Near water ways they hide in embankments, tree hollows, termite mounts, rock piled and dens formerly occupied by small mammals.
- They hunt at dawn or dusk. Near humans, they are attracted by chickens and rats that rummage through garbage or eat the crops.
- Away from humans, they eat rodents, birds, lizards, and amphibians such as frogs. They can go days or months without food depending on how active they are and how big was the last meal.
- In turn, they are eaten by birds of prey, other snakes, and mongoose. A mongoose will bite them in the back of the neck and paralyze them
- Their underside can be yellow, tan, gray, red, brown, or black.
- Their hood becomes wide as they flare the ribs in their neck. The top or back side may be white and black patterned with two black circles connected by a U shaped line that makes it appear as if the cobra is wearing a pair of spectacles (old time glasses).
- Most have light throat colorations above a dark band.

- They are up to 1.5m (4.9ft) in length.
- They are oviparous and lay 10-30 eggs in a rat hole or termite mound. The eggs hatch in 48-69 days and the newborn have venom glands already working.
- The venom paralyzes muscles and their prey dies from respiratory failure or cardiac arrest.
- For humans bitten, symptoms appear in 15 minutes to two hours. With immediate medical attention humans have a 90% chance of surviving the bite.
- Cobras are shy and their first response when confronted is to flee the scene as soon as they feel vibrations on the ground. If they can't escape, the open their hood and hiss.
- They are deaf and snake charmers wave their pipe so the cobra will follow the visual cue. Some snake charmers sell the venom. Others remove the snake's teeth so they can't be bitten, but this ultimately leads to the snake's early death.
- Cobras are vital for keeping the rat population down so that the rats don't eat all the crops, and in turn, locals will have more food to eat. The cobras are protected under the Indian Wildlife act of 1972, but back in the early 1980's wallets, purses, and hand bags were still made out of cobra skins and sold on the black market in secret backroom warehouses to tourists from other countries.
- In the story of Rikki-Tikki-Tavi, Rudyard Kipling wrote about a male cobra named Naga, and a female cobra named Nagami.

# Small Asian Mongoose

| |
|---|
| Kingdom: Animalia |
| Phylum: Chordata |
| Class: Mammalia |
| Order: Carnivora |
| Family: Herpestidae |
| Genus: *Herpestes* |
| Species: *javanicus* |
| **Binomial name:** |
| *Herpestes* |
| *javanicus* |

## Wow Facts

- This mongoose is found from Iraq to Japan and Indonesia, and was introduced to island nations and countries around the world. Including Hawaii, Bahamas, Cuba, Croatia Jamaica, Puerto Rico, Trinidad, and Columbia.
- They live in scrublands, dry forests, or rainforests.
- These **carnivores** eat crabs, frogs, spiders, scorpions, snakes, small mammals, birds, bird eggs, crocodile eggs, and carrion. In St. Croix, they ate all the ground lizards, *Ameiva polops*, and also went after the green Iguana. They also actively hunt for the fawns of white tailed deer. So they are now considered a pet in many countries.
- In Okinawa, they carry antimicrobial-resistant strain of *E. coli* which makes them a health hazard and a pest.
- Early on, countries imported them to eat the rats that ate local sugar cane crops, but the mongoose is active in the day (diurnal) and the rats are active at night (nocturnal) and so they rarely ever meet.
- There are 34 species in the family Herpestidae, which is part of the suborder feliformia which includes the cat, hyena, and civet families. 29 of the species are called mongoose, four species are called kusimanse, and one specie make up the television stars known as meerkats.
- Mongoose like ancestors are first seen in the

Oligocene 35-23 million years ago.

- While many species live solitary lives, other groups such as the popular meerkats live in highly dramatic and sometimes emotionally exhausting social groups.
- Mongoose have non-retractable claws used for digging.
- Males are bigger than females.
- They make 12 different vocalizations.
- Females are pregnant for 49 days then have 2-5 young.
- Similar to pigs, honey badgers, and hedge hogs, a genetic mutation makes them resistant or immune to snake venom.
- They use their speed and agility to bite snakes behind their head and break their spinal cord which paralyzes the snakes. They don't seem to really prefer snake meat over other meat, but to a hungry mongoose, food is food, and you don't pass it up even if it has fangs.
- Life span in captivity is 20 years in captivity and 12 years in the wild.
- In the Jungle Book, Rudyard Kipling wrote about a mongoose named Rikki-Tikki-Tavi.

# Egyptian Exhibit

# Types of Pyramids

## Mastaba 2727 BC

## Step Pyramid 2630 BC

## Bent Pyramid 2600 BC

## Smooth Pyramid 2589 BC

# Social Pyramid

| Pharaoh<br>Pharaoh's Family<br>Pharaoh's Advisors &<br>Priests<br>Officials & Tax<br>Collectors<br>Scribes<br>Skilled Workers<br>Farmers & Peasants | |
|---|---|

# Wow Facts

- Skilled artisans built the pyramids, not slaves.
- These highly skilled workers lived in special villages and had their own cemetery.
- The workers lived on a diet of beer, barley, and fish.
- Working on the Pharaoh's tomb ensured them a better place in the afterlife.
- Pyramids became known as a beacon for looters and thieves, so later Pharaohs were buried underground in the Valley of Kings with no outside visible references as to where each King and their treasure was hidden.
- The Valley of the Kings was guarded, but as time went by, the guards were no longer paid for their services and within 200 years most of the tombs had been looted and everything removed except for the paintings on the walls.

## A Brief History of King Tut

 The three million dollar King Tut exhibit is only one of two sanctioned in the world and handmade in Egypt to ensure authenticity. Had King tut had a pharaoh's typical life and burial his tomb would have been looted within two hundred years after his death and like most of the other pharaohs we would know little about his life or possessions. However, he died unexpectedly at the age of 19 and his burial was far from routine for a typical Pharaoh. At an early age his heretic father Amenhotep IV, in the fifth year of his reign at Thebes changed his name to Ankhanaten and proclaimed that Egypt had a new monotheism religion based on one sun god "Aten" and he built a new royal city called Amarna up north near Karnak. On Tut's boyhood throne a cartouche reads his name as Tutankhaten "Living image of Aten". At nine years of age his father died and his father's vizier Ay, pronounced "eye", became Tut's vizier. Within two years, King Tut moved back to Thebes; now known as Luxor. King Tut renamed himself Tutankhamun, reinstated the old polytheism religion of many gods, restored a fractured country, and reinstated the priests that had previously become enemies of his father. King Tut married his half-sister Ankhesenamun and they had two still born girl babies.

          At the age of 19 Tut suddenly died. Recent CT scans on his mummified remains reveal that the left side of his body showed traumatic injury consistent with a chariot wheel hitting his body as he was kneeling. His remains show that the collision fractured his knee, broke away his left side ribs and his left ileum on the pelvic region, and his sternum was missing.  Tut is curiously the only Pharaoh buried without his heart, perhaps because it was so badly damaged by the accident: Egyptians believed the heart is where the soul resided and crucial for passage into the afterlife. Other scientists believe that most of the bone damage was done after his death. They also believe that it would have been difficult for someone born with a partial club foot to participate in battles. Through DNA tests, scientists think that Tut may have suffered several bouts with malaria during his short life. Could he merely have fallen down from some height and fractured his knee while critically ill with malaria, or was he an unfortunate warrior? And if the majority of these bones were broken after death, was it by accident, or did some unforgiving noble, vizier, or disgruntled priest try their best to make sure that King Tut would never make it to the afterlife?

Unlike any other Pharaoh, Tut was embalmed quickly and this improper haste is the suspected cause for his skin and oil soaked cloth to ignite and slowly burn similar to oil linseed soaked cloths that accidentally catch fire during some modern day painting projects.

Curiously, Tut's sarcophagus and possessions that might come in handy in his afterlife were placed in a tomb built for a nobleman, but not for a king, and a wall had to be chipped and cut back to make his shrine fit inside a small confined room. Instead of many elaborate paintings, the small tomb was minimally painted and the tomb was closed before the paint could dry, allowing this to be the only tomb discovered with mold growing for a brief period of time some 3,159 years ago. The minimal four chambered tomb appears to have been filled quickly and some of the burial items were second hand burial items. Tut's golden death mask was riveted and soldered to a female headdress. Men did not have earrings in ancient Egypt and the earring holes filled or not, were a blatant error or were hastily overlooked by the master craftsmen. The middle coffin is more similar in facial features to his mother Nefertiti's than they are to Tut's. Rather than make things perfect the first time around, the feet on the middle coffin were cut off to make it fit inside the sarcophagus. Some officials suggest that 80% of Queen Nefertiti's afterworld possessions were re-gifted and placed in King Tut's tomb.

Tut had designated Horemheb, Tut's military general,

to become Pharaoh when he died, but Horemheb was away at battle in what is now Syria. Ankhesenamun, Tut's 20 year old wife, sent a message to a Hittite King requesting to marry one of his son's, but the son through some misfortunate adventure or murderously dark unforeseen circumstances never arrived in Egypt and the chief advisor, 61 year old Ay, married the young widowed Ankhesenamun as soon as Tut was placed in his tomb, the door was sealed shut, and even before the paint was dry.

Ay was now Pharaoh of Egypt, and what happened to Ankesenamun is not known for sure, but Ay soon took another wife, but died a mere four years after taking control of Egypt. Soon afterwards, by force, Horemheb became Pharaoh and declared *damnation memoriae* to his predecessors, which means he tried to erase from history all evidence of the heretic Amenhotep or Ankhanaten, Ay, and even King Tut.

It's also important to mention that at the temple of Seti 1 in Abydos 76 kings have cartouches (oval name seals) carved into the first two rows (38 each) and they make up the 1st -19th dynasties. Amenhotep, Ay, and King Tut and a few other pharaoh's who were deemed not legitimate, were erased from history and their cartouches do not appear in the temple of Seti I, and this further helped hide all evidence of the radical one god "Aten" religion, King Tut, and his tomb. Ironically, by trying to erase all evidence of Tut, his tomb is the only tomb that survived looters over the ages, making this boy king that never had a chance to make his mark in life, the most well known pharaoh of all time so far and for many ages to come.

In November 1922 the tomb and treasure was revealed by Howard Carter and his patron Lord Carnarvon. When they entered the tomb chamber, they found that some 60% of the small jewelry had been stolen by two previous break-ins. In a hurry, a bag of rings lying on the floor had been dropped by long ago looters. Scientists believe that Tut was buried in the spring because of the blooming flowers found buried with him, and that the smaller portable items were removed from the tomb within a few months after the burial. The tomb was resealed before a flash flood in autumn buried the tomb with meters of rocks and runoff debris, and left this floor area of the valley looking like a naturally occurring and completely undisturbed bed of a stream.

As for the newspaper coined phrased "curse of the mummy", everyone who first entered the tomb in 1922, as predicted, died at some point in the last hundred years, but this is the predicted outcome from the natural progression of aging and the natural potential for occurring health issues at that time in history, and not so much the mysterious diabolical work of an ancient curse; or was it?

# Geology Room

## (Live Animal)

# Desert Hairy Scorpion

Kingdom: <u>Animalia</u>
Phylum: <u>Chordata</u>
Class: <u>Arachnida</u>
Order: <u>Scorpiones</u>
Family: <u>Caraboctonidae</u>
Genus: *Hadurus*
Species:
**Binomial Name:**

## Wow Facts

- There are eight species of scorpions in the genus *Hadurus*. Only three are considered to be giant hairy scorpions.
- They are found in New Mexico, Arizona, southern Nevada, and southern California. They prefer washes and valleys where they hide in burrows 2.5m (8ft) long, or just under rocks. They come out at night to hunt and find a mate.
- They are a pale yellow or straw color with dark spots on their legs and claws.
- They can reach 15cm (6 inches) in length.
- The hairs on their body can detect/sense prey.
- The eat insects including other species of scorpions, small lizards, and snakes. They get their water from their prey too.
- They molt 6-10 times during their lifetime and they are vulnerable until the next molt hardens: a few days. Females have thinner pincers.
- Females have live young and the young stay on her back for a few weeks.
- Their venom is not that potent, but they can sting like a bumble bee. Some people have allergic reactions and can have difficulty breathing, extreme swelling and intense pain.
- They can live up to 20 years in Captivity and 7-10 years in the wild.

# Geology Room

## (Prehistoric Animals)

# African Elephant
# Loxodonta

Kingdom: Animalia
Phylum: Chordata
Class: Mammalia
Order: Proboscidea
Family: Elephantidae
Genus: *Loxodonta*
Species: *africana*
**Binomial Name:**
*Loxodonta*
*africana*

## Wow Facts

- The habitats occupied by African elephants vary because they can survive long periods of time without water; they occupy deserts, forests, savannas, river valleys and marshes.
- Elephants are **herbivores** and eat vegetation such as leaves, roots, bark, grasses, and fruit. They can use their proboscis (trunk) to breathe, intake water, and collect food.
- African elephants are the heaviest land animal, and the second tallest in the Animal Kingdom. They use their big wide ears to help in thermo regulation.
- Their incisor teeth develop into tusks some 245-250 cm (8 feet) long and the tusks can weigh about 60 kg (130 pounds) each. The only other teeth they have are four molars which are replaced three times throughout their lives after the previous set wears down.
- The matriarch is often the oldest female and she leads a clan of 9 to 11 elephants, but they can join other clans and move in herds from 200-1000 members during the rainy season.
- Adult male bulls live alone or with other males and they can be extremely dangerous or unusually aggressive when in musth: a period at least once a year when testosterone levels are extremely high and males are ready to mate.

- Elephants communicate by touch, sight, and sound and their intelligence level is compared to primates and whales.
- They have self-awareness when looking at mirrors and display empathy for dying, dead, or the exposed bones of former elephants.
- They can hear things through their padded feet.
- Elephants can live up to 70 years in the wild. In many areas they have been decimated by poachers for their ivory tusks.

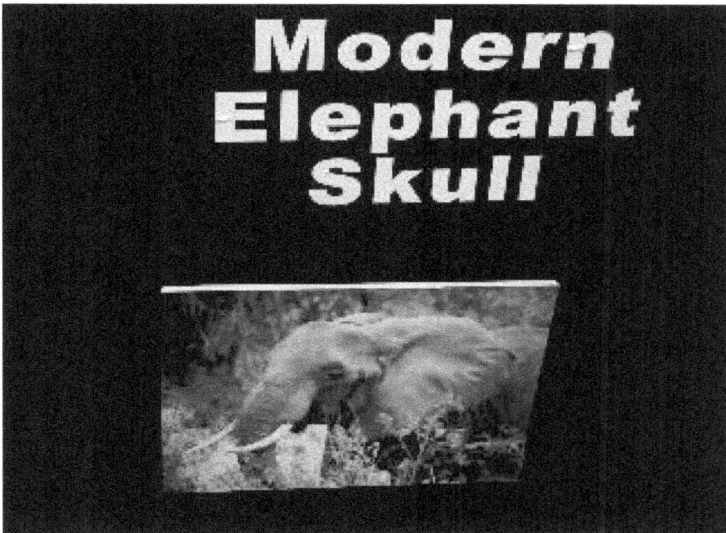

Modern Elephant Skull

# Bison Latifrons

Kingdom: Animalia
Phylum: Chordata
Class: Mammalia
Order: Artiodactyla
Family: Bovidae
Genus: *Bison*
Species: *latifrons*
Binomial name: ***Bison latifrons***

## Wow Facts

- The giant bison lived in plains and woodlands of North America for over 200,000 years. It lived in warmer regions and is found as far south as San Diego.
- It was a **herbivore** with 6 foot wide horns.
- It became extinct 20,000-30,000 years ago.
- It is quite possibly the largest bovid in the fossil record.
- It was replaced by *Bison antiquus* and then evolved into the smaller modern *Bison bison* some 10,000 years ago.

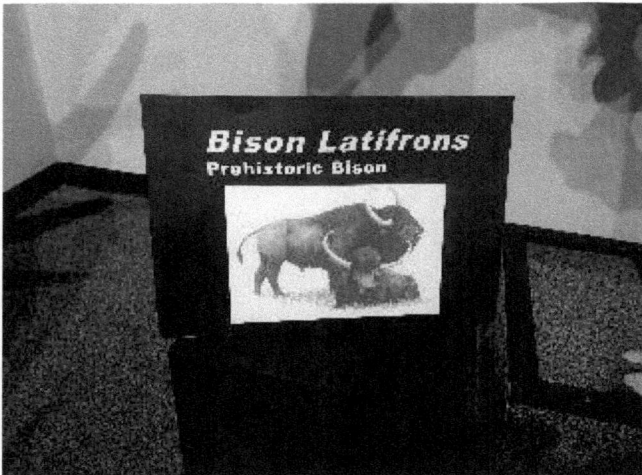

# Giraffe

| | |
|---|---|
| Kingdom: <u>Animalia</u><br>Phylum: <u>Chordata</u><br>Class: <u>Mammalia</u><br>Order: <u>Artiodactyla</u><br>Family: <u>Giraffidae</u><br>Genus: <u>*Giraffa*</u><br>Species: <u>*camelopardalis*</u><br>Binomial name:<br>*Giraffa*<br>*Camelopardalis* | |

## Wow Facts

- This family includes only two living species, the giraffe and the okapi.
- Giraffes are gregarious, living in **herds** of up to 25-32 animals, which occupy large home ranges usually in relatively open savannahs of sub-saharan Africa.
- Giraffes first appeared in the fossil record in the early Miocene.
- Their long necks are brought about by the lengthening of their cervical vertebrae after birth, and not by adding vertebrae. At birth they may be 1.8m (6ft) tall.
- In the upper neck a *rete mirabile* prevents excess blood flow to the brain while they are bending over to drink water.
- Giraffes have short horns that project from the parietals and frontals. These are unique among mammals, consisting of bony cores (ossicones) covered by furred skin.
- Giraffes are **herbivores** and have a four-chambered ruminating stomach.
- They have a long purplish-black colored (possibly for sun protection) prehensile tongue that they use for grasping as well as grooming. The upper lip is also prehensile; the lips and tongue are covered with papillae to protect them from thorns.
- The neck bones work like a ball and socket set to

help slingshot the head and neck into their opponent. Males fight using their necks (called necking) to rub against and/or eventually ram into each other until one submits, disengages, is wounded, or, as witnessed on film, one of them falls unconscious. Sinuses in the head help soften the blows.

- Giraffes either walk or gallop. They can sprint up to 60km/h (37mph) or run at a slower sustained speed for several kilometers at 50km/h (31mph).
- They evolved from the extinct family Palaeomerycidae eight million years ago during the Miocene epoch in central Europe. There are currently nine different subspecies.
- Egyptians kept them as pets and gave them their own hieroglyph "sr" in old Egyptian and later "mmy".
- They live up to 15 years in the wild and 25 years in captivity. The coats of males become darker as they age.

# Hyrax

| |
|---|
| Kingdom: Animalia<br>Phylum: Chordata<br>Class: Mammalia<br>Order: Hyracoidea<br>Family: Procaviidae<br>Genus: *Procavia*<br>Species: *capensis*<br>Binomial name:<br>***Procavia capensis*** |

## Wow Facts

- Occurs throughout most of Africa and the Arabian Peninsula in rocky areas with moderate vegetative cover, and many rock crevices and cavities, the latter of which are used as shelter.

- **Herbivores**

- Fossil remains indicate there was once hyraxes the size of oxen. This may explain a gestation period of 7 to 8 months; unusually long for an animal of its modern small size.

- Hyraxes are the smallest of the sub-ungulate mammals, but in the past they were much larger. We first see them in the fossil record about 37 million years ago with their present form about 2 million years ago.

- They are closely related to elephants and share many characteristics of elephants, manatees, and dugongs.

- They have a single pair of long, strong, tusk-like incisors similar to elephants and molars that are similar to the cheek teeth of rhinoceroses.

- The soles of the feet have soft rubbery sensitive large pads that are kept moist with sweat-like secretions. They have four toes on the front feet and three toes on the back feet. Like elephants the toes have flat stubby nails.

- Their highly-charged myoglobin leads scientists to believe that they derived from aquatic ancestors.

- They live in **harems** of up to 80 individuals with one dominant male.

# Mammoth

Kingdom: Animalia
Phylum: Chordata
Class: Mammalia
Order: Probocidea
Family: Elephantidae
Genus: *Mammuthus*
Species: *primigenius*
Binomial name:
*Mammuthus primigenius*

## Wow Facts

- Mammoths lived in the Miocene epoch (6 million years ago) into the Holocene (4,500 years ago on the plains of North America, Africa, Europe, and Asia.
- The Woolly mammoth was a **herbivore** that grazed on grass. Both males and females had tusks.
- Their tusks alone were longer than a modern elephant.
- The earliest proboscideans existed 55 million years ago around the Tethys Sea. Mastodons are distant relatives that diverged some 25 million years before mammoths evolved.
- Most mammoths died out some 10,000 years ago, but they some lived on in St. Paul Island, Alaska until 3750 BC and on Wrangel Island until 1650 BC. We have found complete specimens buried in Arctic permafrost. Evidence of dwarfing is found in many isolated island populations.
- Thanks to various cave paintings, we know that the Woolly Mammoth was hunted to extinction by the prehistoric human settlers of Eurasia for its tusks to build homes, its meat to eat, and woolly hide to wear.
- President Thomas Jefferson who was interested in paleontology first used the word mammoth as a noun, meaning of giant proportion. The word first became an adjective in phrase "Cheshire Mammoth Cheese," in 1802.
- Some scientists believe it may be possible to clone wooly mammoths using mammoth DNA and modern elephants for gestation.

# Megatherium - Giant Sloth

Kingdom: <u>Animalia</u>
Phylum: <u>Chordata</u>
Class: <u>Mammalia</u>
Order: <u>Pilosa</u>
Family: <u>Megatheriidae</u>
Genus: *<u>Megatherium</u>*
Species: *<u>americanum</u>*
Binomial name:
***Megatherium***
***americanum***

Megather um
Giant Ground Sloth

## Wow Facts

- Woodlands of South America and they pushed into North America when a land bridge appeared.
- **Herbivore**
- Megatherium is the poster mammal for the giant megafauna of the Pliocene and Pleistocene epochs: this prehistoric sloth was as big as an elephant, about 20 feet long from head to tail and weighing in the neighborhood of 4 tonnes (4.4 tons).
- Its long claws forced it to walk on the sides of its feet; similar to a modern anteater.
- Megatherium was much bigger than its contemporary North American relative, *Megalonyx*, the first fossils of which were discovered by Thomas Jefferson.
- Megatherium is also an interesting case study in convergent evolution between dinosaurs and mammals. If you ignore the thick coat of fur, this mammal was anatomically very similar to the tall, pot-bellied, razor-clawed breed of dinosaurs known as therizinosaurs.
- They died out some 10,000 years ago at coincidentally the same time as human hunters expanded their territory.

# Rhynchotherium

Kingdom: Animalia
Phylum: Chordata
Class: Mammalia
Order: Proboscidea
Family: Gomphotheridae
Genus: *Rhynchotherium*
Three Species: *ablicki, falconeri, tlascalae*

**Binomial Name:**
*Rhynchotherium . \*.*

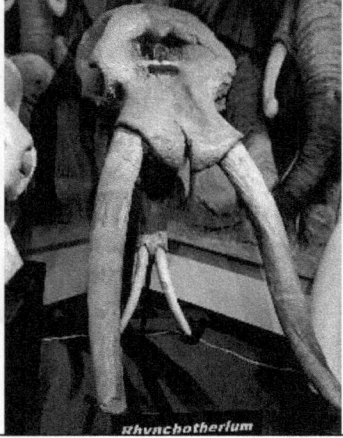

## Wow Facts

- *Rhynchotherium* is an extinct genus of proboscidea (Elephants) endemic to North America and Central America during the Miocene through Pliocene from 13.650—3.6 million years ago, and thrived for approximately 10 million years.
- This gomphothere had two sets of tusks and may have evolved from *Gomphotherium*.

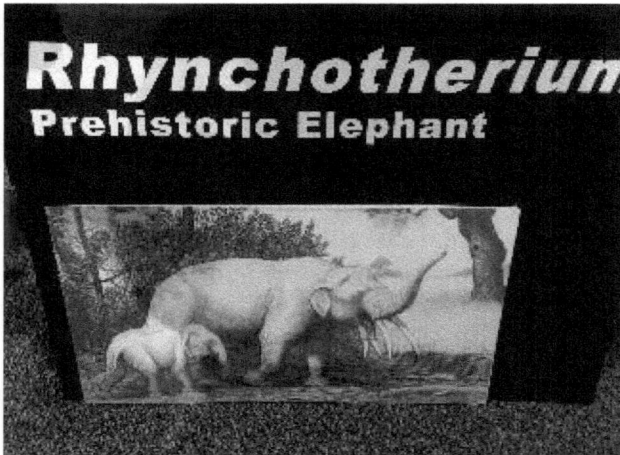

# Sivatherium

Kingdom: Animalia
Phylum: Chordata
Class: Mammalia
Order: Artiodactyla
Family: Giraffidae
Genus: *Sivatherium*
Species: *giganteum*
Binomial name:
*Sivatherium*
*giganteum*

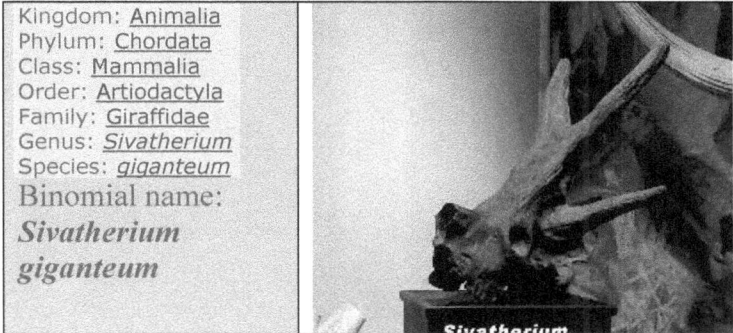

## Wow Facts

- Plains of India and Africa
- **Herbivore**
- The skull has two ossicones above the eyes that are very giraffe-like. It also had two pair of antler like ossicones on its head.
- Although it was directly ancestral to modern giraffes, it looked more like an okapi, but much larger. Sivatherium's squat build and elaborate head display also made it look more like a moose to some.
- Like much of the mammalian megafauna of the Pleistocene epoch, it is thought that early humans hunted Sivatherium to extinction. Pictures of this prehistoric mammal have been found preserved on rocks in the Sahara Desert.

**Sivatherium**
**Prehistoric Giraffe**

# Smilodon

Kingdom: <u>Animalia</u>
Phylum: <u>Chordata</u>
Class: <u>Mammalia</u>
Order: <u>Carnivora</u>
Family: <u>Felidae</u>
Genus: *Smilodon*
Three species: *populator, fatalis, and gracilis*
Binomial name:
*Smilodon . *.*

## Wow Facts

- Plains of North and South America. 2.5 million years ago to 10,000 years ago.
- Smilodon was a large, muscular predator that may well have snacked on early humans as well as young and old Woolly Mammoths and Giant Sloths of the Pliocene and Pleistocene epochs.
- Although Smilodon is referred to by most people as the saber-toothed tiger, this prehistoric mammal wasn't a true tiger at all, belonging instead to an ancient, long-extinct line of cat-like creatures known as "machairodonts".
- Smilodon were heavy, shorter than lions, had a short bobbed tail, and were most likely ambush hunters that leapt out at the last minute and fatally sunk their saber-like teeth into the neck or belly of massive herbivores such as the giant elk *Megaloceros*, prehistoric cows *Auroch*, giant camels, giant bison, and other large megafaunal beasts.
- Saber-toothed lineages also appeared in other mammals of the order Creodonta and marsupials in the upper Miocene to Pliocene and were all examples of convergent evolution.
- Smilodons were very specialized precision hunters that could bring down large prey. They died out about 10,000 years ago when early human hunters began to expand their range and many large

megafaunal animals became extinct.

- In case you're wondering why Smilodons have appeared in so many movies, it may be because thousands of intact Smilodon skeletons have been extracted from the *La Brea Tar Pits* in Los Angeles, a fossilized stone's throw from Hollywood and the California variant of this genus, *Smilodon californicus*, is the official state fossil.
- Some of their bones show signs that they were once wounded and recovered with time, suggesting they might have lived in communities similar to African lions.

*Smilodon*
Saber-Toothed Cat

# Synthetoceras

Kingdom: Animalia
Phylum: Chordata
Class: Mammalia
Order: Artiodactyla
Family: Protoceratidae
Genus: *Synthetoceras*
Species: *tricornatus*
Binomial name:
***Synthetoceras***
***tricornatus***

## Wow Facts

- Lived on the plains of North America during the Miocene epoch 13.6-5.33 million years ago; a total of 8.27 million years
- **Herbivore**.
- Males had a set of normal looking horns behind their eyes, and a long horn on their snout that ended in a Y shape.
- Like modern deer, Synthetoceras seems to have lived in large herds, where the males maintained dominance (and competed for females) according to the size and impressiveness of their horns.
- Synthetoceras was the latest, and largest, member of the obscure family of artiodactyls (even-toed ungulates) known as protoceratids; they lived a few million years after Protoceras and Syndyoceras and was at least double their size.

# Trigonias

| |
|---|
| Kingdom: Animalia |
| Phylum: Chordata |
| Class: Mammalia |
| Order: Perissodactyla |
| Family: Rhinocerotidae |
| Genus: Trigonias |
| Species: osborni |
| **Binomial Name:** *Trigonias osborni* |

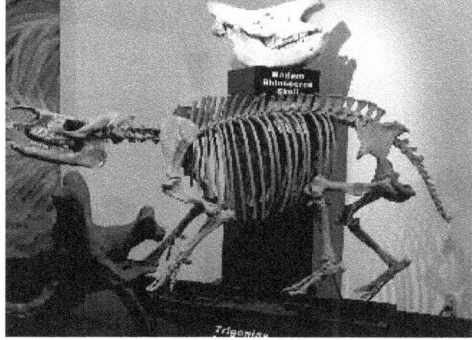

## Wow Facts

- Plains of North America and Western Europe Late Eocene-Early Oligocene (35-30 million years ago).
- **Herbivore**
- It was a prehistoric rhinoceros that lacked a nasal horn.
- It had five-toes on the front feet.

111

# Uintatherium

| |
|---|
| Kingdom: <u>Animalia</u><br>Phylum: <u>Chordata</u><br>Class: <u>Mammalia</u><br>Order: <u>Dinocerata</u><br>Family:<br><u>Uintatheriidae</u><br>Genus:<br><u>Uintatherium</u><br>Species: <u>*anceps*</u><br>**Binomial**<br>**Name:**<br>*Uintatherium*<br>*anceps* |

## Wow Facts

- Plains of North America in the Eocene epoch, 52-37 million years ago.
- **Herbivore**
- Uintatherium was one of the first prehistoric megafauna mammals ever to be discovered in the late-nineteenth-century.
- This plant-eating beast had large upper canine teeth that were larger in males than females and resembled those of saber-tooth tigers.
- Males had six ossicones (Giraffe like horns) that grew in the frontal region of the skull.
- Their cranium walls were thick and had many sinuses to lighten the overall weight, but this thickness left a smaller than average cranial cavity that housed a very small brain.

# International Wildlife Gallery

# Monkey Business Section

# Gelada Baboon

| | |
|---|---|
| Kingdom: <u>Animalia</u><br>Phylum: <u>Chordata</u><br>Class: <u>Mammalia</u><br>Order: <u>Primates</u><br>Family:<br>        <u>Cercopitheci<br>        dae</u><br>Genus:<br>        <u>Theropithec<br>        us</u><br>Species: <u>gelada</u><br>**Binomial Name:**<br>***Theropithecus<br>        gelada*** | |

## Wow Facts

- Gelada baboons live in Northern Ethiopia and Eritrea, especially in the Semien Mountains National Park.
- They prefer mountain grasslands and rocky areas. For safety from predators, they spend their nights sleeping on rocky cliffs and during daylight forage in nearby grasslands.
- Gelada baboons are **herbivores,** and eat grass blades, grass rhizomes, seeds, fruits, tubers, flowers and stems.
- While they live in large groups composed of up to four hundred individuals, their smaller family unit consists of one male, several females, and their offspring.
- They have short brown fur. Both males and females have a hairless patch on their chests, usually triangular in shape, which is outlined by white hairs.
- Males have whiskers and long hair on their head like a rock star, and a brown hairy mantle that hangs down well below their shoulders.
- The dexterity of their opposable first two digits allows them to pick and sort between single grass blades better than other lower primates.
- Life span in captivity is 30 years.

# Barbary Ape
# (Barbary Macaque)

| Kingdom: Animalia<br>Phylum: Chordata<br>Class: Mammalia<br>Order: Primates<br>Family: Cercopithecidae<br>Genus: *Macaca*<br>Species: *sylvanus*<br>Binomial Name:<br>***Macaca sylvanus*** | |

## Wow Facts

- They are found in Northern Africa in Algeria, Morocco, and across the strait in Gibraltar. They prefer forests such as oak, cedar, scrub, high atlas forests, gorges, as well as cliff habitats.
- These **omnivores** eat fruit, young leaves, bark, roots, and invertebrates, and store some food in cheek pouches.
- Their diet changes during the year and they leave the trees to feed on caterpillars in the spring, and eat fallen fruit, roots, and fungi in the summer.
- It is the only primate, other than humans, to live in Europe "Gibraltar" although it was once found all over southern Europe. It is also the only macaque found outside of Asia.
- Barbary macaques in cold climates are covered with thick yellowish-gray to dark grayish-brown fur.
- Their primary predators are eagles.
- Lifespan in the wild is 22 years.

# Anubis Baboons

| | |
|---|---|
| Kingdom: Animalia<br>Phylum: Chordata<br>Class: Mammalia<br>Order: Primates<br>Family: Cercopithecidae<br>Genus: *Papio*<br>Species: *anubis*<br>**Binomial Name:**<br>*Papio anubis* | |

## Wow Facts

- Anubis baboons or Olive baboons are found in savannah, grassland, and rainforest habitats.
- They have an elongated face that makes them resemble the Egyptian god Anubis.
- Males have long canine teeth and a long haired mane.
- These **omnivores** eat seeds, flowers, fruits, grass, rhizomes, roots, tubers, tree gums, insects, eggs, rodents, hares, foxes, antelopes, sheep, goats, other primates, and small vertebrates.
- They have a cheek pouch to store food.
- Baboons communicate with one another by facial expressions as well as by almost a dozen separate vocalizations.
- Members of a **troop** do everything together including travel, eat, fight/defend, and even sleep together. An average troop may consist of 15 to 150 individuals.
- As far as monkeys go, they are one of the largest.
- Average lifespan is 25 years in captivity
- Predators include: Leopards and chimpanzees.

# Vervet Monkeys

| |
|---|
| Kingdom: <u>Animalia</u><br>Phylum: <u>Chordata</u><br>Class: <u>Mammalia</u><br>Order: <u>Primates</u><br>Family:<br>　　　<u>Cercopitheci<br>　　　dae</u><br>Genus: <u>*Chlorocebes*</u><br>Species: <u>*aethiops*</u><br>**Binomial Name:**<br>***Chlorocebus<br>　　aethiops*** |

## Wow Facts

- They are found in Senegal, Somalia, Ethiopia, and down to South Africa.
- They are typically found in wooded areas near water sources such as streams, rivers, and lakes. During the dry season they must drink water daily.
- These **omnivores** eat almost everything and anything including: leaves, young shoots, bark, flowers, fruit, bulb, roots, grass seeds, insects, grubs, eggs, baby birds, rodents, and hares.
- They are known to steal food from human settlements and don't mind raiding human crops.
- These old world monkeys travel together in groups of 10 to 70 members.
- They can be spiteful to one another, and exhibit human-like characteristics such as hypertension, anxiety, and alcohol abuse. Yes, they will steal alcohol too.
- Because of humans transporting them as pets, they are now found in many Caribbean nations such as Bermuda, Bahamas, Cuba, Jamaica, Haiti, St. Kitts and Nevis, and in warmer climate states such as Texas, Florida, Alabama, Louisiana, Arizona, and California.
- Predators include: leopards, snakes, raptors, and baboons.

# GOATS AND SHEEP Section

# Musk Ox

Kingdom: <u>Animalia</u>
Phylum: <u>Chordata</u>
Class: <u>Mammalia</u>
Order: <u>Artiodactyla</u>
Family: <u>Bovidae</u>
Genus: *Ovibos*
Species: *moschatus*
**Binomial Name:**
***Ovibos moschatus***

## Wow Facts

- *The Musk Ox* is a circumpolar species native to Canada and Greenland and up until the late 1800's, Alaska. The musk ox is the poster species of the Arctic tundra.
- They were reintroduced to Alaska from animals captured in Greenland in the 1930's. Musk oxen have also been introduced into Russia, Svalbard, Norway, and Siberia. Some herds have also found their own way from Norway into Sweden.
- These **herbivores** are grazers. In the summer they eat arctic willows, grasses, leafy plants, sedges, mosses, shrubs, and herbs. In the winter they eat willow, dwarf birch stems, and anything they can find under the snow including roots, mosses, and lichens.
- They are related to sheep and goats more than they are to oxen.
- Their thick coat provides excellent insulation. They use their short stocky legs with large rounded hooves to sure footedly move through snow.
- Both males and females have horns that grow longer with age. The cream to caramel colored wide horns grow out from the center of the head, then narrow and flow down the side the head, and then curve back up to end in sharp black tips.
- They are very social and live in harem breeding herds of up to five animals during the summer and they join other groups to form herds of up to 60

members in the winter.
- Musk Ox, bison, and pronghorn sheep represent a few species that survived the cold Pliestocene period. The fossils of two other extinct species of musk ox can still be found south of the Arctic in Montana, and their horns are on display at the Museum of the Rockies in Bozeman.
- Musk ox can run up to 60km/h (37mph).
- Females live 12-20 years. Males live 10-12 years.
- Their known predators are polar bears, grizzly/brown bears, and arctic wolves. Old and young also die due to the harsh environment.

# Tahr (Himalayan tahr)

Kingdom: Animalia
Phylum: Chordata
Class: Mammalia
Order: Artiodactyla
Family: Bovidae
Genus: *Hemitragus*
Species: *jemlahicus*

**Binomial Name:**
***Hemitragus***
       ***jemlahicus***

## Wow Facts

- Tahrs are found on the southern side of the Himalaya Mountains in northern India, Bhutan, and Tibet.
- Tahr were introduced in New Zealand in 1904 and since then, New Mexico, California, Ontario, South Africa, and Argentina in 2006.
- The tahr is an **herbivore**. Similar to a cow, they have a multi-chambered stomach that allows them to regurgitate their food and chew it again to break the food down even further and collect even more nutrients.
- Their hooves have a sharp outer edge and a rubbery core so they won't slip on smooth surfaces.
- They live in herds of 2-23 animals.
- Males have longer horns than females.
- Females live longer than males.
- Average lifespan is 10-14 years in the wild, 15 to 22 years in captivity.
- In the Himalayas, its top predator is the snow leopard. In New Zealand and elsewhere its top predator is humans.

# Altai Argali
# (subspecies of Argali)

| Kingdom: Animalia<br>Phylum: Chordata<br>Class: Mammalia<br>Order: Artiodactyla<br>Family: Bovidae<br>Genus: *Ovis*<br>Species: *ammon*<br>**Binomial Name: *Ovis*<br>*ammon*** | |

## Wow Facts

- They are found in the mountains of central Asia.
- Argali sheep are **herbivorous** and feed on grasses, herbs, and sedges.
- These grazers have adapted to survive in arid, windy and extreme climates of high altitudes above 1000m.
- Altai argali are the largest of all sheep and the horns of males can weigh up to 35kg (75 lb).
- Ewe or females may weigh half as much as a male ram. Females also have smaller horns.
- This species has a wide range with nine localized subspecies recognized. The one on display at the museum is found in the Altai Mountains in Siberia.
- Females are usually found in groups or herds of 2-100 animals. Males may form herds of 3 to 30 individuals. The herds remain separate until the breeding season.
- Their lifespan is 5 to 10 years in the wild, but some may live up to 13 years.
- Predators include: gray wolves, snow leopards, and leopards. Occasionally they are hunted by lynx and wolverines. They have also been heavily hunted by humans for their meat and for their horns which are used in Chinese medicine.

# Mountain Goat

Kingdom: Animalia
Phylum: Chordata
Class: Mammalia
Order: Artiodactyla
Family: Bovidae
Genus: *Oreamnos*
Species: *americanus*

**Binomial Name:**
***Oreamnos americanus***

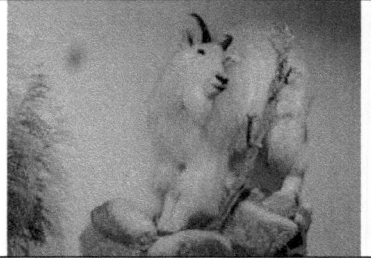

## Wow Facts

- Mountain goats are found in alpine or sub-alpine areas of Alaska, British Columbia down the Cascade mountain range to Oregon State, and over to western Montana, and central Idaho. They prefer steep cliffs, bluffs, and hard to access rocky or broken terrain locations.
- They have also been introduced to parts of South Dakota, Colorado, and re-introduced to parts of Washington State.
- Although their diet varies throughout the year, it generally consists of grasses, ferns, woody plants, mosses, lichens, herbaceous plants, and other vegetation. They get most of their water from their food, and year-round snow banks.
- Mountain goats may converge into large groups in the winter at lower elevations or near salt lick areas in the spring with nursery groups of kids. By late summer they disperse into smaller groups or go their own way with offspring to higher elevations. They are active at dawn, rest mid-day, and then resume activities until dusk.
- Both sexes have beards and horns. The best way to tell them apart at a distance is that females squat to urinate.
- Their horns increase in size every winter after the first year, making it easy to determine their age by counting the number of annual growth rings.
- Life span is 12-15 years in the wild or when their

teeth wear down to the gum line and 16 to 20 years in captivity.

- Known predators include: Cougars, grizzly bears, wolves, golden eagles, coyotes, black bears, and bobcats.

# Saiga Antelope

Kingdom: Animalia
Phylum: Chordata
Class: Mammalia
Order: Artiodactyla
Family: Bovidae
Genus: *Saiga*
Species: *tatarica*

Binomial Name:
*Saiga tatarica*

## Wow Facts

- Saiga antelope were once found all over Western Europe Eurasia, and into Alaska, but are currently found concentrated in central Asia: Mongolia, Kazakhstan, and Kalmykia. They prefer dry steppes and semi deserts where herds feed in large grassy plains.
- Besides grasses, these **herbivores** feed on prostrate summer cypress, saltworts, fobs, sagebrush, and steppe lichens; in all, over one hundred different plant species make up their diet.
- After the day's activities, they dig a shallow hole to rest in for the night.
- Their large flexible nose is used to filter out dust and cool their blood during the summer months when they form herds with thousands of other saiga and dust is kicked up from hooves, fills the air. In the winter their nose is used to warm the air before reaching their lungs. Their fur is longer in the winter and shorter during the summer.
- Males have waxy colored horns that are ringed along their length. During the mating season males are too busy fighting each other to bother with eating.
- One male may lead a herd of 5 to 50 females.
- By the 1920's they were almost hunted to extinction. Chinese use the male's horns for traditional medicine much like rhino horns, and this lucrative practice led to the Chinese population becoming exterminated.
- Life span is 6-10 years in the wild.

# Urial

| |
|---|
| Kingdom: Animalia |
| Phylum: Chordata |
| Class: Mammalia |
| Order: Artiodactyla |
| Family: Bovidae |
| Genus: *Ovis* |
| Species: *orientalis* |
| Trinomial Name: |
| ***Ovis orientalis vignei*** |

## Wow Facts

- Urial sheep are widely distributed in Russia, Pakistan, northern India and Asia. Urial sheep inhabit steep to undulating grassy terrain.
- These sheep are mainly diurnal, and spend most of the day foraging or looking for food.
- Urial are herbivorous consuming mainly grasses, leaves, and shrubs. They will also eat grains.
- Urials are considered to be members of the antelope family.
- They are brown colored with a lighter coat in summer than in winter. They have a distinct white rump patch below the base of the tail and along the back of the hind quarters. Urial sheep have a black and white saddle patch.
- Males have a black neck ruff in the front of the neck area. Males have massive curly horns; female horns tend to be smaller and flatter.
- Males/rams are usually solitary, but during mating season they will band with 4 to 5 females/ewes. Lambs are born five months later.
- Lifespan of urial sheep ranges from 8 to 12 years.

# Gredos Ibex
# (Western Spanish Ibex)

Kingdom: Animalia
Phylum: Chordata
Class: Mammalia
Order: Artiodactyla
Family: Bovidae
Genus: *Capra*
Species: *pyrenaica*

Trinomial Name:
***Capra pyrenaica victoriae***

## Wow Facts

- Found in the Carzorla-Segura and Eastern Sierra Nevada mountain ranges on the Iberian Peninsula, Spain. In northern Portugal only a 100 individuals remain in the Peneda-Geres National Park.
- This subspecies of the Spanish Ibex prefers coniferous and deciduous forested areas with rock outcroppings and rugged terrains with steep slopes.
- This **herbivore** forages for herbaceous plants such as grasses and shrubs, although its diet may vary depending on the availability of resources.
- Gredos Ibex has large flexible cloven hooves that are said to work like suction cups on steep slopes. Their legs are short and extremely maneuverable.
- Their specialized kidneys store fat for winter.
- Males are larger than females. Both sexes have curved horns, but male semi-curved horns are much larger.
- Spanish ibex exhibit herding behavior. They stop and stare at predators, then call out to warn others. They also tend to follow the oldest female when escaping danger.
- A cloned Pyrenean subspecies was born alive in January 2009, unfortunately, it died a few minutes after birth due to lung defects.
- They can live 12-16 years in the wild.
- Predator: Primarily humans.

# Persian Ibex
# (Wild Goat)

| |
|---|
| Kingdom: Animalia<br>Phylum: Chordata<br>Class: Mammalia<br>Order: Artiodactyla<br>Family: Bovidae<br>Genus: *Capra*<br>Species: *aegagrus*<br>Trinomial Name:<br>***Capra aegagrus aegagrus*** | |

## Wow Facts

- This **Herbivore** is also known as the Bezoar Ibex.
- Their preferred habitat is the steep, rocky slopes and the sheer cliffs of countless mountains in Iran, but they are also native to Afghanistan, Armenia, Russia, Georgia, Azerbaijan, Iraq, and from Crete and Turkey to southern Pakistan.
- The Persian ibex is one of the most prized trophies of hunters in the world today.
- In 1970 they were introduced to the Florida Mountains of New Mexico where they thrived and became popular for hunters.
- A few Persian Ibex colonies were later introduced into a few other areas, but many individuals interbred with other species of ibex and so the colonies are less pure as those of New Mexico.
- The horns of the males are scimitar-shaped and can reach 140 cm (4.6ft) long. The female ibex are much smaller and have short horns, rarely more than 20 cm (8 inches) long.
- Ibex that live in the dessert are smaller in size.
- Similar to other animals used in Asian based traditional medicinal use, most body parts of the ibex were once thought to cure ailments and diseases.
- Descendents of the Bezoar goat were domesticated some 10,000 years ago.

# Beceite Ibex
# (Southeastern Spanish Ibex)

Kingdom: Animalia
Phylum: Chordata
Class: Mammalia
Order: Artiodactyla
Family: Bovidae
Genus: *Capra*
Species: *pyrenaica*

Trinomial Name:
***Capra pyrenaica hispanica***

## Wow Facts

- Endemic to Spain. Found in the Carzorla-Segura and Eastern Sierra Nevada mountain ranges above 800m (2600 ft) on the Iberian Peninsula, Spain. Like other ibex, they prefer rock outcrops, sheer cliffs, and rocky areas of coniferous and deciduous forests that are inaccessible to most predators such as humans.
- Spanish ibex feed primarily by browsing. They forage on Holm oaks, acorns, plants and grasses.
- This is a subspecies of the Spanish Ibex which has four subspecies. Of these, two can still be found on the Iberian Peninsula, but the remaining two are now extinct. The Portuguese subspecies became extinct in 1892 and the Pyrenean subspecies became extinct on January 6, 2000.
- A cloned Pyrenean subspecies was born alive in January 2009, unfortunately, it died a few minutes after birth due to lung defects.
- Spanish ibex exhibit herding behavior.
- It is a true wild goat.
- Males are larger than females. Both sexes have horns, but males horns can reach 75cm (2.46 ft) or longer.
- Historically, they were found in southern France and Portugal as well.
- Spanish ibex can live 12-16 years in the wild. Young are hunted by foxes and eagles; adults by hunters.

# Dall's Sheep

| |
|---|
| Kingdom: <u>Animalia</u><br>Phylum: <u>Chordata</u><br>Class: <u>Mammalia</u><br>Order: <u>Artiodactyla</u><br>Family: <u>Bovidae</u><br>Genus: *Ovis*<br>Species: *dalli*<br>**Binomial Name:**<br>***Ovis dalli*** |

## Wow Facts

- Native to North America, Dall's sheep are solid white in color to blend in with the arctic and sub-arctic regions and in high Alpine mountain ranges with steep slopes and rocky cliffs in western Canada such as in the Yukon, British Columbia, and in Alaska in the United States.

- Dall's sheep are **herbivores**, grazing on lowland grasses and sedge meadows in the summer; in winter they eat lichens and moss.

- They are one of two species of thin horn mountain sheep; the other species is Stone's sheep.

- The horns can be either amber or almost transparent. Females/ewes have slender slightly curved horns, while male/ram horns are massive, flaring, and growing fully circular curled by age 7-8.

- Ovis dalli have a well developed social system. Ewes live in flocks with other ewes, lambs, yearlings and immature rams.

- Adult rams live in bachelor groups until mating season in late November to early December. Dominant males breed with multiple females. Lambs are born in late May to early June.

- Rams may live up to 16 years and ewes 19 years, but 12 years is typical.

- Predators include: wolves, coyotes, black bears, grizzly bears, and for small lambs: golden eagles as well.

# Stone's Sheep
# (Ovis dalli stonei)

Kingdom: Animalia
Phylum: Chordata
Class: Mammalia
Order: Artiodactyla
Family: Bovidae
Genus: *Ovis*
Species: *dalli*

Trinomial Name:
*Ovis dalli stonei*

## Wow Facts

- *Ovis dalli stonei* includes populations found in south-central Yukon and north-central British Columbia.
- Dall's sheep are **herbivores**, grazing primarily on grasses and sedge meadows in the summer; in winter lichens and moss.
- This is a subspecies of Dall's sheep and Stone's sheep are darker than the other subspecies of Dall's sheep to blend in with lower level wooded areas.
- Ovis dalli are the only two species of "thin horn" mountain sheep. The horns can be either amber or almost transparent. Females have slender horns, while male horns are massive, flaring, and curled, but thinner than Big Horn sheep.
- Ewes/females live in flocks with other ewes, lambs, yearlings and immature rams.
- Adult rams live in bachelor groups until mating season in late November to early December. Dominant males breed with multiple females. Lambs are born in late May to early June.
- Males treat all sheep with smaller horns as subordinates.
- In the past, gold hunters and road builders hunted them heavily.

# Blue Sheep/Bharal

| |
|---|
| Kingdom: Animalia |
| Phylum: Chordata |
| Class: Mammalia |
| Order: Artiodactyla |
| Family: Bovidae |
| Genus: *Pseudois* |
| Species: *nayaur* |

**Binomial Name:**
*Pseudois nayaur*

## Wow Facts

- Bharals or Himalayan blue sheep are found along the Himalayas of India, Nepal, Bhutan, China, and Pakistan.  They live near rocky cliffs and steppe slopes to escape predators and for this reason they also stay away from forests.
- They feed on dry grasses, forbs, and lichens in the winter, and alpine grasses in the summer.
- Their short dense **coat** is of grayish-brown to slate-blue color, hence the common name blue sheep.
- The bluish color makes them camouflaged and they appear almost invisible as they stand motionless against their native blue-grayish rocky steeps.
- Like bighorn sheep, these **herbivores** can tolerate environmental extremes from searing heat to windy and cold slopes that are inhospitable to most animals. They may come down to lower elevations in search of water.
- Male horns sweep up and outwards, then curve back before curling at the tip. Females have shorter and straighter horns.
- There are now 40 species of caprids (goat-antelopes). They had the greatest diversity in the ice ages. 47 extinct species are known.
- Average lifespan is 12-16 years.
- Predators include:  Snow Leopards and grey wolves. Lambs are hunted by foxes and eagles.

# Desert Bighorn Sheep

Kingdom: Animalia
Phylum: Chordata
Class: Mammalia
Order: Artiodactyla
Family: Bovidae
Genus: *Ovis*
Species: *canadensis*

Trinomial Name:
***Ovis Canadensis nelsoni***

## Wow Facts

- They prefer alpine meadows, high altitude grassy slopes and foothills adjacent to steep cliffs, rocky terrain, and mountain bluffs They cannot live in areas where snow covers the ground vegetation.
- *Ovis canadensis* is found in the Rocky Mountains from southern Canada to Colorado, and as a desert subspecies (O. c. nelsoni) from Nevada and California to west Texas and south into Mexico.
- These **herbivores** eat a variety of desert plants and in the winter they get most of their moisture from the vegetation they eat and/or from water in seasonal rock pools. In the summer they may need to drink water every three days.
- They can become dehydrated and lose up to 30 percent of their body weight, but then recover rapidly after drinking water. Few predators if any can stand or survive such conditions and harsh environments.
- They only need a 5cm (2 inch) wide ledges to gain enough foot hold to jump from ledge to ledge at distances over 6m (20ft) wide.
- They can go 48 km/h (30mph) and run up slopes at 24km/h (15 mph). They are also good swimmers even with heavy horns.
- Male/ **rams** have large set of curling horns while female/ **ewes** have straighter, smaller, and lighter horns. The horns of rams have annual growth rings

that reveal their age, health, and fighting history. The desert subspecies, *Ovis canadensis nelsoni*, is somewhat smaller and has flatter, wider-spreading horns.

- An eight-year-old ram may have horns 1m (3ft) wide and the horns may weigh over 14kg (30lb).
- Both rams and ewes use their horns to rub off sharp spines and break open cacti such as pear cactus, but they prefer to eat grasses if available.
- Rams have double-layered skulls reinforced for hitting one another at up to 32 km/h (20mph).
- The coat of *Ovis canadensis* is bright brown in the summer time and becomes faded by winter.
- Bighorn sheep may gather in **herds** of over 100 individuals, although small groups of 8 to 10 are more common.
- In the wild females may live 10-19 years. Males 6-12 years.
- Predators include: bears, wolves, mountain lions, and eagles for the young.
- Tourists seasonally stop at Hemenway Valley Park near Boulder Dam (Boulder City, NV) in the morning to view and take pictures of a herd consisting of more than 65 members. Many of them wear collars for scientific study; the bighorn sheep that is. They may walk right by you as they have become accustomed to the presence of humans in close proximity, but it is best to keep a safe distance from them as they are wild animals and may act unpredictable if they perceive that they are being threatened or harassed by paparazzi, especially the males; the big horn sheep that is.

# Zebra
# (Hartmann's Mountain Zebra)

Kingdom: Animalia
Phylum: Chordata
Class: Mammalia
Order: Perissodactyla
Family: Equidae
Genus: *Equus*
Species: *zebra*

Trinomial Name:
***Equus zebra hartmannae***

## Wow Facts

- Hartmann's mountain zebras are found in Nimibia, South West Africa and Angola. They prefer dry regions of mountainous slopes and plateaus on the edge of the Namibia Desert.
- They are **herbivores** and primarily eat grass, but will also consume bark, twigs leaves, buds, fruit, and roots.
- Zebras are dark skinned. Their hair is pigmented black forming stripes. Non pigmented hair appears as white bands between stripes. Their belly is white (no stripes).
- The stripes on the head and body are narrow. The stripes are fewer and wider on the rump. The legs are stripped down to the hooves. Their muzzle is black.
- They live in small social groups of either breeding herds (harems) or in exclusive bachelor (all male) groups. Several of the breeding herd home ranges may overlap each other.
- Because they need to drink daily, they will dig in dry river beds to find water.
- Their life span is 20 years in the wild and up to 30 years in captivity.
- Predators include: Crocodiles, Lions, Leopards, Cheetahs, Spotted Hyenas, and Hunting Dogs. However, loss of habitat is their main threat.

# PECCARIES AND PIGS

# JUVENILE PIG

| Kingdom: Animalia |
| --- |
| Phylum: Chordata |
| Class: Mammalia |
| Order: Artiodactyla |
| Family: Suidae |

## Wow Facts

- Sixteen species of pigs and hogs in eight genera make up the modern family Suidae. Suids originally occurred across Eurasia south of 48° N, on islands as far away as the Philippines and Sulawesi, Indonesia, and throughout Africa. Humans have introduced the Eurasian wild boar, from which the domesticated pigs are derived, in a variety of places around the world, including North America, New Zealand, New Guinea, and Hawaii.

- Other related species are the wild boar, peccary, babirusa, and warthog. Males are called boars and females are called sows.

- Fossil suids are known from the Oligocene (33.9 million years ago) of Europe and Asia and the Miocene (23-5.33 million years ago) of Africa.

- They were domesticated 5000-7000 years ago.

- Pigs are **omnivores**, and their diet includes fungi, leaves, roots, bulb, tubers, fruit, snails, earthworms, small vertebrates, eggs, and carrion.

- They use their muscular, mobile snout and forefeet to dig for food. They have a non-ruminating two-chambered stomach.

- Older pigs can drink up to 19 L (5 gallons) of water each day.

- Most species are gregarious and highly intelligent. They cannot sweat, so they take mud baths to cool down.

- The upper canines grow out and backward into large, curved tusks; wear between the upper and lower canines produces sharp edges. The upper canines are ever-growing.

# Peccaries
# (Chacoan Peccary)

| |
|---|
| Kingdom: <u>Animalia</u> |
| Phylum: <u>Chordata</u> |
| Class: <u>Mammalia</u> |
| Order: <u>Artiodactyla</u> |
| Family: <u>Tayassuidae</u> |
| Genus: *Catagonus* |
| Species: *wagneri* |
| Binomial Name: |
| ***Catagonus wagneri*** |

## Wow Facts

- Endemic to the South American Gran Chaco area of Paraguay, Bolivia, and Argentina. They are confined to hot, dry areas impenetrable and untouched by humans.

- These peccaries feed on various species of cacti and gains essential minerals like calcium, magnesium, and chlorine from the salt licks. Their kidneys are specialized to break down acids from cacti.

- These social mammals communicate by various sounds ranging from grunts to chatter of the teeth (tusks).

- They often travel in herds of up to 20 individuals, and even though individuals may occasionally exhibit aggressive behavior like charging and biting, this species is less aggressive than other peccaries.

- They have a tough, leathery snout. They have brown to gray bristle-like fur. A dark stripe runs along the back. White fur may be present on the forehead, the mouth and lower jaw, and white fur may run up along the front shoulders. Tusks are short and straight.

- C. wagneri differs from other peccary species by having longer ears, snout, and tail. C. wagneri also possesses a third hind toe, while other peccaries only have two.

- They are also called Skunk pigs because of their scent glands under their eyes.

# Southern Bush Pig

| Kingdom: Animalia<br>Phylum: Chordata<br>Class: Mammalia<br>Order: Artiodactyla<br>Family: Suidae<br>Genus: *Potamochoerus*<br>Species: *larvatus*<br>Trinomial Name:<br>***Potamochoerus larvatus nyasa*** |  |

## Wow Facts

- The Potamochoerus river pigs range from Somalia to eastern and southern former Zaire, Ethiopia' Southern DK Congo and southwards to Cape Province KwaZulu - Natal province in South Africa as well as Madagascar and the Comoros archipelago.

- Bush pigs are shaggy and inhabit a wide range of habitats from sea-level woodlands, grasslands, and swamps to mountain forests (up to 4,000m (2.5miles).

- These **omnivores** feed on plant roots, water plants, rhizomes, bulb, tubers, fruits, and insect larvae, which are rooted from underground. They also consume a variety of invertebrates, smaller vertebrates, and carrion. Males have warts on their nose and their lower tusks can grow 7cm (3 inches) long.

- Bush pigs have adapted to human agricultural cultivated habitats and they enjoy planted food crops such as potatoes, maize, tomatoes, sugar cane, as well as other vegetables.

- They are mostly nocturnal, but they are known to forage during the day when temperatures are cooler.

- Bush pigs protect their territories vigorously. They have a mane that bristles when they are agitated.

- They live in "sounders" of up to 12 members with one dominant boar and sow, and with other females and juveniles.

- Life span is about 20 years in the wild. Predators include: humans, large cats, spotted hyenas, crocodiles, and pythons.

# MARSUPIALS

# Swamp Wallaby

| | |
|---|---|
| Kingdom: Animalia<br>Phylum: Chordata<br>Class: Mammalia<br>Order: Diprotodontia<br>Family: Macropodidae<br>Genus: *Wallabia*<br>Species: *Bicolor*<br>**Binomial Name:**<br>***Wallabia bicolor*** | |

## Wow Facts

- The swamp wallaby inhabits the east coast of Australia; Queensland down to Victoria. Swamp wallabies live in forests, thick woodlands, and swamp lands. These nocturnal animals may be seen at night in open areas where brush is nearby.
- Swamp wallabies are **herbivores**. Like raccoons, they use their short five digit forefeet to manipulate food. Their diet consists of soft plants such as buds, ferns, leaves, shrubs, bushes, grasses and agricultural crops. They also eat bark, shoots from needle-leaf trees, and plants such as brackens, hemlock, and lantana or shrub verbenas that are poisonous to domesticated animals,
- Swamp wallabies are solitary animals, but may feed in groups. They hop bipedally on their hind feet while holding their head close to the ground and with their tail held out straight behind them. They also use their forefeet to move around on all fours.
- The swamp wallaby has coarse fur that is gray or dark brown in color with darker or black limbs and tail. They may also have light yellowish cheek stripes that extend back to orange fur tufts around their ears.
- Gestation is 33-38 days. Young "joeys" stay in their mother's pouch for 8-9 months. They suckle for 15 months.
- Aboriginal people will not eat them because of their taste and smell after cooking swamp wallabies.
- Average life span is 12 years.

# Virginia Opossum

| |
|---|
| Kingdom: Animalia |
| Phylum: Chordata |
| Class: Mammalia |
| Order: Didelphimorphia |
| Family: Didelphidae |
| Genus: *Didelphis* |
| Species: *virginiana* |
| **Binomial Name:** |
| ***Didelphis virginiana*** |

## Wow Facts

- Common Ringtail opossums are found in North America, down through Mexico to Costa Rica in Central America, and up through southwestern Ontario Canada. Opossums were introduced to the west coast of the United States for food during the great depression.
- They are found in a variety of environments, but they prefer wet areas such as near streams or swamps.
- Opossums are **omnivores**, and include a wide variety of food in their diet. The majority of their diet is composed of insects, carrion, and snakes; they are resistant to snake venom. They also eat plants, including fruits and grains when in season.
- When threatened by dogs, foxes, or bobcats, opossums may feign death or coma, and lie on the ground with their eyes closed or staring fixedly into space for up to four hours.
- Females have a fur-lined pouch to carry their young "baby joey". The color and size of the opossum varies by the region.
- Opossums are nocturnal and have very poor social development. Females tend to live in groups, but the males fight when confined together. Groups of opossums are composed primarily of young because of their short life span two years in the wild and four years in captivity.
- They are preyed on by predators such as coyotes, foxes, large owls, and hawks. As young they may also be preyed on by snakes and smaller birds like falcons.

# Agile Wallaby

| | |
|---|---|
| Kingdom: Animalia<br>Phylum: Chordata<br>Class: Mammalia<br>Order: Diprotodontia<br>Family: Macropodidae<br>Genus: *Macropus*<br>Species: *agilis*<br>**Binomial Name:**<br>***Macropus agilis*** | |

## Wow Facts

- Also known as the Sandy Wallaby for its sandy color. The agile wallaby's range includes the Northern coastal and tropical areas of Australia, southern New Guinea, Southern Papua New Guinea, and neighboring islands. Habitats include open forests, dunes, heaths, adjacent grasslands, regions near rivers and streams, floodplains, and bilabongs.

- This species of wallabies organize into groups called "mobs," which are gregarious groups that are composed of many females that share resting and feeding areas. They are mainly nocturnal.

- Agile wallabies are extremely flexible and opportunistic feeders. During the wet season, agile wallabies eat a variety of native grasses, gumes, shrubs, and bushes. In the dry season they eat flowers, rose tips, azalea tips fruit tree tips and new roots, fruits, twigs, fallen leaves, and bark. They also eat seeds formerly digested through birds and agricultural plants such as sugarcane.

- They dig in holes in dry creeks to find water and thus avoid saltwater crocodiles found along river banks.

- They are yellowish-brown with a white cheek stripe and a white hip stripe.

- Gestation is 30 days. Young stay in mother's pouch 7-8 months.

- Life span in the wild ranges between 11-14 years.

- In New Guinea they are considered bush meat and killed in Australia as agricultural pests.

# PORCUPINES

# North American Porcupine

| Kingdom: Animalia<br>Phylum: Chordata<br>Class: Mammalia<br>Order: Rodentia<br>Family: Erethizontidae<br>Genus: *Erethizon*<br>Species: *dorsatum*<br>**Binomial Name:**<br>***Erethizon dorsatum*** | |
|---|---|

## Wow Facts

- They inhabit North America from the Arctic region down to northern Mexico. Porcupines live at various altitudes in the open tundra, forests, and deserts.
- Porcupines are nocturnal generalist **herbivores**. In the summer they eat twigs, roots, stems, skunk cabbage, clover, flowers, nuts, seeds, and berries. In the winter they eat conifer needles, tree bark, and the cambium layer (a layer beneath the bark) of trees.
- Some 30,000 hardened hairs with barbed tips called quills extend from head to tail on the dorsal surface, but not on the face, feet, or underbelly. Quills on the dorsal/back area are fringed with white, so just like wolverines and skunks, the white line will stand out at night, alerting color blind nocturnal predators of the danger they present. This pattern is visible after porcupines just are three months old.
- Infants are born one at a time and called a porqupette. An infant's quills harden an hour after birth.
- These slow and nearsighted rodents are the only mammal in North America that have antibiotics in their skin; presumably to help if they fall and poke themselves.
- They do not throw quills, they run backwards into a potential predator and the barbs pierce the predator's skin, and once embedded, the quills

detach from the porcupine.

- They are solitary most of the time. They make dens in hollow trees, rocky areas, caves, and inside logs. There is some sharing of dens in the winter. They do not hibernate; they just sleep a lot.
- There are 7 sub-species.
- Their ancestors rafted from Africa to Brazil some thirty million years ago then they wandered up to North America after the Isthmus of Panama rose three million years ago.
- They can live 20-30 years.
- Predators include: lynx, bobcats, coyotes, wolves, wolverines, golden eagles, and great horned owls. Important predators include mountain lions and fishers. Large male fishers will attack from the front repeatedly, avoiding the tail quills, until they are able to flip a porcupine on its back and attack the unprotected underside.
- Starvation and motor vehicles also take a large toll on North American porcupines.

# North African Porcupine

| Kingdom: Animalia |
| Phylum: Chordata |
| Class: Mammalia |
| Order: Rodentia |
| Family: Hystricidae |
| Genus: *Hystrix* |
| Species: *cristata* |
| **Binomial Name:** |
| *Hystrix cristata* |

## Wow Facts

- The North African Crested Porcupine is found in Italy, Sicily, Morocco, and along the Mediterranean coast of Africa to northern Zaire and Tanzania and down to South Africa. *They* are highly adaptable, and found in forests, rocky areas, mountains, croplands, and sand hill deserts.

- This nocturnal **herbivore** eats bark, roots, tubers, rhizomes, bulb, fallen fruits, and cultivated crops. They also consume insects, small vertebrates and carrion. They collect and gnaw on bones for the calcium and to keep frontal teeth sharp. Prehistoric fossils have been found inside their dens.

- They shelter in caves, rock crevices, aardvark holes, or burrows that they dig themselves. They rarely climb trees, but are able to swim.

- They are monogamous and take care to 1 to 3 offspring. Infant spines harden in one week. Small family groups, consisting of an adult pair, infants, and juveniles, share an elaborate burrow system that is used for many years.

- The head, neck, shoulders, limbs and underside of body are covered with coarse, dark brown or black bristles. The quills along the head, nape, and back can be raised into a crest. The stronger and longer quills on the back half of the body are marked with alternating light and dark bands. Tail quills can be rattled to make a warning "hissing" sound. They run backwards into attackers, and the spines are pressed in to the predator's flesh, which include: leopards, birds of prey, and hyenas.

148

# BEARS

# Polar Bear

Kingdom: <u>Animalia</u>
Phylum: <u>Chordata</u>
Class: <u>Mammalia</u>
Order: <u>Carnivora</u>
Family: <u>Bovidae</u>
Genus: *Ursus*
Species: *maritimus*

**Binomial Name:**
***Ursus maritimus***

## Wow Facts

- Polar bears inhabit the circumpolar ice ring also known as the Arctic Circle.
- Polar bears are **carnivores**. They primarily prey on ringed seals. They also hunt bearded seals, harbor seals, harp seals, hooded seals, walruses, belugas, narwhals, sea birds and their eggs, muskox, reindeer, small mammals, fish, crabs, clams, rodents, and scavenge on carrion of seals, walruses, and whales. They can eat and digest higher concentrations of fat than any other terrestrial animal.
- Females may enter a "maternity hibernation" state when pregnant and males may enter a walking hibernation and fast. Their inability to obtain rich fat resources can alter their feeding and fasting behavior as well as drive them to desperate hunting measures such as attacking full groan male walruses with little chance of success.
- They can smell seals a mile away, and three feet under snow and ice. When "still hunting" they just sit patiently for hours next to a seal breathing hole and wait for a seal to pop up and take a quick breath.
- Polar bear skin is black and the fur is actually clear, lacking in pigment. The white appearance is the result of light being refracted from the clear hair strands. Under the summer sun the fur may turn yellowish as the result of oxidation and/or age.

- Polar bears are considered marine mammals as they spend much of their time at sea moving from one ice pack to another. The name *Ursus maritimus* means maritime bear.
- They have been recorded swimming up to 354km (220 miles) at a time. One bear swam for nine days straight. A 10cm (4 inch) layer of blubber helps keep them warm and buoyant.
- They can dive underwater for 3 minutes at a time to reach seals or fish.
- The polar bear is large and stocky, similar to that of a brown bear, except it lacks the shoulder hump. They have large furry feet and short sharp claws, and the paws are covered with dermal bumps (papillae) and used for maintaining traction. The hands are naturally scooped shaped to move large amounts of ice more efficiently.
- Males (boars) are almost twice the size of females (sows). The long hair on the male's forearms is similar to the mane of a male lion and appears to be a desirable trait for females in choosing a suitor.
- Polar bears are solitary except when a mother is caring for her cubs and when couples are mating.
- They can run 40km/h (25mph) for short distances, but their average speed is 5.6 km/h (3.5mph).
- The bear family split 38 million years ago and polar bears and brown bears split 4-5 million years ago. Polar bear mitochondria DNA diverged around 150,000 years ago. The oldest polar bear fossil is considered 130,000- 110,000 years ago. Polar bear teeth changed significantly 20,000 years ago, so they are considered a recently new species and still evolving.
- The extinct species *Ursus maritimus tryrannus* was even larger than the current 19 subspecies of polar bear.
- Near some locations polar bears and brown bears still produce viable hybrid offspring.

- They can live 25 to 32 years in the wild, but one female (sow) in captivity lived to be 42 years of age.
- Humans and other polar bears are their only predators. Their liver is extremely poisonous because of the high concentration of vitamin A. Loss of habitat through global warming, pollution, and the encroachment of civilization are the main issues threatening their long term survival.

# Brown Bear (Grizzly Bear)

| |
|---|
| Kingdom: <u>Animalia</u><br>Phylum: <u>Chordata</u><br>Class: <u>Mammalia</u><br>Order: <u>Carnivora</u><br>Family: <u>Bovidae</u><br>Genus: *Ursus*<br>Species: *arctos*<br>**Binomial Name:**<br>***Ursus arctos*** |

## Wow Facts

- Brown bears have a pronounced hump on their shoulders and are the largest land based predator, but only because Polar bears are considered marine mammals. The Kamchatka Brown Bear is thought to be the ancestor of Polar bears.

- Northern North American Brown bear populations in Alaska and western Canada are doing fine, but populations in the United States have been extirpated, including those of the Sierra Nevada and southern Rockies. There are also small populations in Western Europe, Palestine to eastern Siberia, the Gobi desert and the Himalayan region, and they are now also extinct in Northern Africa.

- Brown bears live wherever human hunters are few or seldom explore. They live in remote diverse habitats from desert edges to high mountain forests, scrublands, open plains, prairies, and ice fields.

- Their biting force may be as much as 7,998 kPa (1160 PSI), which is enough to crush a bowling ball, let alone an animal skull.

- Brown bears are **omnivores**, eating almost anything available and nutritious from berries, crabs, clams, deer, grasses, wild boar, insects, and caribou. Their diet changes with the seasons, but injured, sick, or young bison, big horn sheep, moose, elk, and black bear are prime prey candidates. They dig with their long barely curved claws to find roots and bulb and will scavenge or steal kills made by other bears, wolves, and mountain lions.

- They gather at coastal streams, lakes, rivers, and ponds while salmon are spawning. They only eat the rich fat, eggs, and brains of the fish and leave the rest of the salmon to be scattered around the forest floor and give nitrogen back to the soil, so that the great trees will grow, and forests will be able to accommodate more life. In this way, they are a keystone predator.
- There are now 16 sub species with coastal bears weighing many times as much as smaller inland brown bears.
- They prefer to forage in the morning and evening and rest during the day in thick cover or dug out depressions.
- Because adults are too big to climb trees, they will stand their ground if attacked.
- Brown bears may become inactive from October to December until March or May. They may enter a deep sleep, and their body temperature may drop a few degrees, but they may still awake if confronted. In areas where food is plentiful, they may not feel the need to hibernate.
- Their fur is typically dark brown, but some are cream colored or black. Individuals in the Rocky Mountains have long hairs on their shoulders and back that appears frosted white, golden colored, or grizzled.
- They derived in Asia 800,000 years ago, went into Alaska 100,000 years ago, and down south 13,000 years ago after the extinction of *Arctodu simus*. At least two groups of brown bears entered North America; Grizzlies from Northern Siberia, and Broad skull Kodiaks from Kamchatka.
- Female brown bears usually live longer; up to 47 years in captivity and 20 to 30 years in the wild. Unfortunately, one study showed that 13-49% of cubs die within the first year of life.
- Predators include humans and other brown bears.

# American Black Bear

| |
|---|
| Kingdom: Animalia |
| Phylum: Chordata |
| Class: Mammalia |
| Order: Carnivora |
| Family: Ursidae |
| Genus: *Ursus* |
| Species: *americanus* |
| Binomial Name: |
| ***Ursus americanus*** |

## Wow Facts

- Black bears can be found from Alaska, across Canada to Labrador and Newfoundland, and south through the United States and into central Mexico.
- The densest population of black bears in the world is on Vancouver Island in British Columbia, Canada and this is due to a plentiful rich diet of salmon.
- Black bears eat new shoots, grasses, and forbs in the spring, shrubs, fruits, and berries in the summer, and hazel nuts, oak acorns, and pine nuts in autumn. A small portion of their diet consists of insects such as bees, yellow jackets, ants, and their larvae, and beetles. They also feed on carrion of animals that died during the winter, they will feed on agricultural honey, and they will steal kills from cougars and from hunters; not to mention picnic baskets! These **omnivores** also eat catfish, salmon, suckerfish, elk calves, moose calves, caribou, and bird eggs.
- Black bears are generally crepuscular (active primarily during twilight), although breeding and seasonal feeding activities may alter this pattern. Where human food or garbage is available, Black bears may become distinctly diurnal (on roadsides) or nocturnal (in campgrounds). Where brown bears are present, black bears become nocturnal and stay hidden in dense forest areas.
- Using their nose, they can sense smells seven times greater than that of a bloodhound, so while camping, the only safe place to put food and candy is in a bear

box hung high above the ground and/or suspended between two trees and not in, or next to, trees, tents, or inside unattended vehicles and especially away from occupied open windowed vehicles.

- Wearing a bear bell while hiking will keep you from startling black bears and more importantly keep you from getting between a sow (mother) and her cub.
- The American black bear is the smallest of the three bears species found in North America, and are native to and found only in North America. Black bears have short, rounded, non-retractable claws that give them an excellent tree-climbing ability.
- They can run faster than humans; 55km/h (34mph) for short distances.
- They hibernate in October-November for 3-8 months.
- They usually have a pale muzzle which contrasts with their jet black or dark chocolate color fur and some 25% have a white chest spot. Western populations are usually lighter in color, being more often brown, cinnamon, or blonde.
- The Asian black bear diverged from Sun bears 4.58 million years ago and American black bears diverged from sun bears 4.08 million years ago. From the Holocene onwards black bears have become smaller.
- They can live to 30 years in the wild, but most often live only about 10 years; in captivity up to 44 years.
- Predators include humans, wolves, and brown bears. For cubs: coyotes, cougars, wolverines, and golden eagles as well. Surprisingly, in Nevada the mortality rate in the wild is almost 0% and 83% in developed areas.
- Whinnie the Pooh was based on Winniped who lived at the London Zoo from 1915- 1934. Smokey the bear was named after a cub that survived the 1950 Capitan Gap fire. Yogi bear is in a cartoon class of his own.
- Bird feeders, non bear proof garbage cans, freezers left in open garages, and food left in cars are major league bear attractors.

# BISON

# Buffalo
# (Bison)

| | |
|---|---|
| Kingdom: <u>Animalia</u><br>Phylum: <u>Chordata</u><br>Class: <u>Mammalia</u><br>Order: <u>Artiodactyla</u><br>Family: <u>Bovidae</u><br>Genus: <u>*Bison*</u><br>Species: <u>*bison*</u><br>**Binomial Name:**<br>***Bison bison*** | |

## Wow Facts

- Before the 1800's buffalo numbered above 50 million in North America and were found from grasslands, savannas, subarctic and even in areas with slightly more precipitation than deserts. Bison are now mostly found on private and protected lands in areas of the western United States and Canada. In Utah, they can be found at elevations up to 3km (10,000ft).
- These giant **herbivore** grazers feed on grasses year round, but they will eat sage brush when food is scarce. They will graze for some 2 hours and then rest while chewing their cud. Then they move to a new location.
- When bison travel, they form a line. The traveling pattern of bison is determined by the terrain and habitat conditions.
- The two distinctive features of bison are the shoulder hump and their huge horned head.
- Their fur is shaggy and brown as a winter coat and a lighter shorter length of brown for the summer. The front end tends to be darker than the back end. The difference in hair length is most noticeable in males. The horns are black, curving upward and inward and ending in a sharp tip.
- Calves are reddish-brown and one herd from Seneca, New York has white colored fur, but they are not albino.
- Bison are gregarious animals and are arranged in loose groups according to      sex, age, season, and

habitat. Young males are kicked out of maternal herds at 2-3 years of age and join bachelor groups.

- They are hard to domesticate and difficult to keep fenced in because they can jump 1.8m (6ft) and can destroy almost any fence once their 907kg (2,000 lb) frame hits 56-64 km/h (35-40 mph). They are also good swimmers.
- They almost became extinct because of their meat and fur. Buffalo meat is lower in fat and higher in protein than beef and doesn't become hard as a hockey puck when you over cook it like beef tends to do.
- Sadly, a great number of buffalo were killed for the sole purpose of depriving Native American Indians of a steady food and fur material source, forcing many plains Indians to seek government food supplies and blankets at designated reservations or risk guaranteed harsh winters and/or inevitable starvation.
- Buffalos branched off from Water Buffalo and African Buffalo 5 to 10 million years ago. They came across the Bering Land Bridge to North America. Steepe Bison are the ones typically found in cave paintings and they died out in Eurasia 11,000 years ago and in America 4,000-8,000 years ago.
- In North America Steepe bison, *Bison priscus*, gave rise to the giant *Bison lattifrons* which was replaced by the smaller *Bison antiquus*, followed by *Bison occidentalis*, and finally evolving into *Bison bison* 5,000-10,000 thousand years ago.
- The word "Buffalo" was first recorded in 1625 and the word "bison" in 1774.
- They live 15 to 20 years in the wild and 25 years in captivity.
- Predators besides humans include: Grizzly bears and wolves, which seek out female cows, young calves, and in general, the small, sick or wounded.

# Deer

# White-Tailed Deer

| | |
|---|---|
| Kingdom: Animalia<br>Phylum: Chordata<br>Class: Mammalia<br>Order: Artiodactyla<br>Family: Cervidae<br>Genus: *Odocoileus*<br>Species: *virginianus*<br>Binomial Name:<br>***Odocoileus***<br>        ***virginianus*** |  |

## Wow Facts

- Whitetail deer inhabit most of southern Canada and the entire mainland United States as well as down into Mexico, Central America and the northern coastlands of South America. Whitetail deer prefer to rest and hide in dense thicket, but they may live in woods, grasslands, swamp lands of Florida, farmlands, river valleys, and deserts of Texas and Mexico.

- These **herbivores** have been introduced to New Zealand, Cuba, Jamaica, Hispaniola, Puerto Rico and Bermuda in the Bahamas, as well as Finland, Serbia, and the Czech Republic.

- There are 30-40 subspecies.

- They are extremely agile and can bound at speeds of up to 48km/h (30mph) through tangled terrain in a forest and 75km/h (47mph) elsewhere. They can jump 2.7m (8.9ft). Whitetail deer are good swimmers and often cross streams, lakes, and travel across some 17 islands surrounded by the Atlantic Ocean saltwater in Florida and can be seen swimming in the Pacific Ocean from one cove to another along the Oregon coastline.

- Whitetail deer have four chambered stomachs and feed on a variety of vegetation, depending on where they live. In most cases they eat shrubs, buds and twigs of trees. Unfortunately, they also like agricultural plants, vegetable gardens, and fruit trees

161

from orchards.
- Their coat color varies from one location and subspecies to another. They appear darker in the winter and more reddish brown in the spring. Behind the nose is a white band of fur and white circles around the eyes, inside the ears, on their chin, and the underside of their tail.
- Following Bergmann's Rule they are larger the farther they live from the equator; a buck from colder Canada may weigh four times as much as a buck from the warmer Florida Keys.
- Whitetail deer are extremely nervous and shy and move their tails from side to side when they are startled or fleeing danger. Whitetail deer are usually solitary.
- They have dichromatic (two color) vision and see blue and yellow, but not orange and reds very well, hence the reason hunters can wear red and orange for safety, but not alarm the deer.
- Counting the number of points on one side/branch of the antlers is a common method used to calculate their age; some females "does", have antlers too and they are known to charge.
- In some locations they are carriers of ticks that carry Lyme disease and Rocky Mountain spotted fever.
- Deer increase plant diversity by eating dominant plants and opening up areas where even oak trees will eventually grow.
- They typically live 2 to 3 years. Maximum life span in the wild is 20 years, but few live past 10 years old.
- Predators include: humans, wolverines, wolves, mountain lions, bears, alligators, jaguars, eagles, and coyotes. Collisions with cars are known to cause fatal injuries to both deer and driver.

# Muntjac (Barking Deer)(Reeves's muntjac)

| | |
|---|---|
| Kingdom: Animalia<br>Phylum: Chordata<br>Class: Mammalia<br>Order: Artiodactyla<br>Family: Cervidae<br>Genus: *Muntiacus*<br>Species: *reevesi*<br>**Binomial Name:**<br>*Muntiacus reevesi* | |

## Wow Facts

- Muntjac have a native range that extends throughout the subtropical forests of southeastern China, Taiwan, India, Sri Lanka, Japan, Burma and Indonesian islands. It has also become established in England. There are 3 subspecies.
- They are called the bush huggers because of the paths they create throughout the rainforests.
- Muntjac use their horns to shove an opponent off balance and then inflict a tusk blow to the face or head and try to puncture the opponent's skin.
- These **omnivores** eat bamboo, seeds, bark, fruit nuts, and foliage, like most other deer species, but they also eat eggs, carrion, mice, and ground nesting birds.
- Males are heavier and have short antlers that grow from their pedicles and have long, tusk-like canines up to 5cm (2 inches) long. They grow to .5m (1ft 8 inch) tall at shoulders and .95m (3ft 1 inch) long.
- They are solitary and use their tusk-like canines to defend their territory and gain access to females. They are the oldest known deer: 1.5 to 35Mya. Miocene fossils are found in France, Germany, and Poland.
- Bucks live some 16yrs and Does up to 19 years.
- Predators include: leopards, tigers, dholes, jackals, crocodiles, pythons, and possibly foxes in England. In Ireland they can be hunted year round.

# Brown Brocket

Kingdom: Animalia
Phylum: Chordata
Class: Mammalia
Order: Artiodactyla
Family: Cervidae
Genus: *Mazama*
Species: *gouazaoubira*

**Binomial Name:**
*Mazama gouazaoubira*

## Wow Facts

- Also known as the gray brocket. The word "*Mazama*" comes from the Nahuatl word for deer "Mazame".
- Gray or Brown brocket deer range from the Yucatán Peninsula, southern Central America down through northern South America, and reach as far south as northern Argentina, Bolivia, Uruguay, and also Trinidad. There are 10 species.
- They may be found in very dry areas, in savannas, swamplands, foothills, or at the edge of forests.
- They are **frugavores** in some locations or eat cacti. They are also grazers and browsers. They utilize roots, twigs, flowers, buds, bark and leaves of trees and shrubs.
- The antlers are not always visible and are small spikes. They have a grayish-brown to reddish-brown coat. The males have simple antlers 7-10cm (2.4-2.7 inches) in length.
- Gray brocket deer are generally solitary territorial animals. Rarely have they ever been seen in groups of three. They frequent dense cover during the day, but emerge at night into the open to feed.
- They mature in 19 months and gestation is 7 months.
- The lifespan of the red brocket ranges from 7 to 12 years, so the brown brocket may have a similar lifespan.
- Predators include: ocelots, jaguars, pumas, larger raptors, and humans.

# Roe Deer

| | |
|---|---|
| Kingdom: Animalia<br>Phylum: Chordata<br>Class: Mammalia<br>Order: Artiodactyla<br>Family: Cervidae<br>Genus: *Capreolus*<br>Species: *capreolus*<br>**Binomial Name:**<br>***Capreolus capreolus*** | |

## Wow Facts

- The roe deer is found throughout Europe and eastern regions of Asia. They have also been introduced to Pohnpei in Micronesia and Australia and reintroduced to England through Scotland where they are native.
- Roe deer prefer high grass meadows this shrubs, forest steppes, and small secluded bits of forests isolated by farmlands.
- These **herbivores** are browsers that eat herbs, mushrooms, brambles, ivy, heather, bilberry and coniferous tree shoots. They may seek out and consume approximately 1,000 different plant species in their range. They prefer energy-rich foods that are soft and contain large amounts of water. During winter they may eat the needles of coniferous trees, but only when other food sources are depleted.
- When alarmed, they will bark like a dog and flash out their white rump patch which is heart shaped on does and kidney shaped on males. Males make low grunts.
- Roe deer are either solitary or live in family groups. Does give birth to two fawns of opposite sex in June and by winter she and her fawns will join larger family groups.
- They live up to 15 years in the wild; 17.5 years in captivity.
- The book "Bambi" was based on a Roe deer, but the species was changed for the movie version since most Americans could better identify with a white tail deer than a deer never before seen in North America.

# Indian Hog Deer

Kingdom: Animalia
Phylum: Chordata
Class: Mammalia
Order: Artiodactyla
Family: Cervidae
Genus: *Hyelaphus*
Species: *porcinus*

Binomial Name:
*Hyelaphus porcinus*

## Wow Facts

- The Indian hog deer is found in Southeast Asia from India, Nepal, China, Thailand, Cambodia, and Vietnam. They were introduced to Florida, Hawaii, Australia, and Sri Lanka.
- They are 70cm (2.3ft) high at the shoulders 105cm-115cm (3.5-3.8ft) in body length, and weigh 50kg (110lb).
- These **herbivores** feed on grasses, leaves, and fallen fruits in the morning and late afternoon unless it is too hot, then they will become nocturnal.
- In the winter they are dark brown and reddish brown in the summer. Females have spots on their summer coat. Females and young may stay together in herds of 40-80 individuals.
- Males have antlers with three white colored points. 30-38cm (11.8 inches-1.3ft) long. Males are solitary except for mating season and mark their territory using their preorbital glands. During rutting season males join each other in the meadows to fight.
- They emit a warning bark when danger is near. Their thick fur and short legs make them appear hog like.
- Their head remains low when they run through the underbrush to escape danger.
- Gestation is 220-230 days. They wean in six months, and they are sexually mature in 15 months.
- Their lifespan averages 10 years, but some can live up to 20 years. Predators include: Tigers, dholes, leopards, and pythons.

# Mule Deer

| Kingdom: Animalia<br>Phylum: Chordata<br>Class: Mammalia<br>Order: Artiodactyla<br>Family: Cervidae<br>Genus: *Odocoileus*<br>Species: *hemionus*<br>Binomial Name:<br>***Odocoileus hemionus*** | |

## Wow Facts

- Mule deer are found in North America from Canada down to central Mexico. They inhabit **Canadian boreal forests, Mojave and Baja Californian** deserts, dunes, savannas, Great Plain grasslands, chaparral, forest, and mountain regions. They have also been introduced to Kauai, Hawaii, and Argentina.

- Mule deer are **herbivores**, but have a difficult time digesting high fibrous plant materials. Their diet can consist of twigs, berries, leaves, shrubs, acorns, forbs, grass, bean pods, nuts, and even wild mushrooms.

- Mule deer have no upper teeth in the front region, only a hard pallet. Males are larger and have antlers that fork (bifurcate) as they grow.

- Their fur ranges from dark brown gray, dark and light ash-gray to brown and even reddish. The rump patch may be white or yellow. The throat patch is white. The white tails of most mule deer end in a tuft of black hairs; some tails end in white tufts of hair. Black tail deer are one of the ten subspecies.

- Mule deer prefer home ranges and will move from a winter home range to a summer home range only after the cold temperature becomes uncomfortable, snowstorms are too harsh, or snow deposits make searching for food too difficult.

- Life span in wild is 12 years, but by 9.5 years their teeth are worn down: in captivity 22 years.

- Predators include: wolves, cougars, bears, bobcats, and wolverines.

# Fallow Deer

Kingdom: <u>Animalia</u>
Phylum: <u>Chordata</u>
Class: <u>Mammalia</u>
Order: <u>Artiodactyla</u>
Family: <u>Cervidae</u>
Genus: <u>*Dama*</u>
Species: <u>*dama*</u>
**Binomial Name:**
*Dama dama*

## Wow Facts

- These white spotted deer are native to Eurasia, the Mediterranean region and parts of the Middle East. They have been introduced to some 38 countries: by the Phoenicians to the Western Mediterranean, Romans and Normans to Britain and Europe, and by others to parts of North & South America, southern Africa, Australia, New Zealand, Fiji, the Falklands, and various other islands.
- Their preferred habitat is woodlands for hiding and with grassy clearings for grazing. Fallow deer forage on a variety of vegetation, usually grasses, mast, and browse. Other items in their diet may include herbs, dwarf shrubs, acorns, leaves, buds, shoots, bark and agricultural products such as sugar beets.
- Adult males are solitary. However, at the end of the summer months they may form small bachelor herds of fewer than 6 and begin joining the female groups by early autumn; the beginning of the rut. Females, fawns, and yearlings remain in larger groups of 7 to 14. Fallow deer are active mainly at dusk and dawn, or remain nocturnal in other regions.
- By the age of three, the antlers of bucks change from spikes and grow wide and flat at the ends.
- They can run 48km/h (30 mph) and jump 1.75m (5.74ft) high and 5m (16.4ft) in length.
- They are easily tamed and found semi-domesticated in many parks around the world.
- They have an average life span of 12-16 years.

168

# Caribou (Reindeer)

| | |
|---|---|
| Kingdom: Animalia<br>Phylum: Chordata<br>Class: Mammalia<br>Order: Artiodactyla<br>Family: Cervidae<br>Genus: *Rangifer*<br>Species: *tarandus*<br>Binomial Name:<br>***Rangifer tarandus*** | |

## Wow Facts

- Caribou have a circumpolar distribution similar to polar bears and muskox. (North America and Northern Eurasia). Caribou inhabit arctic tundra, subarctic (boreal) forest, and mountainous regions.
- During the Pliestocene epoch (2.6 million years ago to 11,700 years ago) they were found as far south as Nevada, Tennessee, and Spain in Europe.
- Caribou are grazing **herbivores**. Their diet varies greatly in the summer when these ruminants (they have four chambered stomachs) consume leaves of willows, birches, mushrooms, grasses, and other vegetation. In the winter lichens are an important component of their diet.
- Both males and females have antlers and one of the antler's extensions at the base either on the left or right side juts straight forward towards their nose and is used to scrape away surface snow to help browse during winter. Mature bulls may have large complex shaped antlers, whereas cows and young calves have smaller and simpler formed antlers.
- They can traverse more than 5,000 km (3,107 miles) a year, with extensive migrations in spring and fall. They make a clicking sound when they walk. They may migrate 19-55km (12-34 miles) per day and join in herds of 50,000-500,000 members. They can run 60-80km/h (37-50mph).
- There are 14 subspecies and some are larger or have longer legs than other species. Males of some

subspecies are twice as large as females. The coat of
the caribou is an excellent, lightweight insulation
against the extreme cold temperatures that they
face. The hairs are hollow, air filled, and taper
sharply which helps trap heat close to their body
and also makes them more buoyant in water. Color
varies by subspecies, region, sex, and season from
the very dark browns of woodland caribou bulls in
summer to nearly white coats in Greenland (*R. t.
groenlandicus*) and high Arctic caribou.

- The two cloven toes that they walk on are crescent
  shaped and are good for both walking on snow and
  through swamps, or for swimming.
- Newborns weigh just 6kg (13 lb).
- Santa's Reindeer came from a poem in 1823 called
  "A Visit from St. Nick" and included the names:
  Dasher, Dancer, Prancer, Vixen, Comet, Cupid,
  Dunder, & Blixem. The last two names were later
  changed to Donner & Blitzen which are the German
  words for thunder and lightning; Rudolph came
  later from a rather bright idea.
- They are called Caribou in Canada and the U.S.,
  and Reindeer in Europe where certain species are
  semi-domesticated.
- Average lifespan is 17 years for females and 13
  years for males.
- Predators include: wolves, bears, coyotes, linx, and
  young may be taken by eagles. One whole caribou
  carcass was found as part of the stomach contents of
  a large Greenland shark.

# CAT FAMILY

# Leopard

Kingdom: <u>Animalia</u>
Phylum: <u>Chordata</u>
Class: <u>Mammalia</u>
Order: <u>Carnivora</u>
Family: <u>Felidae</u>
Genus: *Panthera*
Species: *pardus*
**Binomial name:**
*Panthera pardus*

## Wow Facts

- They are found in woodlands, grasslands, savannas, and forests from Sub-Saharan Africa down through south eastern Africa down to South Africa, through the Middle East and up across to eastern Siberia and down through Southeast Asia to Malaysia. During the Pliocene epoch (5.33-2.58 million years ago) they were found in Europe over to Italy.
- These **carnivores** ambush prey such as birds, mammals, reptiles including crocodiles, and fish.
- In warm dry climates they have light yellow or tan coats and reddish-orange coats when living in dark jungles or forests. They are covered with a mosaic of dark, small circlet patterns forming "rosettes."
- They have a long body, short legs, and a broad head with large powerful jaw muscles.
- Their scapula (shoulder blades) have specialized attachment sites giving them extremely powerful climbing muscles.
- To help move in the jungle or forests their ears are small and round and their whiskers on their upper lip and eyebrows are extra long.
- They are usually nocturnal, but they may hunt on cloudy days as long as there are no human settlements nearby.
- They mark their territory with urine, feces, and claw marks.
- They are normally solitary, but they may communicate with one another by growling, roaring, and by spitting

when aggravated, and purring when content.
- There are some eight to eleven subspecies of *Panthera pardus*. In Sri Lanka where there are no lions or tigers, leopards grow larger than anywhere else in the world.
- They can run up to 58km/h (36mph).
- They have been eliminated or exterminated from Hong Kong, Singapore, Kuwait, Syria, Libya, Tunisia, and perhaps Morocco.
- Males are 30% larger than females. Body size and color patterns of leopards vary geographically and most likely reflect adaptations to particular habitats.
- Leopards are one of the five big cats in the genus Panthera.
- Leopards look like a smaller version of the Jaguar and both Jaguars and Leopards may give birth to "melanistic" offspring. These pure black versions are incorrectly, but colloquially both termed Black Panthers. Melanism is a selective advantage for nocturnal ambush predators.
- A rare genetic condition can overproduce red pigment or under produce dark pigment leaving the leopard strawberry colored or looking like a Pink Panther.
- Leopards split from the *Panthera* genus after snow leopards and tigers, but before lions and jaguars.
- DNA studies reveal that leopards are closely related to lions, but mitochondrial DNA studies show that they are also closely related to snow leopards.
- Early extinct leopard species fossils from the Pleistocene and are 2-3.5Mya. Modern leopards evolved in Africa 470,000-825,000 years ago.
- Because of their stealth, people are often unaware how close these big cats may live next to them.
- Lifespan is 24 years in captivity and 12-17 years in the wild.
- Bageera was a black leopard in the Jungle Book.

# Mountain Lion
# (Puma Concolor)

Kingdom: Animalia
Phylum: Chordata
Class: Mammalia
Order: Carnivora
Family: Felidae
Genus: *Puma*
Species: *concolor*
Binomial name:
***Puma concolor***

## Wow Facts

- In North America, they can be found from British Columbia and southern Alberta to California and Texas, but they also extend down to Central and South America to the Andes Mountains. They are nocturnal or crepuscular (feeding dusk & dawn).
- South of Texas, only the jaguar is larger. Mountain lions are related closer to felines such as house cats than they are to other subspecies of lions.
- Mountain lions are **carnivores** that eat moose, elk, white-tailed deer, mule deer, and caribou in North America and brown brocket, lamas, alpacas in South America. They will also eat smaller creatures like squirrels, voles, mice, muskrat, porcupine, beaver, raccoon, striped skunk, coyote, bobcats, other mountain lions, owls, rabbits, opossums, birds, and even snails and fish.
- They may also prey on domestic livestock, including chicken, calves, sheep, goats, and pigs.
- Mountain lions hunt by ambushing prey. If the prey is small they will jump on the prey's back and break its neck with a powerful bite at the base of the skull similar to how a male lion dispatches with a spotted hyena. If the prey is large, they go for a suffocating neck bite like a cheetah performs on an impala.
- They will yield their kills to jaguar, wolves, and bears.

- The mountain lion (*Puma concolor*) is also known as the cougar, puma, panther, and catamount. It has over 40 names just in English and holds the Guiness record for total number of names for just one single species.
- Cougars in eastern North America were exterminated, by early European settlers except for a small population of Florida panthers (*Puma concolor coryi*).
- Recently, cougars have expanded their range into suburban areas on the west coast of North America and even into parks of Los Angeles County in California. Several urbanized puma have been hit by cars as far east as Kansas City, Missouri.
- Mountain lions inhabit mountain forests, tropical forests, grasslands, swamps, and dessert fringes where they can find ample cover and prey. For shelter they prefer caves and rocky crevices, but in urban areas they may rest in intricately designed cement crawl spaces that are so plentiful and precariously secure houses to the slopes of mountain sides surrounding cities like Los Angeles.
- Mountain lions are solitary animals, except for 1 to 8 days of association during mating season.
- Females may have 1 to 6 cubs and by themselves defend and nurture their cubs.
- Cubs are born blind, covered with spots, and rings on their tails. When the eyes first open they are blue.
- Pumas can't roar, but just like a house cat they can hiss growl, purr, chirp, and whistle.
- Found in Asia 11 million years ago, they entered North America 8-8.5 million years ago, and went down into South America 3 million years ago.
- Life span is 18 years in the wild and slightly longer in captivity.

# Jaguar/Black Jaguar

| Kingdom: Animalia<br>Phylum: Chordata<br>Class: Mammalia<br>Order: Carnivora<br>Family: Felidae<br>Genus: *Panthera*<br>Species: *onca*<br>**Binomial name:**<br>***Panthera onca*** |  |
|---|---|

## Wow Facts

- Jaguars are found from southern Arizona and New Mexico south towards northern Argentina and northeastern Brazil.
- They have become extinct or rarely seen in El Salvador, and most of Mexico.
- Jaguars prefer the cover of dense tropical jungles and forests. They are also found in scrublands, reed thickets, coastal forests, swamps, and thickets.
- Jaguars are **carnivores** that prefer to hunt deer, peccaries, and tapirs. They also prey on caimans, turtles, snakes, porcupines, capybaras, fish, and birds. Their teeth can pierce the skull and brain of their prey with one powerful bite.
- Jaguars are excellent swimmers and can be found in habitats near water, such as rivers, slow moving streams, lagoons, waterways, and swamps.
- Jaguars are most active near dusk and dawn, and they like to rest mid-morning and in the afternoon. Jaguars, just like mountain lions, rest in thick vegetation, in caves, or under large rocky outcrops.
- They are only smaller than lions and tigers, and have muscular bodies built for power, not for speed.
- Jaguar coat colors range from pale yellow to reddish brown, with black, rosette-shaped spots. The belly is off white.
- Black, or melanistic, jaguars are fairly common in thick forest habitats and are the result of a single, dominant allele. Their base coat color is black with

black spots that are hard to see without direct sunlight.

- Their name comes from the Amazonian Tupian word "yaguarete" which means "true beast".
- Their common ancestors with lions, tigers, leopards, jaguars, snow leopards, and clouded leopards separated 6-10 million years ago.
- Jaguars can live 11 to 12 years in the wild and up to 20 years in captivity.

# African Lion

| | |
|---|---|
| Kingdom: Animalia<br>Phylum: Chordata<br>Class: Mammalia<br>Order: Carnivora<br>Family: Felidae<br>Genus: *Panthera*<br>Species: *Leo*<br>Binomial Name:<br>***Panthera leo*** |  |

## Wow Facts

- African lions live in plains or savanna habitats.
- The Jaguar and Tiger are their closest relatives and lions evolved in Africa around one million years ago.
- The larger species of cave lions, appeared 500,000 years ago, but died out around 10,000 years ago.
- In the late Pleistocene Epoch, some 10,000 years ago, humans were the only large land mammals more widespread than lions.
- Lions are the only cats that live in groups, which are called **prides**.
- Lions may scavenge up to 50 percent of their food.
- Lions are primarily nocturnal hunters and can sleep some 20 hours a day.
- Female lions are the pride's primary hunters. These **carnivores** often work together to prey upon antelopes, zebras, wildebeest, and other large animals of the open grasslands, but typically an individual lioness does the actual killing.
- A male lion can kill a hyena with one well-placed bite.
- Males are known to kill cubs in newly acquired prides in order to speed up the process of adult females being able to bear the new male's own offspring. Females are known to defend their pride from the advances of unfamiliar male lions to protect their existing young.
- Lions can live up to 14 years in the wild and more than 20 years in captivity.

# South American Puma
# (Jaguarundi)

| | |
|---|---|
| Kingdom: Animalia<br>Phylum: Chordata<br>Class: Mammalia<br>Order: Carnivora<br>Family: Felidae<br>Genus: *Puma*<br>Species: *yagouaroundi*<br>**Binomial name:**<br>*Puma yagouaroundi* | |

## Wow Facts

- The jaguarundi is found from southern Texas and down along the coastal regions of Mexico, through central and down south to Uruguay. South America east of the Andes, and as far south as northern Argentina; also found in southern Texas, Alabama and Florida.
- They prefer brushlands, forests, and grasslands near water.
- Jaguarundis are mostly **carnivores.** They eat small mammals, reptiles, birds, frogs, fish, insects, and some plants including fruits. They have excellent climbing and swimming skills too.
- Their legs are short and they have an elongated body and long tail; making them look like weasels or otters; they are sometimes called "otter cats."
- Length is 137cm (5ft) head to tail. Weight: 8kg (18 lb).
- The ears are short and rounded. Their coat can be hues of black, brown, red, gray, or chestnut.
- They are active in pairs in Paraguay, but solitary in Mexico so they may behave differently depending on the local habitat.
- Like domestic cats they can purr, whistle, yap, chatter, or chirp like birds.
- They are closely related to cougars and secondly to cheetahs. They came across the Bering Land Bridge to the Americas 8.0 to 8.5 million years ago.
- They live 10 years in captivity. Loss of habitat is a major threat.

# Lynx

| Kingdom: <u>Animalia</u><br>Phylum: <u>Chordata</u><br>Class: <u>Mammalia</u><br>Order: <u>Carnivora</u><br>Family: <u>Felidae</u><br>Genus: *<u>Lynx</u>*<br>Species: *<u>lynx</u>*<br>**Binomial name:**<br>*Lynx lynx* | |

## Wow Facts

- Lynx are found typically in high altitude or boreal forests of North America, Europe, and Asia.
- There are four species of lynx: *Lynx lynx, Lynx canadensi, Lynx pardinus, and Lynx rufus.*
- All four of the lynx species have very long legs and evolved from *Issoirlynx* from Europe and Africa. Their coat can be brown, gold, white or somewhere in between and punctuated with dark brownish. They all have white undersides. Bobcats living in desserts have light colored coats, and those living in mountain regions have darker coats.
- These **carnivores** feed on a wide range of animals from white-tailed deer, reindeer, roe deer, red deer, sheep, goats, sheep, and foxes. They also eat smaller prey such as birds, snowshoe hares, jack rabbits, squirrels, mice, and household pets. They also catch fish and are good swimmers.
- A 13.6 kg (30 lb) lynx has bigger feet than a 90 kg (200 lb) mountain lion. Their big feet act like snowshoes, allowing them to hunt even in deep snow. Lynx in colder climates have larger padded feet. The Eurasian lynx at up to 30kg (66 lb) is the largest of all four species. The bobcat at 14kg (31 lb) is the smallest species and has 12 subspecies.
- They have short tails, long whiskers on the face, and elongated wisps of black hair on top of their pointed ears. When present or dark enough, patches under their chin are said to look like a black bowtie.

180

- Lynx are solitary, but may join in small groups to hunt.
- They mate in late winter and after 70 days of gestation give birth to two to six kittens. They stay with their mother until after the next winter.
- Mothers let their kittens play with their "live" food to develop better hunting skills.
- Lynx are similar to cougars in that they make their dens in crevices or under ledges; only on a smaller scale.
- Lynx in captivity live up to 26 years, and average 14.5 years in the wild.
- Known predators include: coyotes, wolves, cougars. Also killed by hunters for sport and ranchers for livestock protection.

# Caracal

| | |
|---|---|
| Kingdom: <u>Animalia</u><br>Phylum: <u>Chordata</u><br>Class: <u>Mammalia</u><br>Order: <u>Carnivora</u><br>Family: <u>Felidae</u><br>Genus: *Caracal*<br>Species: *caracal*<br>**Binomial name:**<br>*Caracal caracal* | |

## Wow Facts

- Caracals are found in Africa, and central and southwestern Asia. They live in forests, grasslands, woodlands, thickets, plains and rocky terrain.
- These nocturnal **carnivores** eat rabbits, hyraxes, rodents, small sized antelope species, monkeys, lizards, snakes, insects, birds, and fish. Larger prey they bite on the throat and suffocate; similar to a cheetah.
- Their long powerful legs allow them to be excellent climbers, swimmers, and jumpers. They can leap 3m (9.8ft) when catching birds. The record for a single leap, is swatting down 12 pigeons.
- They may growl, hiss, purr, and also make a "warning" barking sound.
- They have brown or reddish brown hair and lighter or white on the underside like African golden cats. They have black markings especially on their chin cheeks, and nose. Eyes are gray, green, golden or copper colored. They have long black tufts of hair on their ears and their tail is short, so they are said to be the African Lynx.
- The Turkish word "Karakulak" means "Black ears".
- They are solitary, except when mating and rearing **kits**. They are territorial, and males are larger.
- They are closely related to the African Golden Cat and split off from their common ancestor 5 Mya.
- Lifespan is 20 in captivity and 12 years in the wild.
- Known predators are lions, hyenas, and leopards. Habitat destruction and human hunting are major detrimental issues.

# Tiger

| | |
|---|---|
| Kingdom: <u>Animalia</u><br>Phylum: <u>Chordata</u><br>Class: <u>Mammalia</u><br>Order: <u>Carnivora</u><br>Family: <u>Felidae</u><br>Genus: <u>*Panthera*</u><br>Species: <u>*tigris*</u><br>**Binomial name:**<br>***Panthera tigris*** | |

## Wow Facts

- From Russia, China and India they inhabit scrub oak, birch woodlands, tall grass jungles, mangrove swamps, and forests such as taiga, evergreen, tropical lowland, monsoonal, and deciduous. Yet despite all these habitats, they have lost 93% of their home range in the last 100 years. From 1850-2006 tiger populations decreased from some 100,000 down to under 4,000 individuals.

- Tigers are strong swimmers and catch prey, as well as bathe, in rivers, lakes, and ponds. Their burst speed is 49-65 km/h (30-40 mph). Using their fangs, they can bite the throat and suffocate large animals or bite the nape of the neck and break the spine of smaller prey. One swipe of their paw can break the back of smaller prey.

- Older tigers that have lost their fangs may look for easy prey and sometimes become man eaters.

- Tigers prefer to hunt at night, when large mammals such as deer and bovid prey are most active. Like cougars and leopards, tigers prefer to hunt in dense vegetation or along animal paths, and even frozen waterways where they can move silently across the ice and ambush prey.

- There are ten recognized subspecies of *Panthera tigris*.

- They have a reddish-orange coat with vertical black stripes along the flanks and shoulders and black bands on their tail. They have a white spot on the back of each ear. Their skin is striped too. Like human finger prints, each tiger has their own unique pattern of stripes. Males are 1.7 times bigger than females. Tigers from colder regions such as Siberia are much larger than tigers found in warmer regions such as Japan and Sumatra.

- All white tigers are produced from Bengal tigers with rare recessive alleles for white fur, but for some reason white tigers have shorter life spans.
- Tigers are solitary; the only long-term relationship is between a mother and her offspring. Males have a territorial range that overlaps the range of several females.
- In one case, a male shared his kill with a female and her cubs but male/ male encounters can lead to territorial disputes and end in death or serious injury of either one or both males.
- Tigers split from a common ancestor with snow leopards 2.88 million years ago. A primitive tiger was found living in China 2 Million years ago, and a true tiger was found living in Java 1.6-1.8 millian years ago.
- Male lions crossed with female tigers produce large "Ligers". Female lions crossed with male tigers produce smaller "Tigons". Male Lion Growth Hormone is a key ingredient to growing larger than life.
- Shere Khan was the tiger in Rudyard Kipling's 1894 classic "The Jungle Book". Tigger was in Winnie the Pooh, and Tony the tiger was used on the cover of Kellogg's frosted flakes cereal. A tiger also starred in the 2001 movie "Life of Pi".
- Tigers live 8 to 10 years in the wild and up to 26 years in captivity.
- Mortality of cubs is 50% in the first two years. Habitat destruction and poaching for fur and body parts used for traditional Chinese medicine have decimated tiger populations.

# DOGS

# Black/Gray Timber Wolf

Kingdom: Animalia
Phylum: Chordata
Class: Mammalia
Order: Carnivora
Family: Canidae
Genus: *Canis*
Species: *lupus*

**Binomial name:**
*Canis lupus*

## Wow Facts

- Gray wolves were once found worldwide except for southern Africa and South America. They currently inhabit small pocket regions of the mainland United States, Alaska, Canada, Mexico (a small population), and Eurasia. They inhabit the arctic tundra, forests, prairies, grasslands, and arid landscapes.

- Gray wolves are **carnivores**. Wolves hunt in packs for large hoofed herbivores: moose, elk, bison, musk ox, and reindeer. They may hunt smaller prey such as rabbits and mice by themselves, steal kills made by other predators, or scavenge carrion. They can follow fresh tracks or if downwind, they can scent carrion up to 3 km (1.8 miles) away. Prey varies from one geographic region to the next.

- To "wolf" down your food is to eat 15-19% of your body mass in one short quick feeding.

- The main social difference between the wolf and coyote is that a wolf follows a very strict set of pack rules when hunting large prey or around the den. A coyote with fewer rules is seen more as a scavenger or predator of urban house pets. Wolves do interbreed with coyotes especially in parts of the eastern United States where true wolf populations are almost non-existent or have been exterminated.

- Wolves are the largest of some 37 wild species of canids. Gray wolves vary in size based on geography and the related climate and follow Bergmann's rule. In colder Alaska or Canada, they may be three to six times larger in size than in the warmer Middle East or south Asia.

- Arctic wolves are solid white colored, while blends of gray, brown, cinnamon, and white in other geographic regions give them the local name of Timber Wolves.
- Black colored wolves came about due to hybridization with dogs 10,000 to 15,000 years ago. Half the wolves in Yellowstone Park are black wolves. Their howls can be heard 129.5 sq km (50sq miles).
- Wolves can put their head between there back legs and cover their face with their tails and with the added help of their dense fur they can withstand temperatures down to minus 40°.
- Western dogs diverged from a common ancestor with wolves 14,900 years ago. Dogs have pointed ears, wolf ears are more rounded. Wolves also have longer legs and in their loping pace they put one paw in front of the others to move through snow more quickly with less effort. They can travel for hours at 8-9 km/h (5 mph) or run fast at 55-70km/h (34-44 mph) for a mere twenty minutes.
- Gray wolves can snap bones with a bit force of 1,500 psi; a German Sheppard has a bite force of only 750psi.
- Gray wolves live in packs of two to thirty six individuals. The average is five to nine members and pack size is usually correlated to local prey population size.
- The alpha male is the pack leader and the alpha female is second in command. All other pack members know their place and who is above or below whom in a strictly followed social hierarchy.
- Aesops Fable: *The boy who cried wolf*. A wolf played the villain in *Little Red Riding Hood*.
- They may live thirteen years in the wild, though average lifespan is 5 to 6 years.

- Predators include: humans, gray wolves, and coyotes. 14-65% of wolves are killed by wolves in other packs in territorial fights.

# Coyote

| | |
|---|---|
| Kingdom: <u>Animalia</u><br>Phylum: <u>Chordata</u><br>Class: <u>Mammalia</u><br>Order: <u>Carnivora</u><br>Family: <u>Canidae</u><br>Genus: <u>*Canis*</u><br>Species: <u>*latrans*</u><br>**Binomial name:**<br>***Canis latrans*** | |

## Wow Facts

- Coyotes are found in forests, grasslands, deserts, swamps and near human settlements in North and Central America and even up into Alaska and northern Canada.
- They don't mind living next to humans and these nocturnal hunters are known to hunt stray cats and neighborhood dogs.
- On the outskirts of Las Vegas, you may see them in the daytime only on rare occasions when they have been flushed out of the storm drains by heavy rains.
- They are **carnivores**; 90% of their diet consists of mammals, although they consume fruits and vegetables during the fall and winter months.
- They prefer to expand on existing formerly occupied burrows made by other animals such as badgers, than dig their own burrows. They will build several entrances to the den and then use the den for as many years as they can.
- Their earliest ancestors are from the group of Eocene Miacids (extinct carnivores) 38-56 million years ago.
- They diverged from gray wolves 1-2 million years ago and are a more primitive line and are evolutionary placed somewhere between the golden jackal and gray wolf. They were once larger, but they became smaller as giant megafaunal herbivores became extinct and the gray wolf filled the void left by the extinction of the dire wolf. This is similar to

the sabre toothed lion extinction giving way to the smaller sized cougar and the even smaller Linx or bobcat adapting to a niche habitat where a larger sized cat could not survive on such small and infrequent prey.

- Coyotes usually hunt as individuals or in pairs because of prey scarcity, but they are also known to hunt in packs where food is plentiful.
- They are still expanding into new territories: Costa Rica in the 1970's and Panama in the early 1980's and they are expected to reach into South America soon if they are not already there. Currently there are 19 subspecies.
- The black tipped bottle shaped tail makes up half their body length.
- Hybrids of coyotes with wolves and dogs are becoming more common and the white coyotes of Newfoundland get their color from genes inherited from golden retrievers.
- Eastern wolves and red wolves show heavy influence of coyote genes.
- One mysterious animal called a Chupacabra was examined and using DNA tests was found to be a hybrid of a male Mexican gray wolf and a female coyote.
- Coyotes are known to live 10 years in the wild, and 18 years in captivity.
- Predators include: humans, wolves, and mountain lions.

# Gray Fox

| |
|---|
| Kingdom: Animalia |
| Phylum: Chordata |
| Class: Mammalia |
| Order: Carnivora |
| Family: Canidae |
| Genus: *Urocyon* |
| Species: *cinereoargenteus* |
| **Binomial name:** |
| ***Urocyon cinereoargenteus*** |

## Wow Facts

- They inhabit forests and woodlands from southern Canada down to South America in Venezuela and Columbia.
- Gray foxes are **omnivores**. They hunt rodents, voles, shrews, rabbits, birds, fruits, nuts, corn, berries, birds, and insects. They store extra food.
- The Gray fox and the raccoon dog are the only two canids that can climb trees.
- Adult gray foxes may have mixtures of white, red, black, silver, or gray stiff fur. Some have a grizzly "salt and pepper" appearance. Their tail has a black line across the top and ends in a black tip. The tail is one third of the body length.
- Gray foxes are solitary for the majority of the year. They mate for life and during winter, they socialize with their mate. They are primarily nocturnal, but are occasionally spotted at dusk, dawn, or during the daytime.
- Gray foxes prefer to make a den with one opening.
- They appeared in the Pliocene epoch about 3.6 million years ago.
- Lifespan for wild gray foxes ranges from 6 to 8 years and up to 15 years in captivity.
- Coyotes can displace gray foxes in an area, and in turn gray foxes can displace red foxes in an area.
- Predators include: bobcats, golden eagles, great-horned owls and coyotes.

# Kit Fox

Kingdom: <u>Animalia</u>
Phylum: <u>Chordata</u>
Class: <u>Mammalia</u>
Order: <u>Carnivora</u>
Family: <u>Canidae</u>
Genus: *Vulpes*
Species: *macrotis*

**Binomial name:**
*Vulpes macrotis*

## Wow Facts

- Kit foxes inhabit arid regions of eastern Oregon down to central and Baja Mexico in areas with desert scrub, chaparral, and grasslands.
- Kit foxes look like miniature gray foxes with large tall ears, which help them locate prey. No fox member in the family Canidae in North America is smaller.
- Kit foxes have a dark grayish back and light yellowish colored face, neck and legs, a light colored underside, and dark patches on the cheeks and end of the tail.
- These **carnivores** eat mice, kangaroo rats, rabbits, squirrels, gophers, birds, and lizards.
- Kit foxes rest in one of their many dens during hot days. They usually hunt alone at night when most of their prey is active, but sometimes they hunt at dusk or dawn (crepuscular).
- Pups are independent in 5-6 weeks and adults by 10 months. 74% of pups die within the first year.
- Average lifespan in the wild is 5.5 years and 14 years in captivity.
- 75% of kit foxes are preyed upon by coyotes, which not only eat them, but may take over and remodel the den. Other predators include bobcats, red foxes, American badgers, feral dogs, and large raptors. Habitat loss is another major long term survival issue.

# Arctic Fox

| Kingdom: <u>Animalia</u><br>Phylum: <u>Chordata</u><br>Class: <u>Mammalia</u><br>Order: <u>Carnivora</u><br>Family: <u>Canidae</u><br>Genus: *Vulpes*<br>Species: *lagopus*<br>**Binomial name:**<br>*Vulpes lagopus* | |

## Wow Facts

- Arctic foxes are found in the circumpolar barren and alpine arctic regions of Eurasia, North America, Greenland, and Iceland. There are four subspecies.

- Their multilayered fur changes color twice every year. The winter fur is white, and the summer coat ranges from grey to brown on the back, to somewhat lighter on the belly. Arctic foxes may remain dark colored in regions where the climate is warmer.

- Their paws are sheathed in dense fur during the winter, unlike other canids giving it the name "lagopus", which means, "Rabbit footed". They also have a unique counter current heat exchange system in their paws to keep them from freezing. A rounded body shape also lowers their surface area to volume and along with extra body fat, minimizes overall heat loss.

- They only start to shiver when the temperature goes down below -94°F (−70°C). They live in dens with multiple entrances and tunnels that may extend out some 30 square meters (99 sqft).

- The arctic fox will hunt or feed on almost any animal on the smaller size; dead or alive. Besides their favorite, ringed seal pups, these **omnivores** will eat other small mammals such as lemmings, birds, eggs, insects, berries, and seaweed, carrion left by wolves and polar bears, and even the stool left by these larger mammals or by humans.

- Their winter coastal diet consists of marine mammals, invertebrates, sea birds, fish, and seals. Their inland summer diet consists mostly of lemmings. Surplus food is often buried or placed under stones for later retrieval.
- Besides a nomadic life, they also form small bands to scavenge the countryside for food. A family band consists of one adult male, the litter of pups, and two vixens; one of the vixens is a non-breeding female born the previous year that stays to help care for the next litter.
- They have the largest litters in the order Carnivora. 5-8 kits on average, but they may have up to 25 kits in one litter.
- Like other foxes, they do not hibernate.
- The Arctic fox is the only land animal native to Iceland.
- Arctic Foxes live 3-4 years in the wild and up to 16 years in captivity.
- Predators include wolves and bears.

# Side-Striped Jackal

Kingdom: Animalia
Phylum: Chordata
Class: Mammalia
Order: Carnivora
Family: Canidae
Genus: *Canis*
Species: *adustus*
**Binomial name:**
*Canis adustus*

## Wow Facts

- Side-striped jackals inhabit central and southern tropical Africa. They live in wooded areas, savannas, marshes, bush lands, scrublands, grasslands, farmlands, swamps and mountainous areas up to 2,700 meters (1.7 miles) in altitude.
- They are nocturnal.
- They tend to live in pairs, but may form packs of up to 16 members. They are adults by 11 months old.
- Side-striped jackals are **omnivorous** and eat insects, fruits, plant vegetation, vertebrates, and carrion.
- They have shorter legs and ears than other jackals. Their colors are light gray to tan and they have a dark tail with a white tip. They may have a white stripe from elbow to hip and a black stripe on each side of their body, which may not always stand out.
- There are seven subspecies.
- Lifespan: 10-12 years.
- Predators include: hyenas and large wild cats.

# Bengal (Indian) Fox

Kingdom: Animalia
Phylum: Chordata
Class: Mammalia
Order: Carnivora
Family: Canidae
Genus: *Vulpes*
Species: *bengalensis*

**Binomial name:**
*Vulpes bengalensis*

## Wow Facts

- They are native to India, Nepal and Pakistan. They prefer foothills, grasslands, scrublands, and semi-desert habitats.
- Over half their body length is made up of their black tipped bushy tail.
- They are **Omnivores** that feed on termites, beetle, spiders, birds, eggs, small mammals such as gerbils and mice, reptiles, snakes, crabs, and fruits such as mango.
- Bengal foxes are not afraid of humans making them easy to hunt. They hunt in the daytime if not too hot or there are clouds, unless they are near human settlements, then they hunt in the evening and early morning, or hunt nocturnally.
- They hunt alone by themselves.
- They reach sexual maturity in one to two years. Gestation is 50-53 days. They may have 2-6 offspring and the young are independent in four months.
- Lifespan in captivity 6-8 years; 10 years in the wild.
- Predators include: tigers, Asiatic wolves, and feral dogs. Lack of habitat is another threat.
- Hunted by local tribes for food and the body parts are also used for traditional medicine.

# Red Fox

| | |
|---|---|
| Kingdom: <u>Animalia</u><br>Phylum: <u>Chordata</u><br>Class: <u>Mammalia</u><br>Order: <u>Carnivora</u><br>Family: <u>Canidae</u><br>Genus: <u>*Vulpes*</u><br>Species: <u>*vulpes*</u><br>**Binomial name:**<br>*Vulpes vulpes* | |

## Wow Facts

- Red foxes are found from the Arctic Circle to Central America, Eurasia, northern Africa, and they were introduced to Australia. They inhabit forests, tundras, prairies, deserts, mountains, farmlands, urban areas, and even city centers as they adapt to almost any environment.
- Red foxes for the most part live solitary lives and there are 45 subspecies.
- They are **omnivores**. They eat rodents, rabbits, reptiles, birds, insects, and fruit. In England, people are known to leave food out for them at night.
- Coloration of red foxes ranges from pale yellowish red to deep reddish brown on the upper parts and white, ashy or salty colored on the underside. The lower part of the legs is usually black and the tail usually has a white or black tip. All white and all black versions are also known to exist. Red foxes are the largest of the Vulpes species. They are larger in northern regions and smaller in southern regions.
- They colonized North America in at least two waves, and they have been genetically separate from other regions for over 400,000 years.
- They can live 10 to 12 years in captivity, but average three years in the wild. Predators usually go for the young.
- Predators include: wolves, coyotes, golden eagles and large wild cats. Their long soft winter fur makes them irresistible to hunters.

# Antelope

# Klipspringer

Kingdom: Animalia
Phylum: Chordata
Class: Mammalia
Order: Artiodactyla
Family: Bovidae
Genus: Oreotragus
Species: otragus

Binomial name:
***Oreatragus oreotragus***

## Wow Facts

- They are found in South Africa to the highlands of Ethiopia.
- Klipspringers prefer, rocky terrain, cliffs, steep mountains and difficult to access river gorges.
- The klipspringer is an **herbivore** that eats shoots and leaves. Also, fruits, berries, and succulents and derives most of their water from the food they eat.
- It is said that when standing on the tips of their hooves, they may take up no more flat surface area than a dollar coin, allowing them to climb and thrive where few other creatures can reach.
- Their loosely connected hollow hair stands straight up when they want to cool off. Their hair is unique among bovids, but found in pronghorns and the white tailed deer.
- Klipspringers are monogamous animals that are nearly always seen in pairs, usually with one offspring.
- Males are territorial and mark their area with dung.
- Maximum lifespan 14 years.
- They mate for life and while one is eating, the other stands as a lookout for predators such as eagles, leopards, caracals, and humans.

# Kudu

| Kingdom: <u>Animalia</u><br>Phylum: <u>Chordata</u><br>Class: <u>Mammalia</u><br>Order: <u>Artiodactyla</u><br>Family: <u>Bovidae</u><br>Genus: <u>*Tragelaphus*</u><br>Species: <u>*strepsiceros*</u><br>**Binomial name:**<br>***Tagelaphus strepsiceros*** |  |

## Wow Facts

- Greater kudus inhabit woodlands and bush lands. Lesser kudus are found in acacia and thickets in arid savannas. For safety and security reasons, both species avoid open areas.
- Greater kudu are **herbivores**. They eat sprouting grass, leaves, herbs, fruits, vines, flowers, and they love oranges and tangerines.
- When the rains come greater kudu move into the deciduous woodlands. As the lands dry up, they move to the banks of the rivers to look for plants and vegetation along the banks.
- They can survive in waterless areas.
- The body color of the greater kudu varies from reddish brown to blue-gray, with the darkest individuals found in the southern populations.
- Their natural colors and markings camouflage them from most predators and there first response if they sense trouble is to stand still and become essentially invisible by blending in with the local background.
- Adult males have horns averaging 120cm (4ft) in length and the horns are used to make Shofars which are ceremonial blown for Rash Hashanah.
- Females live in herds of 1-3 adults and all their offspring. Female groups may combine to form larger groups, but these groups are not permanent. Males live in bachelor herds, which range from 2 to 10 males.
- Lifespan: 7-8 years in the wild or up to 23 years in captivity.

# Maxwell Duiker

Kingdom: Animalia
Phylum: Chordata
Class: Mammalia
Order: Artiodactyla
Family: Bovidae
Genus: *Philantomba*
Species: *maxwellii*

**Binomial name:**
*Philantomba maxwellii*

## Wow Facts

- They are found in western Africa in Senegal and Gambia to Nigeria. Maxwell's duikers inhabit anything related to rainforests, secondary growth forests, and clearings in rainforests.
- Maxwell's duikers are **herbivores** and eat the leaves of small forest plants, herbs, shrubs, fruits, forest vegetation, flowers discarded by monkeys, ants, plus young birds are eaten in captivity.
- Maxwell's duikers have small horns around 18cm (7 inches) long and both males and females have horns. The horns bend backwards so they won't snag in the underbrush. Females are larger in length and are overall, bigger than males.
- They are either solitary or live in pairs, but where territories overlap or when placed in captivity, duikers can live together in socially harmony.
- They are mostly nocturnal, but sometimes they may be seen in the early morning, late afternoon, and evening.
- They are always on guard and fidgety and constantly flick their tail up and down. They rarely venture more than 30m (90 ft) from thick underbrush.
- They are sexually mature in 3 years and then they may have one offspring each year.
- They are known to live as long as 10 years in captivity.
- Predators include: crowned eagles, pythons, leopards and other wild cats. Humans eat them as bushmeat.

# Ogilby's Duiker

Kingdom: <u>Animalia</u>
Phylum: <u>Chordata</u>
Class: <u>Mammalia</u>
Order: <u>Artiodactyla</u>
Family: <u>Bovidae</u>
Genus: *<u>Cephalopus</u>*
Species: *<u>ogilbyi</u>*

**Binomial name:**
***Cephalophus ogilbyi***

## Wow Facts

- Ogilby's Duiker is found on the equatorial coast of Africa from Sierra Leone, Liberia, over to Nigeria, Cameroon, down to Gabon, and across the gulf of Guinea to Equatorial Guinea's Bioko Island.
- Ogilby's Duikers live in high altitude rainforests and return nightly to the same area to sleep.
- In the wild they are diurnal. They like to forage in the morning and late afternoon. These **herbivores** follow monkeys to feed on fallen fruits, seeds, leaves, and flowers.
- They can be heard making a "wheet" call.
- This small short legged antelope varies in color from light brown to dark brown. Young have spotted coats. Like other duikers they have large hindquarters. A thin black strip runs down their back to their tail.
- Both sexes have short curved spike horns, but male horns can be twice as long as females.
- They have large pre-orbital scent glands in front of their eyes.
- Since 2011 they no longer have subspecies.
- Other duikers are known to live 10 to 15 years in captivity.
- Leopards, Lions, small cats, and pythons are common predators. Humans hunt them for bushmeat.

# Northern Gerenuk

| |
|---|
| Kingdom: <u>Animalia</u><br>Phylum: <u>Chordata</u><br>Class: <u>Mammalia</u><br>Order: <u>Artiodactyla</u><br>Family: <u>Bovidae</u><br>Genus: <u>*Litocranius*</u><br>Species: <u>*walleri*</u><br>**Binomial name:**<br>***Litocranius walleri*** |

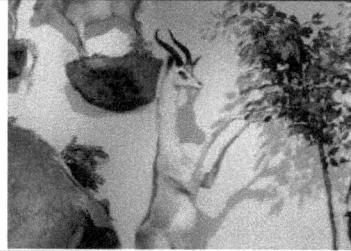

## Wow Facts

- Gerenuk means "giraffe neck" in the Somali language. They are also called Waller's Gazelle.
- They inhabit shrublands, scrublands, and the dry brushy regions of northeast Africa from the Serengeti plains of Tanzania north along the coast through Kenya, Ethiopia, Eritrea, and into southern Somalia. The habitat includes the treeless plains of Tanzania in the southern reaches of its range to the dry high deserts of Kenya.
- These **herbivores** eat flowers, fruits and buds. Their long necks, long legs, and the ability to stand on their hind legs allow them to obtain tree leaves that are out of reach for most other antelope species. Over 80 different species of plants have been found in a single individual's stomach.
- Their big ears and v-shaped face is very distinguishable.
- They do not need to drink water as they get their water content form the plants they eat.
- Males have curved horns.
- Females may form groups of up to ten individuals. Males are solitary and very territorial; they only associate with females when young and during mating season when they are older.
- Their lifespan is 8 years in the wild and 13 years in captivity.
- Predators include: cheetahs, leopards, lions, hyenas, hunting dogs, hyenas, jackals, and eagles.

# Steenbok

Kingdom: <u>Animalia</u>
Phylum: <u>Chordata</u>
Class: <u>Mammalia</u>
Order: <u>Artiodactyla</u>
Family: <u>Bovidae</u>
Genus: *Raphicerus*
Species: *campestris*
**Binomial name:**
*Raphicerus campestris*

## Wow Facts

- Also known as the steinbuck or steinbok.
- They are found in central and southern Africa in Kenya, Tanzania, Angola, Namibia, and South Africa to name a few countries.
- Steenbucks prefer open savannahs with acacia trees and bushes for nearby cover.
- These **herbivores** eat fruits, roots, tubers of plants and sometimes grass; they get most of their water from their food. They prefer the shoots of bush land trees and shrubs and use their sharp hooves to dig them up.
- They are most active during cool periods of the day.
- The steenbok is one of the dwarf antelopes. The short smooth pointed 7-19cm (2.8-7.5 inches) long horns are only found on males.
- They appear reddish-fawn or orange, with a white throat and belly. They also have large, finger lined ears and their slight V shaped face looks similar to a gerenuk, but with a shorter neck.
- Steenbucks are usually found single or in pairs, and they are a territorial species.
- If they perceive the presence of danger, they will initially lay still in the grass. If this strategy fails, they will spring up and run away in zig zag patterns.
- Lifespan: about 7 years.
- Predators include: African wild cat, caracal, jackal, leopard, eagle, and python.

# Harar Dik Dik

Kingdom: Animalia
Phylum: Chordata
Class: Mammalia
Order: Artiodactyla
Family: Bovidae
Genus: *Madoqua*
Species: *saltiana*

**Trinomial name:**
*Madoqua saltiana*
*hararensis*

## Wow Facts

- They are found from Ethiopia, south of Chercher Mountains, to western Somalia on the south side of the Golis Mountains.
- These **herbivores** eat leaves of scrub, bushes, buds, plants, flowers, fruits, berries, and herbs. They use their four-chambered stomach to ruminate and chew cud and they can get all the water they need from the food they eat.
- They tend to live far away from water sources where few predators can survive, so dry mountain slopes and areas with acacia trees and dense underbrush are ideal habitats.
- They are closely related to Salt's Dik Dik.
- The Harar Dik-dik has the reddest coloration of all dik-diks.
- They are a mere 30-40cm (12- 16 inches) tall and weigh 3-6kg (7-16 lb). Only males have (small) horns.
- They are fast and can run 42km/h (26mph).
- Females are larger than males and females are known for emitting the "Dik Dik" sound when alarmed.
- They live alone or in pairs in territorial areas.
- They can live up to 10 years.
- Predators include: lions, hyenas, wild dogs, hawks, eagles, baboons, cheetahs, leopards, and pythons, just to name a few.

# Kirk's Dik Dik

Kingdom: Animalia
Phylum: Chordata
Class: Mammalia
Order: Artiodactyla
Family: Bovidae
Genus: *Madoqua*
Species: *kirkii*

**Binomial name:**
*Madoqua kirkii*

## Wow Facts

- Kirk's Dik-diks are found in extreme southeastern Somalia, central and southern Kenya, northern and central Tanzania, southwestern Angola, and Namibia. Dik-diks inhabit arid bush country, with grass short enough so they can view all around them.
- Dik-diks hide in brush during the warm part of the day. When startled, they take off in a series of zigzag leaps and may call out "zik-zik" or "dik-dik," when disturbed, hence their name. They can run 42km/h (26mph).
- These **herbivores** eat herbs, leaves, berries, and fruit high in water content and can live far from water sources. They prefer vegetation easily digested and low in fiber. 80% of their diet comes from the leaves of trees and shrubs; 17% comes from grasses; and the remainder comes from herbs and sedges.
- Males may have up to 7.6 cm (3 inch) long horns; the small horns are ringed and stout at the base. The horns slant backwards and may be hidden by a tuft of hair on the Dik dik's forehead.
- In the wild they live 5-10 years; 18.4 years in captivity.
- Because of their small size of 35-45cm (14-18 inch) tall, they are preyed upon by wild cats, jackals, leopards, cape hunting dogs, eagles, baboons, crocodiles, and cheetahs. Humans will use an entire hide to make one suede glove. Their bones are used to make jewelry.

# Lelwel Hartebeest

Kingdom: Animalia
Phylum: Chordata
Class: Mammalia
Order: Artiodactyla
Family: Bovidae
Genus: *Alcelaphus*
Species: *buselaphus*

**Trinomial name:**
*Alcelaphus buselaphus lelwel*

## Wow Facts

- They are found in Cameroon, Central African Republic Chad, Sudan, Ethiopia, Uganda, Kenya, and down to Tanzania. They are extinct in five other African countries and their fossils are found in Israel.
- This **herbivore** prefers open plains, grasslands, and savannas.
- They are not aggressive, but will fight to protect young.
- They can run up to 80km\h (48mph).
- They are social and may be found in herds of 20 to 300 individuals; the largest known herd had 10,000.
- Female have more slender horns than males.
- The hartebeest is diurnal and grazes in the cool early morning and late afternoon. They rest in the shade during the hottest part of the day. While feeding, a sentry watches for potential signs of predators, and may be seen standing on a termite mound or other high spot in order to increase their viewing range.
- At 3-4 years of age, males attempt to hold a territory, but usually lose out to 4-5 year old males. Winners lose their territory by the time they reach 8 years old.
- They live 11-20 years in the wild and 19 years in captivity. Hartebeest are first seen in fossil record 4.4 million years ago.
- Predators include: Lions, leopards, hyenas, wild dogs, cheetahs. Juveniles: jackals.
- Other issues: Habitat destruction and displacement by domestic cattle.

# Harvey's Red Duiker

| |
|---|
| Kingdom: Animalia<br>Phylum: Chordata<br>Class: Mammalia<br>Order: Artiodactyla<br>Family: Bovidae<br>Genus: *Cephalophus*<br>Species: *harveyi*<br>**Binomial name:**<br>***Cephalophus harveyi*** |

## Wow Facts

- Harvey's Red Duiker is one of 19 species of duiker found in East Africa namely Tanzania, southeastern Kenya, southern Somalia, and in the Bale Mountains National Park in Ethiopia.
- Duiker is Dutch for "diver" as they dive into the brush if they feel threatened.
- Harvey's Duikers live and stay hidden most of the time in thick brush in mountains, lowlands, and riverside forests, and therefore are hard to study.
- The **omnivores** eat leaves, twigs, fruit, insects, birds eggs, and carrion.
- Harvey's Red Duiker are least concern threatened and not endangered, but they inhabit forested lands that are becoming smaller in number and size as they are harvested for timber.
- They have a chestnut colored coat with patches of black on their face, forehead, and on parts of their legs.
- Females are larger than males, but have smaller horns.
- They are 45-50cm (18-20 inches) tall and weigh 13-16kg (30-35 lb).
- Other species of duikers are known to live 10-15 years.
- Predators include: just about everyone from the cat family, jackals, birds of prey, pythons, and anything else looking for a quick snack.

# Springbok

| Kingdom: <u>Animalia</u> Phylum: <u>Chordata</u> Class: <u>Mammalia</u> Order: <u>Artiodactyla</u> Family: <u>Bovidae</u> Genus: *Antidorcas* Species: *marsupialis* **Binomial name:** *Antidorcas marsupialis* |  |
| --- | --- |

## Wow Facts

- Springbok are found in the south and southwestern African countries of Namibia, Botswana, Angola and the Republic of South Africa. They gravitate to grass savannas near the edges of dry lake beds.
- The springbok has a white colored face with a dark stripe running from their mouth to their eye. They have a reddish-brown coat with a wide dark chevron stripe that runs from their lower front shoulder to a higher point on their back hip. Their lower sides, belly, and tail are white. The tip of the tail is dark colored.
- They have a flap of skin on their back that they use like a flag (crest of white hair) to bring attention to themselves as they repeatedly leap; this is called "pronking" or "stotting".
- This diurnal **herbivore** eats both grass and leaves.
- Females live in herds with their offspring and a few dominant males. Springboks traveled and lived in mega-herds, some million members strong known as "treks," but because they are now mostly confined to private farms and game reserves, treks are few and are limited to remote areas of Angola and Botswana.
- At 97km/h (60mph) they are one of the top 10 fastest land animals. Historically, they first show up in the fossil record in the Pliocene; 3 million years ago. Their modern form goes back to 0.1 million years ago.
- They can live 7-9 years. Predators include Leopards, lions, cheetahs, hyenas, caracals, jackals, pythons, and eagles for small members.

# Zebra Duiker

| |
|---|
| Kingdom: Animalia |
| Phylum: Chordata |
| Class: Mammalia |
| Order: Artiodactyla |
| Family: Bovidae |
| Genus: *Cephalophus* |
| Species: *zebra* |
| **Binomial name:** |
| *Cephalophus zebra* |

## Wow Facts

- Also called the striped-back duiker, they are found in forest areas in the mid-western part of Africa. It inhabits mostly national park regions of Sierra Leone, Côte D'Ivoire (the Ivory Coast), Guinea, and is commonly found in Liberia.
- The zebra duiker inhabits forests in river valleys, rain forests, and hill-forests.
- They remain solitary except when mating and raising an infant.
- They are nocturnal in the wild, but diurnal in captivity.
- These **omnivores** eat leaves, shoots, seeds, fruits, and even rodents. They prefer eating fruits and leaves thrown down or discarded by monkeys, bats, or birds.
- They have 12-16 black vertical stripes over a cream colored area on the sides of their body. The underside or ventral surface is a solid cream color. The head, neck, rump, and limbs are red-brown, and patches of black are found near the joints of their limbs.
- Both sexes have short horns. Females are slightly larger than males. Their markings look similar to the now extinct Tasmanian tiger.
- They live 11-13 years in captivity.
- Predators include: leopards. African gold cats, African rock pythons, crowned eagles, and bushmeat for humans.

# Red Flanked Duiker

| |
|---|
| Kingdom: <u>Animalia</u> |
| Phylum: <u>Chordata</u> |
| Class: <u>Mammalia</u> |
| Order: <u>Artiodactyla</u> |
| Family: <u>Bovidae</u> |
| Genus: *Cephalophus* |
| Species: *rufilatus* |
| **Binomial name:** |
| ***Cephalophus rufilatus*** |

## Wow Facts

- Red-flanked duikers are found in Gambia and Senegal on the west side of Africa over to Sudan and the Nile Valley to the east. They prefer transition zones near open savannas, woodlands, and forests.
- They are **herbivores** and their diet consists mainly of leaves and fallen fruits, but also includes flowers and twigs. They are major players when it comes to eating and later dispersing seeds of the Cape figs, African peaches, and wild dates.
- The duiker's wedge-shaped body with a narrow head and neck gradually widening to the hips is common to many other unrelated species around the world, and this phenomenon is called convergent evolution.
- Red-flanked duikers have a reddish orange coat with a dark greyish stripe on their dorsal midline. The lower legs are bluish grey to dark grey-black. They have large preorbital glands.
- If present, females have smaller horns than males.
- They stand some 35cm (15 inches) tall and weigh 14kg (31 lb).
- Red-flanked duikers feed during the early morning and late evening. They like to reside in one place for a few months before moving on.
- Lifespan in the wild is 5 years and 15 in captivity.
- Predators include: leopards, eagles, rock pythons, and humans. Humans are the greatest predator of all as the use them for bush meat and the hide for leather goods.

# Blackbuck

| Kingdom: Animalia<br>Phylum: Chordata<br>Class: Mammalia<br>Order: Artiodactyla<br>Family: Bovidae<br>Genus: *Antilope*<br>Species: *cervicapra*<br>**Binomial name:**<br>*Antilope cervicapra* |  |

## Wow Facts

- They are native to the India subcontinent and migrated to Pakistan and southern Nepal. They live in open woodlands, semi-desert areas, and dry deciduous forests. They were introduced to Argentina and Texas.
- They prefer to live near grasslands and rest in the shade on hot days.
- These **herbivores** are grazers; they feed on short grass as well as occasional pods, flowers, and fruits. Unfortunately, they also love agricultural crops such as sorghum and millet and that puts them in direct conflict with farmers.
- The blackbuck males have long spiraling horns and turn dark brown on their upper sides with age, while females are tan or fawn colored and no horns. Both sexes have white under sides, insides of the legs, and a white circular patch around each eye.
- They are gregarious social animals and may live in herds of 5 to 50 animals, but herds may gather in groups by the thousands. Each herd is a harem consisting of one dominant male and any number of adult females and their young.
- They can run 80km/h (50mph) or gallop at 64km/h (40mph) for up to 24km (15 miles).
- They can live 12-16 years.
- Predators include: Wolves, and previously, the extinct Asiatic cheetah. Fawns fall victim to jackals. Domestic livestock destroy Blackbuck habitat and introduce bovine diseases.

# Nyala

| | |
|---|---|
| Kingdom: <u>Animalia</u><br>Phylum: <u>Chordata</u><br>Class: <u>Mammalia</u><br>Order: <u>Artiodactyla</u><br>Family: <u>Bovidae</u><br>Genus: *Tragelaphus*<br>Species: *angasii*<br>**Binomial name:**<br>*Tragelaphus angasii* | |

## Wow Facts

- Nyala are found in southeastern Africa. They inhabit dry thickets of savanna woodlands, in close proximity to grasslands and fresh water, but they can also survive in areas where water is only available seasonally. At the hottest part of the day they remain in shaded thicket areas and then eat during the cooler evening or early morning.

- These **herbivores** graze or browse on leaves, twigs, flowers, and fruits. In the rainy season they feed on fresh grass and plants.

- When in danger they make a "dog-like" bark alarm call and they react to impala, baboon, and kudu calls.

- Nyala are medium sized antelopes. Males are larger and turn slate gray or bluish as adults and are tan below the knees. Males have spiral horns with one to two twists and are yellow tipped. Females and juveniles are rusty red in color. Both males and females have a ridge of hair that runs from the back of the head to their tail and patterns of white vertical stripes and spots. Males also have fringing hair on their chin, chest, and stomach areas.

- Nyala are gregarious, and live in groups of 2-30 individuals. Old males live alone.

- They are known to live just under 19 years. They are first seen in the fossil record 5.8 million years ago.

- Predators include: lions, leopards, and cape hunting dogs. Juveniles: also baboons and birds of prey. Adult males are in high demand by big game hunters.

# Sable

| Kingdom: Animalia<br>Phylum: Chordata<br>Class: Mammalia<br>Order: Artiodactyla<br>Family: Bovidae<br>Genus: *Hippotragus*<br>Species: *niger*<br>**Binomial name:**<br>***Hippotragus niger*** | |

## Wow Facts

- Sable live in the southern woodlands, grasslands and savanna of Africa from southeastern Kenya, eastern Tanzania, and Mozambique to Angola and southern Zaire. In South Africa they are raised commercially and on reserves.
- Sables are ruminating **herbivores** and feed 85% on grass. They also feed on foliage and herbs, especially those growing on termite mounds.
- Sable antelope are both nocturnal and diurnal, although they prefer to feed just until dark, because of a high risk of predation at night. Most sable will travel roughly a mile a day for food and less during the dry season.
- Sables are powerfully built and have a strong thick neck. Male ringed horns grow out more and curve more than female horns. Males and females are appear similar until 3 years of age when males become darker and grow bigger in size than females. They are then exiled from the herd, of one male and 10-30 females and calves, and form bachelor groups.
- Sable can live 13-16 years, if they don't starve from ground down teeth, or up to 19 years in captivity.
- Lions rarely attack adults, because of their size and their ability to defend themselves. Humans are the only real threat to adult sable. Young calves are preyed upon by lions, leopards, hyenas, African hunting dogs, and crocodiles.

# Livingstone Suni

| |
|---|
| Kingdom: Animalia<br>Phylum: Chordata<br>Class: Mammalia<br>Order: Artiodactyla<br>Family: Bovidae<br>Genus: *Neotragus*<br>Species: *moschatus*<br>**Trinomial name:**<br>***Neotragus moschatus***<br>***livingstonianus*** | |

## Wow Facts

- They inhabit dense under bush and thicket areas in the Kwazulu-Natal Province of South Africa, Mozambique, Zambia, and Zimbabwe.
- They are one of the smallest antelopes at 30-43cm (12-13 inches) tall and weighing 4.5-5.4kg (10-12lb).
- Females don't have horns, but are slightly larger.
- This **herbivore** eats, shoots, and leaves. They also eat fruits, mushrooms, and flowers and require very little water to drink. They prefer to eat in the morning and late afternoon.
- Named after the missionary and explorer Dr. David Livingstone (1813-1884).
- Livingstone suni are larger than East African suni and they have longer, thicker horns; 8-13cm (3-5 inches). They are reddish brown in color with a white underside. The back, neck, and top of the head may be darker than the sides. The tail is relatively long, dark, but has a white edge. The upper lip protrudes over the lower lip.
- They make barking and whistling sounds.
- They may live up to 7 years in the wild.
- Predators include: lions to birds of prey, just about any predator in Africa is large enough and strong enough to catch these little antelopes. They prefer well used trails and are easy to catch in traps. Trophy hunters use a shotgun as they only get one shot before they're gone.

# BIRDS

# India Blue Peacock

| | |
|---|---|
| Kingdom: <u>Animalia</u><br>Phylum: <u>Chordata</u><br>Class: <u>Aves</u><br>Order: <u>Galliformes</u><br>Family: <u>Phasianidae</u><br>Genus: *Pavo*<br>Species: *cristatus*<br>**Binomial name:**<br>*Pavo cristatus* | |

## Wow Facts

- Indian blue peafowl (also known as peacocks) is one of three species of peafowl. *Pavo cristatus* are native to Sri Lanka and India, but can also be found naturally in Pakistan, Kashmir, Nepal, and many other regions. The green peafowl, *Pavo muticus* is found in Burma, Indochina, and Java in Indonesia. *Pavo congensis* is found in Africa in the Congo. They are most common in deciduous, open forest habitats.

- Males are called peacocks, females are peahens, and chicks are peachicks.

- Blue peafowl necks and breasts are a bright blue, golden feathers line their sides and backs, and their trains are an iridescent arrangement of multiple colors featuring ocelli (eye-spots).

- Blue peafowl are **omnivores**. They consume insects, worms, lizards, frogs, small mammals, and snakes. Termites are their food of choice. They also feed on tree and flower buds, petals, grain, grass and bamboo shoots.

- Peafowl are prized possessions and therefore can be found in any country in captivity through trade with India. Indian blue peafowl do not migrate or travel widely, but can adapt to harsh climate once relocated even as cold and as far north as Ontario, Canada.

- Indian blue peafowl are known best for their exquisite train and plumage. If the length of the tail and wing span is included, the peafowl is considered one of the largest flying birds. Females are brown, grey, and cream-colored. Chicks are usually a light yellow to brown color. The males have a long train, about 1.2m in length on average, from June to December. The train is discarded in January, but is grown again at a rapid pace when breeding season approaches.

- Charles Darwin studied them to find out why peacocks evolved to stand out so much, and why peahens evolved to blend in so well.
- It is said that the bright coloration of the male peacock is a handicap or liability for survival as they standout for prey, but female peahens lose interest in males that have had their eye spots on their trains cut off.
- White peacocks with pink eyes are albino and lack melanin, where white peacocks with blue eyes have leucism; a genetic mutation that reduces pigment.
- Indian blue peafowl prefer a mostly solitary and isolated lifestyle. During the breeding season, a male will defend its territory and females will seek them out as mates. A single male can have a harem of six females. They nest on the ground, but roost in the trees.
- *Pavo cristatus* can live up to 25 years in the wild, but the average 20 years due to predation, diseases, electrocution from flying into power lines, pesticide poisoning, and destruction of their natural habitat.
- Predators include: civets, tigers, and leopards.

# Great Horned Owl

| |
|---|
| Kingdom: Animalia |
| Phylum: Chordata |
| Class: Aves |
| Order: Strigiformes |
| Family: Phasianidae |
| Genus: *Bubo* |
| Species: *virginianus* |
| **Binomial name:** |
| ***Bubo virginianus*** |

## Wow Facts

- Great horned owls are found in North, Central, and South America. They inhabit pampas, rain forests, deserts, swamps, dense woodlands of hardwoods and conifers, along cliffs, rocky fringes of canyons, and in forest openings. They will inhabit just about anywhere, but will not colonize islands and they don't build their own nests. There are 20 species.

- The great horned owl is solitary and inhabits areas away from human settlements.

- Owls as a group eat their prey whole and some 6-10 hours later regurgitate the unwanted parts (bones, fur, and feathers) in the form of pellets.

- For smaller prey, they stab them with their talons and/or constrict their prey so it can't breathe with a strong force of 13,000g (29lb). Large prey is decapitated and may be torn in strips to swallow and they may cache/store extra prey in trees for eating later.

- By studying the prey remains in these regurgitated pellets scientist have counted some 500 different species of prey.

- They hunt mostly at night, preferring to feed on small mammals, such as rabbits, woodchucks, mice, rats, squirrels, skunks, porcupines and coyote pups. The great horned owl is also known to feed on some 250 species of birds such as crows, ravens, ducks, game birds, quails, and occasionally geese or turkeys. Crabs, scorpions, bats, and frogs are also on the menu. In all they eat approximately 87% mammals, 6.1% birds,

1.6% reptiles and amphibians, and 4.7% insects and invertebrates.

- Great horned owls have short wings and slow maneuverability at 40mph (65km/h), but they are the fiercest and most powerful of the common owls. They can take on any bird talon to talon and only eagles have a slight advantage in battle. Red tail hawks rule the sky most of the day, but great horned owls take over when night falls. Their large eyes, great night vision, and silent soft feathered wings turn them into powerful stealth fighters on the prowl at a time when their prey is most active.

- They can also hunt during the day, but if they do, they are more likely to be mobbed by crows and ravens or attacked by defending territorial red tailed hawks or eagles.

- They are sometimes called the cat owl because of their catlike ears, eyes, shape of head, and appearance when huddled up on its nest. They are also recognizable for the feather tufts on their head that resemble horns. Their large eyes do not move from side to side, but rather the whole head can turn 270°.

- Cold Alaska and Ontario, Canada have the largest great horned owls, and they are smaller in warmer California and Texas, but they are the smallest in even warmer Baja California and the Yucatan Peninsula of Mexico. Pleistocene fossils are larger than modern day remains/skeletons of great horned owls.

- As adults they are shot, trapped, electrocuted, hit by cars, attacked by eagles, or caught unaware by a mountain lion. Juveniles, as well as eggs, are taken by foxes, bobcats, feral cats, ravens, crows, and snakes.

- In the wild they can live 13 years, and 38 years in captivity.

# Ring Necked Pheasant

| | |
|---|---|
| Kingdom: <u>Animalia</u><br>Phylum: <u>Chordata</u><br>Class: <u>Aves</u><br>Order: <u>Galliformes</u><br>Family: <u>Phasianidae</u><br>Genus: *Phasianus*<br>Species: *colchicus*<br>**Binomial name:**<br>***Phasianus***<br>     ***colchicus*** | |

## Wow Facts

- Their native range extends from the Caspian Sea, east across central Asia to China, and includes Korea, Japan, and former Burma. They were introduced to Europe, North America, New Zealand, Australia, Hawaii, South Africa, and South America. In many places they are bred to be hunted.
- In North America, *Phasianus colchicus* populations have been established on agricultural lands and grasslands from southern Canada to Utah, California to New England states, and south to Virginia.
- They prefer relatively open cover, such as grass and stubble fields and are found in habitats with grass, ditches, hedges, marshes, and tree stands or bushes for cover.
- Pheasants are dietary generalists, eating a wide variety of plant matter, such as grain, seeds, shoots, and berries, as well as insects and small invertebrates.
- They are mostly ground dwelling and scratch for food in the undergrowth with their bill. Pheasants prefer to roost in trees at night if trees are available.
- Like Roadrunners, Pheasants would rather run from trouble and dash for cover, but if need be, they will noisily take off and fly for short distances.
- Common pheasants are medium-sized birds with

deep, pear-shaped bodies, small heads and long, thin tails. They are sexually dimorphic, with males being more colorful and larger than females; similar to peacocks. Males have spectacular, multi-colored plumage with long, pointed and barred tails and fleshy red eye patches.

- Common pheasants are social birds. In the autumn, they flock together, sometimes in large groups in areas with food and cover. Usually the core home range is smaller in the winter than during the nesting season. Flocks formed in the winter may be mixed or single-sexed and may have up to 50 pheasants. Common pheasants are social birds. In the autumn, they flock together, sometimes in large groups in areas with food and cover. Usually the core home range is smaller in the winter than during the nesting season.
- Nearly all wild birds die by age three.
- Predators include many types of carnivores, but most pheasants are hunted by humans.

# Lady Amherst Pheasant

| Kingdom: Animalia<br>Phylum: Chordata<br>Class: Aves<br>Order: Galliformes<br>Family: Phasianidae<br>Genus: *Chrysolophus*<br>Species: *amherstiae*<br>**Binomial name:**<br>*Chrysolophus*<br>    *amherstiae* | |

## Wow Facts

- They are native to southwestern China and Myanmar, but they have been introduced to other regions.
- William Pitt Amherst, Governor General of India and husband of the countess of Amherst (1762-1838), sent the first birds to London in the early 1800s.
- They have a black and silver head, long grey tail and rump, and red, blue, white and yellow body plumage.

# Golden Pheasant

| Kingdom: Animalia<br>Phylum: Chordata<br>Class: Aves<br>Order: Galliformes<br>Family: Phasianidae<br>Genus: *Chrysolophus*<br>Species: *pictus*<br>**Binomial name:**<br>*Chrysolophus pictus* | |

## Wow Facts

- They are native to forests in mountainous areas of western China and have been introduced to the rest of the world.
- Males have a golden-yellow crest with a hint of red at the tip. The face, throat, chin, and the sides of neck are rusty tan. Females appear similar to the female common pheasant.

# Mongolian Pheasant

| Kingdom: Animalia<br>Phylum: Chordata<br>Class: Aves<br>Order: Galliformes<br>Family: Phasianidae<br>Genus: *Phasianus*<br>Species: *colchicus mongolicus*<br>**Trinomial name:**<br>***Phasianus colchicus mongolicus*** | |

## Wow Facts

- This subspecies is native to cold regions of Turkistan and Mongolia. Now found even in Oregon.
- It has a broad white neck ring and white coverts on wings; other body colors brown to copper colored.

# Silver Pheasant

| Kingdom: Animalia<br>Phylum: Chordata<br>Class: Aves<br>Order: Galliformes<br>Family: Phasianidae<br>Genus: *Lophura*<br>Species: *nycthemera*<br>**Binomial name:**<br>***Lophura nycthemera*** | |

## Wow Facts

- They are found in mountain forests of Southeast Asia, and eastern and southern China, and introduced in Hawaii as well as various other locations in the US mainland.
- They are well known in ancient Chinese art and poetry.
- The male is black and white, while the female is mainly brown. Both sexes have a bare red face and red legs (the latter separating it from the greyish-legged Kalij Pheasant).

# Canada Goose

| | |
|---|---|
| Kingdom: <u>Animalia</u><br>Phylum: <u>Chordata</u><br>Class: <u>Aves</u><br>Order: <u>Anseriformes</u><br>Family: <u>Anatidae</u><br>Genus: *Branta*<br>Species: *canadensis*<br>**Binomial name:**<br>***Branta***<br>　　　***canadensis*** | |

## Wow Facts

- Canadian geese, as many Americans call them, are found throughout North America in arctic temperate regions, Northern Europe and they have even reached china and Japan. They have been also introduced to countries such as New Zealand, Argentina, and the Falkland Islands. They are found near waterways in open, grassy habitats such as grasslands, chaparral, and arctic tundra.
- They enjoy feeding in man-made habitats that are open and grassy, such as golf courses, agricultural land, airports, and parks. They also appear to enjoy defecating on docks, yachts, and expensively groomed shoreline properties most profusely and with great regularity to the great displeasure of surrounding homeowners.
- Migration begins in the fall and takes place in large flocks. Many Canadian geese living in warm places with abundant water such as Florida have given up the whole migration thing altogether. Meanwhile further north, large winter aggregations of geese form while on lakes, coastal waters, and mudflats. In flight, flocks form large aerodynamic V formations to reduce drag and change places as they travel on.
- When on land, they eat a variety of grasses including Bermuda grass, salt grass and wild barley.

Geese are able to grab a hold of each blade and pull it out with their bills by jerking their heads. They also eat wheat, beans, rice, corn, seaweed, insects, and fish.

- They have a black neck, bill, and head with a white chin strap plus occasional white patches elsewhere. The body is usually brownish-gray although colors vary in some of the 7 subspecies.
- They are reported to live up to 24 years in the wild and up to 31 years in captivity.
- Many die within their first year of life, as nestlings, fledglings, and during their first migration. Canada geese are highly social, being found in flocks at all times of the year except when they are nesting.
- Unguarded nests and eggs are targets for predators such as gulls, common ravens, American crows, skunks, domestic dogs, raccoons, wolves, coyotes, owls, falcons, and many others. Canada geese are also a common game bird, hunted regularly by humans, but should not be consumed in some areas due to built up toxins, and ingested residual chemicals. Not only do many people consider them a pest, but they are a major hazard for humans in the form of accidental hits "airstrikes" on planes.

# King Vulture

| | |
|---|---|
| Kingdom: Animalia<br>Phylum: Chordata<br>Class: Aves<br>Order: Falconiformes<br>Family: Cathartidae<br>Genus: *Sarcoramphus*<br>Species: *papa*<br>**Binomial name:**<br>*Sarcoramphus papa* | |

## Wow Facts

- King vultures are found in the southern part of Mexico and on the east side all the way down through Central America and down to Argentina. They generally live in undisturbed forests in the lowland tropics.

- The most noticeable difference between king vultures and other vultures is that they are mostly covered with white plumage. Their wings are half white and black tipped. The ruff, flight, and tail feathers are gray to black; the black areas have an almost opalescent sheen. Their bare head, neck, beak and muttle are reddish orange and yellow. Their eyes are straw, white, or silver in color. Their beaks have a hooked tip and cutting edges, which are very strong. Their feet are gray.

- They are scavengers. Their main source of food is dead animals, and sometimes fruit. Their sense of smell is limited; therefore, they follow other smaller species of vultures to the site of the carrion and then take over as if they were king, but otherwise are non-aggressive.

- King vultures stay in family units and do not congregate in large groups. They remain out of sight for the most part, sitting high in the canopy or flying and soaring high in the air looking for food. They try to minimize flapping their wings and prefer to glide. They mate for life. They are not migratory and are seen in the same areas all year long.

- They can live 30 years in captivity. Their closest living relative is the Andean Condor. Jaguars may catch an adult, but snakes kill the young.

# Wild Turkey

| |
|---|
| Kingdom: <u>Animalia</u><br>Phylum: <u>Chordata</u><br>Class: <u>Aves</u><br>Order: <u>Galliformes</u><br>Family: <u>Phasianidae</u><br>Genus: *Meleagris*<br>Species: *gallopavo*<br>**Binomial name:**<br>*Meleagris gallopavo* |

## Wow Facts

- They are found everywhere in North America and northern Mexico and introduced to Hawaii and New Zealand.
- They prefer wooded forests with scattered openings such as cow pastures, fields, orchards, swamps, and marshes.
- They are swift runners and fast fliers. Turkeys have been recorded flying at 55mph (88.5 km/h).
- These **omnivores** eat acorns, nuts, seeds, berries, buds, leaves, roots, grasses, and fern fronds. They also eat ground-dwelling insects, lizards, and salamanders, which account for about 10% of their diet.
- Males are called "toms" and have dark iridescent plumage. Their flight feathers are black with brown stripes and are barred with white. They have a red wattle (a fleshy lobe that hangs down from the chin or throat). Females are called "hens" and are brown and gray. Juvenile males are called "Jakes"
- Wild turkeys are diurnal and non-migratory. They can be seen grazing in fields and woodlands. At night, they roost in trees.
- The lifespan for wild turkeys is 1.3 to 1.6 years.
- Humans are the primary predator of adult wild turkeys. Other predators include coyotes, wolves, bobcats, raccoons, bears, mountain lions, golden eagles, and great horned owls. Eggs are eaten by smaller mammals, birds, and snakes.

# Emu

| Kingdom: Animalia<br>Phylum: Chordata<br>Class: Aves<br>Order: Struthioniformes<br>Family: Dromaiidae<br>Genus: *Dromaius*<br>Species: *novaehollandiae*<br>**Binomial name:**<br>***Dromaius novaehollandiae*** | |

## Wow Facts

- Found in Australia in all areas except rainforest and cleared land; rare in deserts and the extreme north.
- Found in desert areas only after heavy rains have caused growth of herbs and grasses and heavy fruiting of shrubs.
- The emu is the second largest living bird. They are flightless and shaggy birds. Their necks and legs are long, but their wings are tiny. After molting the birds are dark, but as sunlight fades the melanins that give the feathers their brown color, the birds become paler. They have three toes like *T. Rex* and velociraptors.
- These omnivores eat wheat, seeds, fruits, flowers and young shoots. They disperse seed too. They will also eat insects and small vertebrates when available.
- Emus ingest large pebbles up to 46g (1.6 ounces) to help their gizzards grind up food. They also often eat charcoal.
- The males sometimes make calls which sound like "e-moo" and can be heard over long distances. Females make characteristic resonant, booming sounds.
- The emu is a good swimmer and a fast runner at 30mph (50 km/h).
- Females court males. Males make nests, incubate eggs, and raise the young.
- Live 19 years in the wild and 40 in captivity.
- Predators include: dingos for adults, and monitor lizards and red fox for young.

# Chilean Flamingo

| Kingdom: Animalia<br>Phylum: Chordata<br>Class: Aves<br>Order: Phoenicopteriformes<br>Family: Phoenicopteridae<br>Genus: *Phoenicopterus*<br>Species: *chilensis*<br>**Binomial name:**<br>*Phoenicopterus*<br>*chilensis* | |

## Wow Facts

- Found in temperate South America from Peru, Chile, Argentina, Brazil, and introduced to Germany, Netherlands, Utah, and California. Chilean flamingos inhabit muddy, shallow alkaline and brackish lakes.
- They live in warm and tropical environments, and range from sea level, along the coast, to high altitudes up to 4,500m (13,123ft) in the Andes.
- Like all adult flamingos, Chilean flamingos have pink plumage, but the plumage is mostly whitish with a faint pink tinge. In addition to the pink plumage, they have black primary and secondary wing feathers lined with bright crimson along the edge. Chicks are born gray.
- They have small heads, long necks in proportion to their bodies, bare faces, linear nostrils, pale yellow irises, long legs, and three webbed front toes, which help support them in mud.
- Their long necks are formed from the elongation of their 19 cervical vertebrae similar to giraffes.
- The bill of Chilean flamingos consists of two main colors: the terminal half is black and the rest is white.
- This **carnivore** eats insects, mollusks, aquatic or marine worms, aquatic crustaceans, other marine invertebrates, and zooplankton.
- Chilean flamingos are gregarious social birds that

feed and nest together in flocks ranging from a few individuals to tens of thousands. They have to nest in crowded conditions to stimulate breeding.

- They are good swimmers and migrating groups fly in skeins (V-formation), with their long necks and feet held straight out. They communicate in flight with loud, goose-like calls, which are important in keeping the flock together. On the ground, they stand on one leg to conserve body heat, drawing the other leg close to the body and tucking the head under a wing.
- It is not unusual to find 50 year old Chilean flamingos in the wild. In captivity, the average life span is around 40 years.

# Ostrich

| | |
|---|---|
| Kingdom: <u>Animalia</u><br>Phylum: <u>Chordata</u><br>Class: <u>Aves</u><br>Order: <u>Struthioniformes</u><br>Family: <u>Struthionidae</u><br>Genus: *Struthio*<br>Species: *camelus*<br>**Binomial name:**<br>***Struthio camelus*** | |

## Wow Facts

- Ostriches are currently restricted to drier and sandy regions of central and southern Africa. They became extinct in China at the end of the Ice age where they are still seen on petro glyphs and prehistoric pottery. There are five sub-species.
- They are the tallest terrestrial bird and have the largest egg of any living bird.
- Ostriches are **herbivores** eating mostly plant matter such as shrubs, grass, fruit, and flowers, but they occasionally eat insects such as locusts, and animal remains left by predators. They are very selective feeders, taking the seed heads of grasses and certain flowers. An ostrich in captivity requires 3.5 kg (7.7 lbs) of food per day. They use "gastroliths" stomach stones to help grind food in their gizzards.
- They can survive without water for long periods of time and can lose up to 25% of their weight in water, but they love to take baths when possible.
- Males are black and white, females gray brown.
- They live in flocks of 5 to 50, and they are normally found in the company of grazing animals like antelope and zebras. Smaller groups of 2-5 members are formed outside of the breeding season.
- Sometimes, in order to escape detection, ostriches may lie on the ground with their necks outstretched. This peculiar behavior most likely gave rise to the myth that ostriches bury their heads in the ground.
- They have the fastest land speed of any bird and can

run short periods up to 70km/h (43mph) using their
wings as rudders to change direction. They can run
a steady pace of 50km/h (31 mph) for longer
periods. Their strong legs can kick a man to death,
but only in a forward direction.

- They are farmed for their eggs, meat, and as a
tourist attraction not only in Africa, but in Australia,
Israel, New Mexico, and Curacao in the Dutch West
Indies.

# Humboldt Penguin

| Kingdom: Animalia<br>Phylum: Chordata<br>Class: Aves<br>Order: Sphenisciformes<br>Family: Spheniscidae<br>Genus: *Spheniscus*<br>Species: *humboldti*<br>**Binomial name:**<br>***Spheniscus humboldti*** | |
|---|---|

## Wow Facts

- They inhabit the coastal regions of Peru and Chile. They spend most of their time at sea. On land, they live in burrows composed of soil, rock, or guano, and they may live in large colonies.
- They are black and white in color with pink around the eyes and on the beak. The feet are webbed and serve as rudders. They have claws at the end of their toes for climbing.
- The feathers are in two layers. The top layer is flat and overlaps the second layer to stop the wind and water from penetrating to the body. The second down layer is for insulation. The wings evolved into flippers for flying through the water. Their bones are solid and act as ballast while diving.
- The feathers must be groomed to prevent water infiltration as maintaining a high degree of air insulation is important. Before their early feeding in the morning, they preen. They gather oil from the preening gland located in the rump where the tail originates. The oil is applied to the feathers and edges of the flippers. They also preen each other.
- They eat small fish and crustaceans. They have spines on their tongue to help hold on to their catch.
- The average life span is 15 to 20 years. In water, they are eaten by leopard seals, fur seals, sea lions, sharks, and killer whales. On land foxes, snakes, and introduced predators such as cats and dogs prey on the eggs and chicks.

# Adelie Penguin

| Kingdom: Animalia<br>Phylum: Chordata<br>Class: Aves<br>Order: Sphenisciformes<br>Family: Spheniscidae<br>Genus: *Pygoscelis*<br>Species: *adeliae*<br>**Binomial name:**<br>*Pygoscelis adeliae* | |
|---|---|

## Wow Facts

- Adelie Penguins are found only in the Antarctic..
- Adelie penguins are social hunters. They typically stay in groups as it reduces risk of predation and increases efficiency of finding food. They can dive to 175m (575ft) deep.
- The primary food source for Adelie penguins is krill, but they also like squid, and silverfish. They can swim up to 72km/h (45mph).
- Living in the Antarctic region, Adelie penguins must withstand very cold temperatures.
- Adelie penguins are one of the smaller species of penguins in Antarctica; just above 60.96 cm (2ft) tall. Their back, long tail, head and face are black. They have a white belly and a white ring around their brown eyes. Their feathers cover half of their bill, which is black with an orange base. They have dull white to pink legs and feet with black soles.
- They are constantly interacting with others in their small group or colony. They also travel together from pack ice to their nesting beach when breeding season is about to begin. There is no known social structure within their colony, but mated pairs are protective of their nest site made out of stones and grass which are frequently stolen by their neighbors. Parents take turns nesting on 1 to 2 eggs.
- They live 5 to 20 years.
- Typical predators are leopard seals, killer whales, and south polar skuas.

# Osprey

| |
|---|
| Kingdom: <u>Animalia</u><br>Phylum: <u>Chordata</u><br>Class: <u>Aves</u><br>Order: <u>Accipitriformes</u><br>Family: <u>Pandionidae</u><br>Genus: *Pandion*<br>Species: *haliaetus*<br>Binomial name:<br>***Pandion haliaetus*** |

## Wow Facts

- They are also known as the Sea Hawk, river hawk, fish hawk, and fish eagle. There are four species. *Aspriet* is an old Anglo-French word for *bird of prey*.
- They are found in every continent except for Antarctica. They are found near rivers, ponds, streams, estuaries, and coral reefs, as far remote as the Solomon Islands, and their fossils have been found in Tonga. The oldest known fossils are from the Oligocene (35-23 million years ago) in Egypt.
- They have a black bill and white feet. The eyes are golden or brown with a pale blue nictitating membrane. Like an owl, their out toe is reversible and they can grasp prey with two front and two back toes.
- They can close their nostrils to keep out water.
- Seen in the air, they seem to have bent or "M" shaped wings. The male is slimmer than the female.
- They migrate from as far away as Norway to India, and spend winter in Africa, South America, South East Asia, Malaysia, and the Philippines.
- They predominantly eat fish, but will eat small mammals, frogs, or reptiles if the fishing is poor.
- They hunt by eyesight from 10-40m (30-131ft) high. They dive feet first down on a fish near the surface.
- They mate for life. The female stays on the nest, the male brings food, and the female feeds the juveniles.
- Life span averages 7-10 years, but one lived 30 years.
- They are preyed on by great horned owls, golden eagles, and bald eagles.

# Main Hall

# African Lion

| | |
|---|---|
| Kingdom: <u>Animalia</u><br>Phylum: <u>Chordata</u><br>Class: <u>Mammalia</u><br>Order: <u>Carnivora</u><br>Family: <u>Felidae</u><br>Genus: *Panthera*<br>Species: <u>Leo</u><br>Binomial Name:<br>*Panthera leo* | |

## Wow Facts

- African lions live in plains or savanna habitats.
- The Jaguar and Tiger are their closest relatives and lions evolved in Africa around one million years ago.
- Larger species of cave lions, appeared 500,000 years ago, but died out around 10,000 years ago.
- In the late Pleistocene, some 10,000 years ago, humans were the only large land mammals more widespread than lions.
- Lions are the only cats that live in groups, which are called **prides**.
- Lions may scavenge up to 50 percent of their food.
- Lions are primarily nocturnal hunters and can sleep some 20 hours a day.
- Female lions are the pride's primary hunters. These **carnivores** often work together to prey upon antelopes, zebras, wildebeest, and other large animals of the open grasslands, but typically an individual lioness does the actual killing.
- A male lion can kill a hyena with one well-placed bite.
- Males are known to kill cubs in newly acquired prides in order to speed up the process of adult females being able to bear the new male's own offspring. Females are known to defend their pride from the advances of unfamiliar male lions to protect their existing young.
- Lions can live up to 14 years in the wild and more than 20 years in captivity.

# Albertosaurus

Kingdom: <u>Animalia</u>
Phylum: <u>Chordata</u>
Order: Saurischia
Family: Tyrannosauridae
Genus: *Albertosaurus*
Species: *sarcophagus*

Binomial Name:
*Albertosaurus sarcophagus*

## Wow Facts

- 71-68 Million Years Ago; Late Cretaceous period.
- Greek for "Alberta lizard". Sarcophagus means "flesh eating".
- First found in 1884 in the Horseshoe Canyon Formation in Red Deer River, Alberta Canada. Twenty-six of the known thirty fossils are from this one area and thought to have come together due to rising flood waters.
- The largest found was 28 years old and 10m (33ft) long. The smallest was 2yrs old and 2m (6.6ft) long. By the age of two they were one of the largest predators in the area. Adults could weigh 1.7 tonnes (1.9 tons).
- They were more slender and smaller than *T. rex,* their legs were longer, and had a smaller head 1m (3.3ft) long.
- They had a bony crest above their eyes that may have been used for species identification or for mating purposes.
- Like *T. rex*, they had 58 banana sized teeth except the front teeth were slightly smaller.
- Their bite force of their back teeth was 3,413 Newtons.
- Adults are thought to walk 14-21km/h (8-13mph). Juveniles are thought to have been much faster.
- Like *T. rex* they had two digits with claws on their hands and three toes for walking on their feet and a smaller dewclaw that does not reach the ground. Healed ribs and shoulder bones show that they could take a bad fall and keep on going.
- These **carnivores** disappeared from the fossil record at the same time that *T. rex* first appeared in the area.

# Archaeopteryx

Kingdom: <u>Animalia</u>
Phylum: <u>Chordata</u>
Order: Saurischia
Family: Archaeopterygidae
Genus: *Archaeopteryx*
Species: *lithographica*

Binomial Name:

*Archaeopteryx*
*lithographica*

## Wow Facts

- 150.8-148.5 Million Years Ago; Late Cretaceous period.
- Greek for "ancient wing" Pronounced ark-e-op-ter-ix.
- 51cm (20 inches) long; about the size of a raven.
- It was thought to be the oldest bird, but now thought to be a close relative of some of the most primitive birds, as three other species have been recently identified.
- The first fossil was found in Solnhofen in southern Germany in a lagoon when Europe was a series of arid islands near the equator; similar to islands near Baja California, Mexico today.
- Archaeopteryx was a primitive bird and like modern birds they had flight feathers, hollow bones, and a wishbone. (furcula). They also had a long bony tail with a frond shaped group of feathers at the end unlike the fantail of feathers found in modern birds.
- They had predator teeth and three claws on the fore limbs (each wing) that were similar to those of the **carnivore** *Deinonychus.* On their three toe feet they had a killing claw; a hyper extensible second toe.
- They are thought to have been warm blooded, but with a slow growth and metabolic rate similar to a flightless Kiwi bird.
- Because of their flat sternum keel, they are thought to have weak flight muscles similar to Grebes. They may have required a long take off path like Grebes, a jump to start their flight, or they may have climbed trees or rock cliffs then slowly sailed down towards prey over lagoons with slight down strokes of the wings.

# Blue Duiker

Kingdom: Animalia
Phylum: Chordata
Class: Mammalia
Order: Artiodactyla
Family: Bovidae
Genus: *Philantomba*
Species: *monticola*

Binomial Name:
*Philantomba monticola*

## Wow Facts

- They live in habitats from sea level to 3,000m (9,800ft). Montis is Latin for "mountain", colo means "I inhabit".
- They are found in at least 18 countries from western and eastern Africa; anywhere with dense brush or understory.
- Besides east and west, there are two sub groups; a gray legged northern species, and a red legged southern species. In all there are 16 sub species with coat colors ranging from blue, gray, brown, and black.
- They are 32-41cm (13-16 inches) at the shoulder, 55-90cm (22-35 inches) long, and weigh some 3.5-9kg (7.7-19.8lb). Females are larger than males.
- They have spiky horns 5cm (2 inches) long.
- Their white hair fringed dark tail is 10cm (3.9 inches) long.
- The blue duiker branched off from Maxwell's duiker 2.68-5.31 million years ago.
- They use their orbital glands to mark territory.
- They are known to chirp like birds and whistle.
- These diurnal (daytime) feeders are mostly **herbivores** that eat fallen fruits, leaves, flowers, bark, and fungi, but also like to lick up ants.
- Gestation is 4-7 months. Newborns can walk within 20 minutes and are weaned within 2.5-3 months.
- As the smallest duiker, every predator larger than them is a possible threat, but their greatest threat is humans hunting for bush meat.

# Cape Grysbok

| Kingdom: Animalia |
| Phylum: Chordata |
| Class: Mammalia |
| Order: Artiodactyla |
| Family: Bovidae |
| Genus: *Raphicerus* |
| Species: *melanotis* |

Binomial Name:
***Raphiceras melanotis***

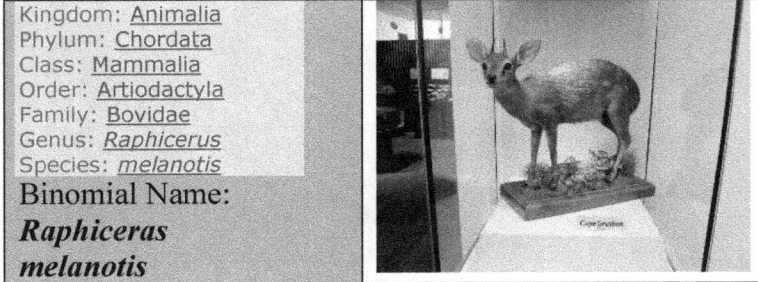

## Wow Facts

- Endemic (native) to South Africa and found along the western and eastern cape provinces.
- 45-55cm (1.5-1.8ft) tall at shoulder. Weight: 8-10kg (18-22lb). Tails 4-8cm (1.5-3 inches) long.
- They have large ears, and males have horns 8-13cm (1.5-5 inches).
- They have white and reddish hair on their back that gives them a grizzled appearance which makes them blend in or appear invisible.
- They are nocturnal and hide in dense brush during the day and come out at night to browse and forage.
- They require very little water and can therefore live in savannahs, river beds, reed beds, scrub forests & scrub lands.
- These herbivores eat fruit and leaves, but they have become urbanized and now live on the fringe regions of vineyards and orchards where one of their favorite foods is new grape vine shoots, which puts them directly at odds with humans.
- Predators include: leopards, jackals, crowned eagles, and pythons.
- Gestation is 6-7 months, weaned in 3 months, and sexually matures in 18-24 months.
- Oldest known lived 7.7 years in captivity.

# Deinosuchus

Kingdom: Animalia
Phylum: Chordata
Class: Reptilia
Order: Crocodilia
Superfamily: Alligatoroidea
Genus: *Deinosuchus*
Species: *rugosus*
Binomial Name:
*Deinosuchus rugosus*

## Wow Facts

- 80-73 Million Years Ago; Late Cretaceous period.
- Name means "terrible crocodile". The first fossil was found In North Carolina and now they have been found in ten states and Mexico, including both sides of the Western Interior Seaway.
- 10.6m (35ft) long. There were four other crocodilian forms thought to be the same size. *D. riograndensis* was 12m (39ft) long.
- The skull was 1.5m (4.9ft) long and the lower jaw was 1.8m (5.9ft) long.
- They had a broad snout like an alligator.
- They had a bite force of 10,000-100,000 Newtons which was more powerful than *T. rex*. Modern 6m (20ft) long saltwater crocodiles have a bite force of 16,414 Newtons.
- Because of their size and bite force they were one of the largest apex predators on the eastern side of the Western Interior Seaway.
- They are found and therefore they are thought to have lived in marine and brackish water.
- Their bite marks have been found on hadrosaurs to sea turtles, with bites of sea turtle shells found in their coprolites, (fossilized dung or poody poo).
- By examining the large scutes (osteoderms) on their back, scientists have determined that these large predators could have lived up to 50 years.

# Gastornis (Diatryma)

Kingdom: Animalia
Phylum: Chordata
Class: Aves
Order: Anseriformes
Family: Gastornithidae
Genus: *Gastornis*
Species: *parisiensis*

Binomial Name:
*Gastornis gigantea*

## Wow Facts

- 56-45 Million Years Ago; Eocene epoch.
- The fossil of *G. parisiensis* was first found near Paris France, and later in Belgium, Germany, England, North America, and China.
- Is was called Diatryma in North America, but the similarities to *Gastornis* prompt scientists to include the junior synonym "Diatryma" in this genus.
- There are five species in the *Gastornis* genus.
- The largest species *G. gigantea* from North America was 2-2.14m (6.6-7ft) tall. The skull was .5m (1.5ft) in length. They weighed around 170kg (385lb).
- Their foot prints have been found outside of Paris France and Washington State near Bellingham.
- Foot prints suggest that they did not have hooked claws typically found in predators. Their beaks were not hooked like predators as well.
- They may have eaten occasional small mammals, but they were built for tearing off foliage and cracking nuts, so they are more likely to have been a **herbivore** than a carnivore.
- They had small wings like a modern-day cassowary and they could not fly, but their large pointed beak and strong neck gave them considerable protection against predators for over eleven million years.
- Eggs were 24 by 10cm (9.5 by 4 inches). Shells 2.3-2.5mm (.09-.1 inch) thick.

# Giraffe

Kingdom: <u>Animalia</u>
Phylum: <u>Chordata</u>
Class: <u>Mammalia</u>
Order: <u>Artiodactyla</u>
Family: <u>Giraffidae</u>
Genus: *Giraffa*
Species: *camelopardalis*
Binomial name: *Giraffa Camelopardalis*

## Wow Facts

- This family includes only two living species, the giraffe and the okapi.
- Giraffes are gregarious, living in **herds** of up to 25-32 animals, which occupy large home ranges usually in relatively open savannahs of sub-saharan Africa.
- Giraffes first appeared in the fossil record in the early Miocene.
- Their long necks are brought about by the lengthening of their cervical vertebrae after birth, and not by adding vertebrae. At birth they may be 6 feet tall.
- In the upper neck a *rete mirabile* prevents excess blood flow to the brain while they are bending over to drink water.
- Giraffids have short horns that project from the parietals and frontals. These are unique among mammals, consisting of bony cores (ossicones) covered by furred skin.
- Giraffes are **herbivores** and have a four-chambered ruminating stomach.
- They have a long purplish-black colored (possibly for sun protection) prehensile tongue that they use for grasping as well as grooming. The upper lip is also prehensile; the lips and tongue are covered with papillae to protect them from thorns.
- The neck bones work like a ball and socket set to

help slingshot the head and neck into their opponent. Males fight using their necks (called necking) to rub against and/or eventually ram into each other until one submits, disengages, one is wounded, or as witnessed and filmed, one of them falls and goes unconscious. Sinuses in the head help soften the blows.

- Giraffes either walk or gallop. They can sprint up to 60km/h (37mph) or run at a slower sustained speed for several kilometers at 50km/h (31mph).
- They evolved from the extinct family Palaeomerycidae eight million years ago during the Miocene epoch in central Europe. There are currently nine different subspecies.
- Egyptians kept them as pets and gave them their own hieroglyph "sr" in old Egyptian and later "mmy".
- They live up to 25 years in the wild. The coats of males become darker as they age.

# Gray Duiker

| Kingdom: Animalia |
| --- |
| Phylum: Chordata |
| Class: Mammalia |
| Order: Artiodactyla |
| Family: Bovidae |
| Genus: *Sylvicapra* |
| Species: *grimmia* |
| Binomial Name: |
| ***Silvicapra grimmia*** |

## Wow Facts

- Found in eastern, western, and southern Africa.
- Silva is Latin for "Forest", and Capra means "she goat". Duiker (DIKE-er) is Afrikaans for "diver".
- There are 19 subspecies. Those in the forest are more reddish brown colored and those in the northern savannah are more grizzled gray in color.
- Their nose, nose bridge, and forelegs are black.
- Height 45-60cm (1.5-2ft). Length 80-115cm (2.6-3.8ft). Tail 10-20cm (4-8 inches). Weight 10-20kg (22-44 lb).
- Females are larger than males.
- Males have horns 7-18cm (3-7 inches) long with tufts of hair between the horns and mark their territory with their preorbital gland secretions.
- These **omnivores** eat foliage, fruits, and seeds. They are also known to eat insects, frogs, small birds, small mammals, and even carrion.
- They can go a long time without drinking water.
- Near human settlements, they are nocturnal. In other areas they feed at dusk or dawn. The rest of the time they dive and hide in bushes or grass.
- Gestation is 6-7 months. Weaning in 2 months. Females mature in 8-10 months and males mature in 12 months.
- Predators include cats, baboons, crocodiles, pythons, and eagles.
- They are known to live up to 14 years in the wild and 25 years in captivity.

# Hadrosaurids

Kingdom: Animalia
Phylum: Chordata
Clade: Dinosauria
Order: Ornithischia
Superfamily: Hadrosauroidea
Family: Hadrosauridae
Genus: *Brachylophosaurus*
Species: *candensis*

Binomial Name:
***Brachylophosaurus***
***canadensis***

## Wow Facts

- 90-66 Million Years Ago; Late Cretaceous period.
- In Greek: Brachy "short", lopho "crested", saurus 'lizard".
- Their front legs were shorter than their back legs, and while adults walked on all four legs, they could stand to increase their feeding range similar to gerenuk antelopes do today.
- The mummified body of Leonardo is 77 million years old. He died at around 3 years of age and already 6.7m (22ft) long; adults could range up to 10-11m (30-36ft).
- It is surmised that he received a fatal bite on his ribs and stomach from a predator then managed to escape only to be caught in a flood of water where he was buried quickly.
- Not only can we see his short triangular crest that ran from the top of his head down his back to his tail, muscle tissue, skin and foot pads, but we can see that he had a bird like crop, and a hard keratin beak like cover over the end bones that formed his flat duck bill facial appearance. Inside his mouth, a unique grinding plate was full of multiple rows of replaceable teeth.
- Leonardo is the most complete (90%) mummified dinosaur ever found; the end of his tail was missing.
- X-rays have revealed his internal organs such as his liver, lungs, and heart. Ground up leaves, flower pedals, and 40 different types of pollen were found in his stomach.
- Hadrosaurids are descendants of Iguanodons.

# Harvey Red Duiker

Kingdom: Animalia
Phylum: Chordata
Class: Mammalia
Order: Artiodactyla
Family: Bovidae
Genus: *Cephalophus*
Species: *harveyi*

**Binomial name:**
*Cephalophus*
*harveyi*

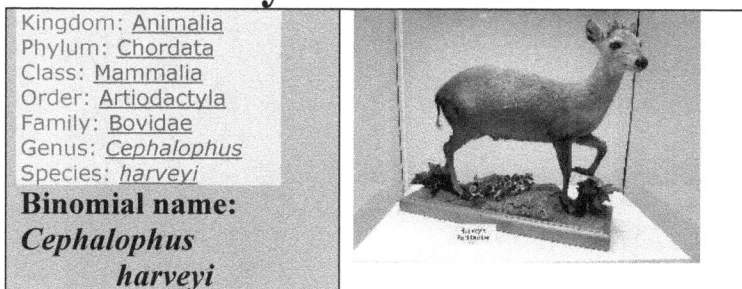

## Wow Facts

- No matter where you go on the internet, the information on Harvey's Red Duiker is the almost identical word for word. They are not rare, but not very well studied either. They are hard to study as they remain hidden in brush most of the time to elude predators.
- Harvey's Red Duiker is one of 19 species of duiker found in East Africa namely Tanzania, southeastern Kenya, southern Somalia, and in the Bale Mountains National Park in Ethiopia.
- Harvey's Duikers live in thick brush and cover of mountain, lowlands, and riverside forests, where they eat leaves, twigs, fruit, insects, birds, eggs, and carrion.
- Although this duiker is not endangered, it is dependent on protected forestland and has lost habitats where timber is harvested.
- They have a mostly chestnut coat, but their legs and face are black.
- Females are larger, but have smaller horns.
- They are 45-50cm (18-20inches) tall and weigh 13-16kg (30-35lb).
- Other species of duikers may live 10-15 years.
- Predators include: just about everyone from the cat family, jackals, birds of prey, pythons, and anything else looking for a quick snack.

# Klipspringer

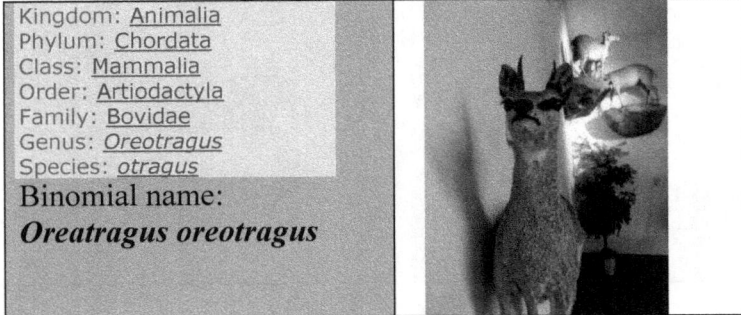

Kingdom: <u>Animalia</u>
Phylum: <u>Chordata</u>
Class: <u>Mammalia</u>
Order: <u>Artiodactyla</u>
Family: <u>Bovidae</u>
Genus: *Oreotragus*
Species: *otragus*

Binomial name:
***Oreatragus oreotragus***

## Wow Facts

- The klipspringer is an **herbivore** that eats shoots and leaves. Also fruits, berries, and other succulents. They mainly derive their water from the food they eat.
- They are found from South Africa to the highlands of Ethiopia.
- Klipspringers live in steep, rocky terrain and are most common in mountain ranges and gorges of major rivers.
- Their loosely connected and hollow hair type is unique among bovid and found only in pronghorns and the white tailed deer.
- They stand on the tips of their hooves and can fit all four hooves in a space no bigger than a Canadian Dollar coin.
- Klipspringers are monogamous animals that are nearly always seen in pairs, usually with one offspring.
- Males are territorial and mark their area with dung.
- Maximum life span 14 years.
- They mate for life and while one is eating, the other stands as a lookout for predators such as eagles, leopards, caracals, and humans.

# Oribi

Kingdom: <u>Animalia</u>
Phylum: <u>Chordata</u>
Class: <u>Mammalia</u>
Order: <u>Artiodactyla</u>
Family: <u>Bovidae</u>
Genus: *Ourebia*
Species: *ourebi*

Binomial Name:
***Ourebia ourebi***

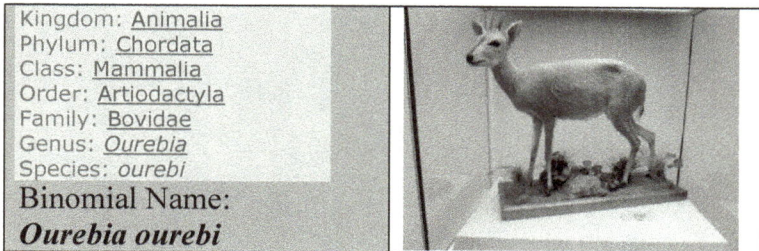

## Wow Facts

- Found in eastern, western, and southern Africa.
- Live in savannahs, flood plains, and grasslands up to 2,000m (6,000ft).
- Height is 50-67cm (20-26 inches) at shoulder. Length is 92-110cm (36-43 inches). Weight 12-22kg (26-49 lb).
- They have a long neck and an arched back. Their coat is yellow to brown in color. They have a white chin, throat, underbelly and rump. Their tail is brown or black.
- Males have horns 8-18cm (3-7 inches) long.
- There are 8 sub species and in most, males are smaller than females.
- They have 6 different scent glands.
- These **herbivores** are active in the day and eat 90% grasses, but also flowers and mushrooms.
- Gestation is 6-7 months. Most births take place in August to September or November to December in South Africa when it is summer on the southern hemisphere. They wean for 4-5 months. Sexually mature 10-14 months.
- They whistle when alarmed and live in small herds of four individuals; either male of female or mixed groups.
- They live 8-12 years in the wild and 12-14 years in captivity.
- Poaching by humans, agricultural expansion, and livestock encroachment are their most pressing problems.

# Royal Antelope

Kingdom: Animalia
Phylum: Chordata
Class: Mammalia
Order: Artiodactyla
Family: Bovidae
Genus: *Neotragus*
Species: *pygmaeus*

Binomial Name:
*Neotragus pygmaeus*

## Wow Facts

- The world's smallest antelope is found in West Africa in dense warm moist forest lowlands.
- Neo "new", tragus "he goat", pygmaeus "as small as a fist".
- 25cm (10 inches) high at shoulder. Body length 40cm (16 inches). Weight 2.5-3kg (5.5-6.6 lb). Males have (spikes) horns 2.5-3cm (1-1.2 inches).
- They have reddish to golden coats with a white color on their neck, underbelly, and under their 5-8cm (2-3 inch) long tail that ends with a white tuft. There are two sub species. Females are larger than males. They have small ears and large brown eyes.
- The most recognizable feature of this species is that their hind slender legs are twice as long as their front slender legs; similar to a rabbit. They can leap 2.8m (9ft) and 55cm (22 inches) off the ground.
- They are active at night (nocturnal) and this herbivore eats leaves and shoots as well as some fruits and fungi.
- They mark their territory with dung.
- Six months until sexually mature. Most give birth in November-December.
- They have ancestors in common with klipspringers and duikers.
- Life span in captivity less than 7 years.
- Human settlements, destruction of habitats, and use as bush meat are their main threats.

# Salt's Dik Dik

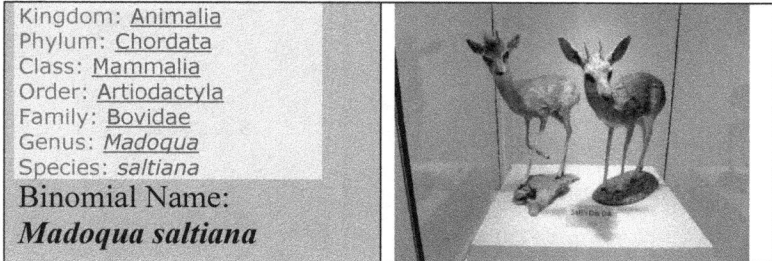

Kingdom: Animalia
Phylum: Chordata
Class: Mammalia
Order: Artiodactyla
Family: Bovidae
Genus: *Madoqua*
Species: *saltiana*

Binomial Name:
*Madoqua saltiana*

## Wow Facts

- Found on the Horn of Africa in northern Kenya, eastern Sudan, Ethiopia, Somalia and Eritrea. The live in semi-desert, bush lands, and thickets.
- 52-67cm (20-26 inches) long. 33-41cm (13-16 inches) tall. Weight 2.5-4kg (5.5-8.8 lb.
- They are reddish gray, ginger red with gray, brown gray and silver with orange sides (flanks). There are five sub species.
- Males have small horns with tufts of hair between them.
- They are active in the morning, at dusk, and at night.
- When it comes to acacia trees, they eat shoots and leaves. These **herbivores** also eat flowers, fruits, and herbs.
- They can give birth twice a year. Newborns are .5-.8kg (1.1-1.8 lb) and after one week can eat solid food, but wean for 3-4 months.
- After one month males grow horns, but males don't sexually mature until 8-9 months and stop growing after 12 months. Females sexually mature after 6-8 months.
- Found in groups: usually parents and two youngest calves.
- They use runs (paths) in thickets and run in zig-zag patterns when chased and when alarmed, make the sound "dik-dik".
- Life span is 3 to 4 years in the wild.
- Besides any predator larger than themselves, they are hunted by humans for their fur to make gloves.

# Steenbok

Kingdom: <u>Animalia</u>
Phylum: <u>Chordata</u>
Class: <u>Mammalia</u>
Order: <u>Artiodactyla</u>
Family: <u>Bovidae</u>
Genus: *Raphicerus*
Species: *campestris*

Binomial Name:
***Raphicerus campestris***

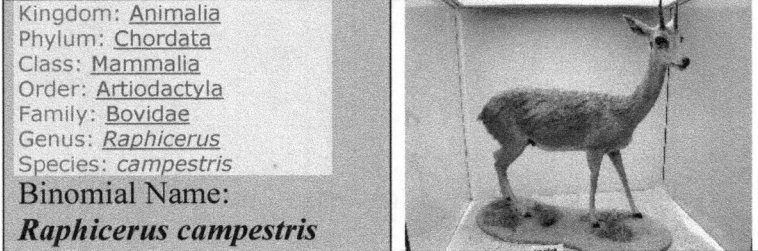

## Wow Facts

- Found in southern and eastern Africa. They live in savannahs, plains, and grasslands.
- In Greek: Raphis "needle", ceras "horn", campestris "countryside or plains".
- Height 45-60cm (16-24 inches) at shoulders, body length 70-95cm (2.3-3.2ft). Males have horns 7cm (2.8 inches) long; the record is 19cm (7.5 inches). The tail averages 4-6cm (1.6-2.4 inches) long.
- Their coat is golden brown to orange. The underside is white and so is the ring around their eyes. They have a black elongated triangle on their nose. There are two sub species.
- They have large ears with inner ear ridges.
- These **herbivores** eat leaves, shrubs, roots, tubers, and fruits and get most of their water from the food they eat.
- These Solitary antelopes are active in the day but rest during the hottest periods of the day.
- Gestation is 170 days. They wean in 3 months. Newborns are usually born November to December and can walk within minutes after birth. Females sexually mature in 6-8 months; males in 9 months. Life span 10-12 years.
- If in danger, they lay down first, then zig-zag run if discovered, or hide in aardvark burrows.
- Predators for young include baboons, ratel, and monitor lizards. Adults fear wild cats, jackals, pythons, and eagles.

# Suni

| Kingdom: Animalia<br>Phylum: Chordata<br>Class: Mammalia<br>Order: Artiodactyla<br>Family: Bovidae<br>Genus: *Neotragus*<br>Species: *moschatus*<br>**Binomial Name:**<br>***Neotragus moschatus*** | 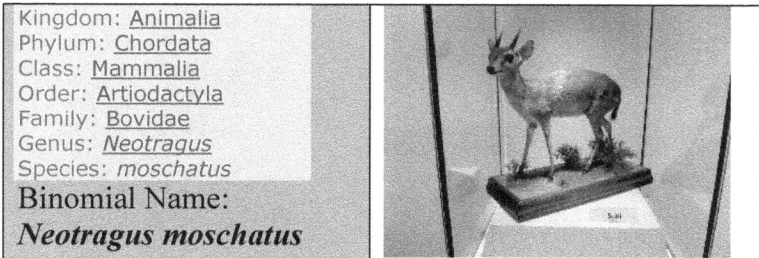 |

## Wow Facts

- Found in southeast Africa. They live in areas with lots of shrubs and thick brush.
- Height is 30-43cm (12-17inches) at the shoulder. 57-62cm (26-24 inches) long. Weight 4.5-7kg (10-15 lb).
- Chestnut on back, lighter on flanks and legs, white on undersides, black ring around eyes and a black band above hooves. There are four sub species.
- Males have horn that thrust backward; 8-13cm (3-5 inches) long. Males also scent mark their territory with preorbital glands and leave dung piles at edges of territory.
- These herbivores eat fresh leaves, fruits, flowers and fungi on the forest floor and get most of their water from these food sources.
- They are active evening, night, or in the early morning.
- Gestation is 183 days and then they have one newborn .9kg (2lb).
- Suni are in the genus *Neotragus*, as are the Royal antelope (*N. pygmaeus*) and Bates pygmy antelope (*N. batesi*), but Suni (*N. moschatus*) are larger.
- They are known to bark and whistle.
- Poaching and predation by dogs are more detrimental to their species than predation by crowned eagles and pythons.

# Water Chevrotain

Kingdom: Animalia
Phylum: Chordata
Class: Mammalia
Order: Artiodactyla
Family: Tragulidae
Genus: *Hyemoshus*
Species: *aquaticus*

Binomial Name:
***Hyemoshus aquaticus***

## Wow Facts

- Found in tropical lowland forests of Sierra Leon to Western Uganda and within 250m (820ft) from fresh water rivers, streams, marshlands, and lakes.
- Length 60-102cm (2-3.3ft) long. Height 30-40cm (1.2-1.3ft) at the shoulders. Tail is 10-15cm (4-6 inches). Weight 7-16kg (15-35 lb). Females are larger than males by at least 2kg (4.4 lb). There are three sub species.
- They have a chestnut coat with horizontal lines in the form of dashes and dots with a white underside.
- No horns, but males may bite one another with their elongated canine teeth that look like tusks. Females have slightly shorter and blunter canines.
- Their back end is higher than the front end giving then a wedge shape. They walk with their head held low. They also have thicker skin on their back so they can ram their way through the underbrush without getting too beat up.
- These mostly solitary animals are nocturnal and you can see them on the open banks of the river or near a pond in an open area at night. If in trouble they will freeze or run and dive underwater.
- A large proportion of their **Omnivore** diet is fruit and leaves, but they also lick up ants, eat crabs, fish, and carrion.
- Gestation is 7 months. Weaning 3-6 months. Sexually mature 9-26 months.
- Life span 8 years. Record: 13 years. Many predators.

# Wildebeest

Kingdom: <u>Animalia</u>
Phylum: <u>Chordata</u>
Class: <u>Mammalia</u>
Order: <u>Artiodactyla</u>
Family: <u>Bovidae</u>
Genus: *Connochaetes*
Species: *C .gnou and C. taurinus*

**2 species**

## Wow Facts

- The Blue Wildebeest "*C. taurinus*" is found in plains, grasslands, and woodlands south of the Sahara Desert in Africa. They may go on annual migrations of up to 1609km (1000 miles). These **herbivores** prefer grasses rich in phosphorous and nitrogen.

- Wildebeest became two separate species over a million years ago. Both species have wide noses, manes, and beards.

- The Black Wildebeest "*C. gnou*" is found in the grasslands of South Africa and is considered nomadic or non-migratory. Their horns go forward, then down, then curl up like letter U's on the sides of their head.

- Blues are larger than Black Wildebeest, and Blues have horns that go out and curl up like a letter C resting on its back on top of their head. Blues have 5 sub species.

- Gestation is 250-260 days. Most calves are born during a three-week period. The light-colored newborns can stand within minutes. Adults can run 80km/h (50mph).

- Wildebeest herds display "swarm intelligence". They can overcome situations like crossing rivers filled with crocodiles by moving as one unit over a more confined period of time. Large herds are also less likely to be attacked in general. Some wildebeest sleep while others stay alert. They also remain alert for calls from zebras and baboons. Predators prefer the sick, young, or old.

- Life span 20 years. Record: 40 years. Fences placed between migratory routes have reduced some populations by 90%.

# Marine Room

# American Lobster

Kingdom: Animalia
Phylum: Chordata
Class: Mammalia
Order: Carnivora
Family: Felidae
Genus: *Panthera*
Species: *leo*

Binomial Name:
***Panthera leo***

## Wow Facts

- They are also known as Maine lobsters and are mainly found along the Atlantic coast from Canada to New Jersey and sometimes found down to North Carolina.
- They are typically bluish green or brown with red spines but 1 in 2 million is blue, 1 in 10 million is red,1 in 30 million is yellow, 1 in 30 million is calico (orange and brown), and 1 in 100 million is albino or lack color pigments.
- One of their large claws has rounded nodule ridges and is used for crushing prey while the other large claw has sharp inner edges and is used for cutting or tearing prey.
- They use their sense of smell for finding food.
- For 10-11 months, females are "in berry" if they are carrying eggs. After a few molts in the egg, the young hatch. For 10-20 days they are part of the plankton where only one in a thousand survives. After a few more molts they look like 25-38mm (1-1.5 inch) long tiny adults. After one more molt they sink and begin life on the substrate (sea floor). Average depth is 4-50m (13-64ft), but they can go down to 480m (1,570ft).
- They eat mussels, echinoderms, polychaetes, other crustaceans, brittle stars, cnidarians, and herring.
- If they have a hard shell, they can live out of water 5 days if kept cool; if soft shelled (recently molted) they can live only a few hours out of water.
- Only 6% of the lobsters that enter traps are actually caught.

# Atlantic Blue Marlin

Kingdom: <u>Animalia</u>
Phylum: <u>Chordata</u>
Class: <u>Actinopterygii</u>
Order: <u>Perciformes</u>
Family: <u>Istiophoridae</u>
Genus: *Makaira*
Species: Negricans

Binomial Name:
*Makaira negricans*

## Wow Facts

- The Sailfish is a bill fish that inhabits warmer waters worldwide. There are two species. During the colder months, they are found near the equator.
- They hunt near the surface. They use their bill to stun, injure, or kill small prey fish before they eat them.
- They feed on mackerel, tuna, squid, white marlin, yellow fin and big eye tuna.
- Females may weigh four times as much as males; 818kg (1,803kg) and 5m (16.4ft) long. When they are over 1,000 lb. they are called "granders"; the current record is 636kg (1,402 lb).
- *Machaira* is the Greek name for short sword; *negricans* is Latin for becoming black.
- They can quickly change colors. They are blue black on top and silvery white on the ventral side. They also may have 15 lightly colored blue stripes or dotted lines.
- Tagged marlins have swum 14,893km (9,254 miles) from the Pacific to the Indian Ocean and from Delaware to Africa.
- Males live 18 years and females up to 27 years.
- Called "a'u" in Hawaii, they are typically smoked.
- They are a bycatch in tuna lines and a multimillion sports fishing operation from boat operators, boat builders, marinas, dealerships, fishing tackle, hotels, and airlines.
- Earnest Hemmingway wrote about Santiago fighting a Blue Marlin for three days in "The old Man and the Sea".

# Atlantic Spotted Dolphin

Kingdom: Animalia
Phylum: Chordata
Class: Mammalia
Order: Artiodactyla
Infraorder: Cetacea
Family: Delphinidae
Genus: *Stenella*
Species: *frontalis*

Binomial Name:
*Stenella frontalis*

## Wow Facts

- Atlantic spotted dolphins are found in the Atlantic Ocean from the United States and Canada over to Europe and down to west Africa, and over to Brazil.
- Pantropical spotted dolphins, *Stenella attenuata*, a close cousin species, are found worldwide and look similar to Atlantic spotted dolphins, but are more slender and have a longer nose.
- The robust Atlantic dolphin change colors as they age and as claves they are gray-white, by 3-4 years when weaned they become speckled, 8-9 years old become mottled with blended gray and white spots on the dorsal (top) side and black spots on the ventral (lower belly) side, and as they get older they appear black with white spots.
- Adults average 2.26m (7'5") long and weigh 140kg (310lb); females are slightly smaller than males.
- They have 35-48 conical teeth on each upper side of the jaw, and 34-47 teeth on each lower side.
- They make ten vocalizations such as whistles, buzzes, squawks, and barks.
- They feed on fish and squid and are known to swim with yellowfin tuna and because of this habit; they have an 80% mortality rate when caught in purse seine nets that are meant to catch tuna.
- From 1959-1978, more than four million spotted dolphins lost their life in nets, but now due to consumer pressure this number is down to 20,000 dolphins a year.

# Baleen Whales

Kingdom: Animalia
Phylum: Chordata
Class: Mammalia
Order: Artiodactyla
Infraorder: Cetacea
Parvorder: Mysticeti

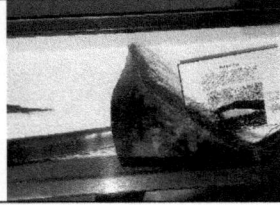

## Wow Facts

- They prefer to live in colder oceans worldwide. There are 15 species in four families: Baleanopteridae or rorquals, Balaenidae or right whales, Cetotheriidae or pygmy right whales, and Eschrichtiidae or gray whales.
- The largest baleen whale is the blue whale measuring over 34m (112ft) in length and the smallest is the pygmy right whale at 6m (20ft) long. Females are typically larger than males.
- They feed on tiny krill, copepods, small fish, and sometimes birds.
- Instead of teeth they have baleen plates made from a keratin material and skin derivative similar to hair, fingernails, and horns that hang like a set of combs from each side of the roof of their mouth. These plates are reinforced with calcium and known as whalebone.
- On larger baleen whales the plates may weigh 90kg (200lb) and measure 3.5m (11ft) long.
- The plates act like a giant sieve. The whale brings food and water into its mouth, then closes the mouth and by pushing its tongue against roof of the mouth forcing all the water to pass out through the baleen plates and trapping all the food inside the mouth where it is then swallowed.
- Baleen whales have a three-chambered stomach.
- Rorquals lung at their food which automatically expands their throat pleats increasing the volume inside their mouth. Rorquals and right whales spit from the main group 20 million years ago.
- Right whales, gray whales, pygmy whales, and sei

whales skim feed, but sei whales can also lunge feed.

- Gray whales skim and sift through substrate sand for amphipods.

- Baleen whales split from toothed whales 28-17Mya. One of their early ancestors *Janjusetus hunderi* had both teeth including incisors, canines, molars, premolars, and small baleen plates. At first baleen whales were small species.

- Baleen whales have two blow holes instead of one found in toothed whales. The blowholes converge towards one another on the front, anterior, end and diverge or get wider apart at the back, posterior, end and look something like a camel or deer hoof print. This shape causes them to spout a V-shaped cloud of water when their lung warmed exhaled air hits the cold ocean air. The septum, wall between the blow holes, has coverings that plug the two holes when they dive.

- The fin whale is the fastest and can swim at speeds up to 37 km/h (23mph). The fin whale can also dive down to 470m (1,540ft) deep.

- Unlike humans that only extract some 20% oxygen out of the air with each breath, whales can extract 80% oxygen with each breath.

- A blue whale heart may weight 454kg (1000lb). Their resting heart rate may be 60-140 beats per minute. A human's resting heart rate is 60-100 beats per minute, but a diving whale can reduce its heart rate down to 4-15 beats per minute.

- Their red and white blood cells are the largest of any animal on the planet.

- Baleen whales use eyesight for navigation and do not possess echolocation. Their eyes are spherical and see better above water than below. They also lack s-cone cells that make it difficult to see in color.

- They use their fins for steering and move their tail or fluke up and down for propulsion. They may have a small dorsal fin and their hind legs are enclosed inside their body or vestigial.

- Their brain is small compared to their body mass, but they can keep one side of their brain active while the other side remains in slow wave sleep mode.
- They have good hearing, but sound does not pass through the lower jaw.
- Their larynx has U-shaped folds that they use to make vocal sounds. Humpback songs are the most famous underwater vocal sounds and can be heard hundreds of kilometers away.
- They have a vomeronasal organ with which they can detect chemicals and pheromones of prey. They have an olfactory tract, but no olfactory bulb, so they have an impaired sense of smell and they have a few taste buds to detect salt.
- They migrate from the poles in the spring and summer to go to calving grounds in tropical waters. Some gray whales are known to go 23,000km (14,000 miles) from the sea of Okhotsk to Baja Peninsula.
- Life span for blue whales is 80-90 years. In 5-10 they are up to 24m (79ft) long. They become too large to be captive for very long. Also, it is expensive to feed them as a gray whale calf can eat 215kg (475lb) of fish each day.
- Predators of calves include dusky sharks, and orcas. Prehistoric predators include Megalodon sharks and prehistoric killer sperm whales. Currently, only cookie cutter sharks and human prey on adults. Natives harvest baleen whales in Iceland, Norway, and Japan.
- Japan may kill hundreds of minke and fins whales each year in Antarctica under the pretext of scientific research.
- They are also caught as bycatch, struck accidentally by ships, victims of nets, and susceptible to pollution such as PCBs, as well as noise pollution.
- Whale watching is a worldwide billion-dollar tourist industry and the proceeds go to local taxes in the form of boat charter operations, hotels, restaurants, and other tourist related activities and amenities.

# Beluga Whale

Kingdom: Animalia
Phylum: Chordata
Class: Mammalia
Order: Artiodactyla
Family: Monodontidae
Genus: *Delphinapterus*
Species: *leucas*

Binomial Name:
***Delphinapterus leucas***

## Wow Facts

- They are found in the circumpolar arctic and sub-arctic regions, which includes North America, Russia and Greenland. They live in fjords, bays, inlets, channels, and in polynyas "holes or openings in the ice" in the winter.
- In the summer, they travel south to the river gravel beds to have young, shed their outer skin layer, and hunt salmon.
- Their name comes from the Russian word "белуха" *Belukha,* which is derived from the word "белый" white.
- *Delphinapterus* means dolphin without a fin" although they do have a slight crest on their back that they can use to break ice 8cm (3 inches) thick without getting hurt.
- Length 5.5m (18ft) long. 1600kg (3,500 lb). Their body fat ratio is 40-50% which is higher than any other whale but it gives them some 15cm (5.9inches) of fat insulation to keep comfortably warm in ice cold conditions.
- They swim 3-9km/h (1.9-5.6mph), but can reach speeds up to 35km/h (22mph) for up to 15 minutes.
- They have a thyroid gland three times the weight of a horse thyroid to help regulate their body temperature during the summer months in the warmer rivers.
- They have no olfactory bulb and no sense of smell.
- The large melon chamber on their head is used for

echolocation with which they can tell distance to, speed, size, shape, and even internal structure of their prey.

- They have a hearing range of 1.2-120kHz. Humans hear sounds in the range of .02-20kHz. These "canaries of the sea" sing to each other and can imitate human speech sounds.
- Unlike most other species of whale and dolphins, their seven neck vertebrae are not fused, allowing them to turn their head without turning their entire body. They can also swim backwards.
- They can dive to depths of 700m (2,300ft), but usually do 30-50 shallow dives per day for 3-5 minutes per dive as they hunt for invertebrates such as clams, crabs, shrimp, worms, squids, octopus, as well as fish from flounder that they may hunt alone to salmon that they may hunt as a coordinated group.
- When diving, their heart rate goes from 100 beats per minute down to 12-20 beats per minute, and they can store more oxygen in their muscles than most mammals.
- They have 36-40 teeth that they use to hold prey before swallowing it.
- They live in small groups of up to ten individuals led by a dominant male, but in the summer time they group together in the rivers by the thousands. They are known to travel thousands of kilometers/miles up rivers.
- One beluga swam in the Champlain Sea after the melting of the ice age 12,000 years ago, when seas were higher. After its death and thousands of years later, it was found buried in an area that had dried out and become a Vermont field.
- Males are larger than females by about 25%. Newborn calves are born gray and females turn white by age 6 and males by age 9, and they are full grown by age 10.

- Mature females have one calf every three years. Newborns are 1.5m (4.9ft) long
- They are in the Monodotidae family along with narwhals.
- They diverged from cetaceans 30 million years ago, and separated from Delphinoidea 11-15 million years ago. Their ancestors were first seen 9-11 million years ago.
- Lifespan is 70-80 years.
- Predators include polar bears in the winter when their ice holes shrink in size and in the summer when the ice melts and killer whales can more readily hunt them.
- They have a higher rate of cancer than humans, and they are susceptible to PCBs and other toxic chemicals.

# Bigeye Thresher Shark

Kingdom: Animalia
Phylum: Chordata
Class: Chondrichthyes
Order: Lamniformes
Family: Alopiidae
Genus: *Alopias*
Species: *superciliosus*
Binomial Name:
*Alopias superciliosus*

## Wow Facts

- They live in tropical to temperate waters worldwide.
- Their tail makes up half their body length. They use their heterocercal tail to thresh or whip and stun prey such as bluefish, tuna, mackerel, squid, and sea birds.
- They are diel and may dive down to 500m (1,600ft) to a max of 723m (2,372ft) during the day, then they swim closer to the surface during the night.
- They are prey to marine mammals and other sharks.
- They have a *rete mirabile* vascular heating exchange system around their brain and eyes. Their eyes are in a keyhole style oval bracket and are 10cm (3.9 ") wide to make it easier to see prey above them.
- They have a deep lateral V shaped ridge on their head. They get their species name from the Latin words *super* "above" and *ciliosus* "eyebrow".
- The largest known Bigeye so far was 4.9m (16ft) long.
- They are a purple brownish colored on top and cream colored on the underside.
- Their fossilized teeth are first seen in the middle Miocene 16-11.6 Mya. Males have more slender teeth than females. In the Indian Ocean males and females are found at different depths and may eat different prey.
- Lifespan for females is 20 years and 19 for males. Females are ovoviviparous and have two pups at a time and only twenty total pups over their entire lifetime.
- These game fish have a mushy meat. They are a bycatch of long lines and quite often are caught by their tail as they try to stun fish already caught on the hooks.

# Blind Cave Fish

Kingdom: Animalia
Phylum: Chordata
Class: Actinopterygii
Order: Characiformes
Family: Characidae
Genus: *Astynax*
Species: *mexicanus*

Binomial Name:
*Astynax mexicanus*

## Wow Facts

- Mexican Tetra are native to Texas, Mexico, and Central America. Some tetras have good eyesight while some from caves may have limited sight (Micos Cave) or no eye sight (Pachón Cave) and appear as albino to pinkish white. There are some 29 different cave populations in Northeastern Mexico.
- These **carnivores** eat crustaceans, insects, and worms. Max length is 12cm (4.7 inches).
- They use their lateral lines to feel pressure waves from nearby objects.
- Blind cave fish have better olfactory senses and have taste buds on their head. They can also store four times the regular amount of energy as fat. Females are larger and plumper than males. They can lay 100 eggs. Fry hatch in 2-3 days.
- Some believe that this going blind phenomenon shows regressive evolution in cave species. Others point out that this is natural selection versus genetic drift, but the lack of eyes is not an advantage or a disadvantage in a world always dark, and being blind has no effect on the fitness of the population. It is just less complex or easier if you don't have to spend energy making something that can't be used in a perpetually dark environment.
- In some groups of cave fish, the eyes atrophy after birth and in others a skin flap grows over the eyes as they grow.
- Life span is five years.

# Blue Shark

Kingdom: <u>Animalia</u>
Phylum: <u>Chordata</u>
Class: <u>Chondrichthyes</u>
Order: <u>Carcharhiniformes</u>
Family: <u>Carcharhiniformidae</u>
Genus: *Carcharhinus*
Species: *obscurus*

Binomial Name:
*Carcharhinus obscurus*

## Wow Facts

- They are a requiem shark and are found in tropical to temperate oceans worldwide from as far north as Norway and as far south as Chile. They are known to migrate from as far away as New England down to South America.
- Their head and face are long and cone shaped like a missile and they are fast.
- They are 3.82m (12.3ft) long and weigh 391kg (862 lb); females are larger than males.
- They are counter shaded deep blue on top and white on the underside.
- They eat squid, cuttlefish, pelagic octopus, crabs, shrimps, fish, sea birds, and small sharks. They are known to work together to coral groups of fish before attacking.
- They usually only last 30 days in captivity but one lasted 3 months until eaten by a bull shark, and one lasted 7 months until dying from a bacterial infection.
- They are viviparous and give birth to 25-80 live pups; the max is 134 pups.
- Lifespan is 20 years.
- Juvenile blue sharks are eaten by great whites, tiger sharks, killer whales, and even California sea lions, but gill nets appear to be their worst enemy.

# Bonito

Kingdom: Animalia
Phylum: Chordata
Class: Actinopterygii
Order: Perciformes
Family: Scombridae
Genus: *Sarda*
Species: Four main species
Binomial Name:

## Wow Facts

- There are four main species. *Sarda sarda* is found in the Atlantic and Mediterranean. *Sarda orientalis* is found in the Indo-Pacific. *Sarda chilensis* in the eastern Pacific, and *Sarda australis* in Australia and New Zealand.
- "Bonito" means *good* in Italian, and *handsome* in Spanish and Portuguese.
- Cooks like this fish because it has a firm texture and adults have a dark colored meat.
- They are best when grilled, pickled, or baked.
- Bonito have striped sides and silver bellies.
- The species are further divided by regions they live in.
- They eat anchovies, sardines, crustaceans, and squid; depending on where they live and what food source is seasonally available.

# Cichlids

Kingdom: Animalia
Phylum: Chordata
Class: Actinopterygii
Order: Perciformes
Family: Cichlidae
Genus: Too many
Species: thousands
Binomial Name:

## Wow Facts

- There are over 1600 species of cichlids in Africa, another 120 species in Mexico, and Central & South America, and nine species in Asia.
- 2.5cm (1 inch) to1m (3.3ft) long depending on species.
- The most known species include Oscars, Angelfish, and Tilapia. Tilapia are farmed worldwide and are considered the "aquatic chicken". They are worth $1.8 Billion dollars per year which is about even with sales of trout and salmon.
- Cichlids are found near the surface down to 150m (490ft) in Lake Malawi. A blind cichlid *Lamprologus lethops* lives at 160m (520ft) in the Congo River.
- Cichlids even live in Lake Abaeded in Eritrea in water 29-45°C (84-113°F).
- Many of them are herbivores and eat algae or small organic particles, while others eat snails, sponges, fish eggs, young fish, fish scales, fins, and insects.
- Cichlids have a second set of pharyngeal teeth located in their throat that help them pulverize their food.
- Some species lay eggs (brood their young) in the open, some are cave brooders, some incubate the eggs in their mouth (Ovophile mouth brooding), and some guard young hatchlings in their mouth (Larvophile mouth brooding).
- Aquarium hybrids consist of several species combined. Blood parrot cichlids, Love heart parrot cichlids, flowerhorn cichlids, convict cichlids, Texas red cichlids and leucistic (albino) long finned cichlids are just a few of the popular hybrids.

# Colorado River Toad

Kingdom: <u>Animalia</u>
Phylum: <u>Chordata</u>
Class: <u>Amphibia</u>
Order: <u>Anura</u>
Family: <u>Bufonidae</u>
Genus: *Incilius*
Species: *alvarius*

Binomial Name:
*Incilius alvarius*

## Wow Facts

- They are also known as the Sonoran Desert toad.
- These amphibians are found in deserts, semi-arid lands, grasslands, and woodlands of Southeastern California, Nevada, Southern Arizona, New Mexico and Northern Mexico. They inhabit the Colorado River, Gila River, streams, springs, canals, reservoirs, dams, drainage ditches, and even underneath water troughs.
- They can dig, but their favorite place to live is inside a rodent hole or burrow, and they come out at night (nocturnal) to feed or mate.
- These **carnivores/insectivores** feed on termites, butterflies, crickets, wasps, ants, beetles, grasshoppers, centipedes, millipeds, spiders, other insects, snails, mice, other rodents, small mammals, small lizards, and small toads.
- They are most active during the rainy season when they come out to spawn in the pools of water created by the monsoon rains (May-September). Females can lay over 8,000 eggs as a black jelly like strand. Tadpoles hatch in 2-12 days and in 30days become a froglet. The tadpoles eat algae and aquatic bugs.
- Average size is 19cm (7.5 inches) long and they are the largest native toad in the United States.
- They don't drink water, but use osmotic absorption to bring water across their skin through and area of their stomach called "the seat patch".

- They make a low pitched "hoot" noise.
- They are green or brown and have golden eyes with horizontal pupils. Females can be recognized by their red warts in strait lines on their back.
- The white wart and white glands on their legs secrete toxins that can paralyze or kill a dog. Raccoons will pull on the back of their legs to turn them over and feed on just the belly region
- Their secretions are toxic if taken orally, but harmless if smoked and they produce warm sensations and auditory hallucinations.
- They live 2-4 years near the Adobe Dam in Arizona, but this is short for a toad species.
- They are endangered in California and threatened in New Mexico and you may not legally remove them. Many died from pesticides used after World War II.
- In Arizona you can bag up to 10 if you have a fish and game license, but they are illegal if the intents is to smoke their venom/poison.
- They are eaten by raccoons, birds, mammals, and reptiles.

# Dusky Shark

Kingdom: Animalia
Phylum: Chordata
Class: Chondrichthyes
Order: Carcharhiniformes
Family: Carcharhiniformidae
Genus: *Carcharhinus*
Species: *obscurus*

Binomial Name:
*Carcharhinus obscurus*

## Wow Facts

- They are a requiem shark and are found in tropical to temperate coastlines and out to the continental shelves of Africa, Australia, North America, South America, Indian Ocean, and the east and west pacific.
- They migrate towards the poles in the summer, and then back to the warmer equator regions during the winter.
- Dusky grow up to 4.2m (14ft) long and weigh up to 347g (765 lb).
- They are typically found in 1080m (33-262ft) of depth, but they may dive to 400m (1249ft) deep.
- They are counter shaded with a blue/gray or golden colored on top with a white underside.
- They have a short round nose and sickle shaped pectoral fins, and a prominent ridge between the dorsal fins. Their upper teeth are triangular shaped and the lower teeth are pointed and narrower. Their teeth first appear in the Miocene epoch 23-5.3 Mya.
- They eat fish, squid, crustaceans, and larger ones eat other sharks, sea turtles, sea mammals, carrion, and manmade garbage.
- They don't mature until 20 years old and gestation takes up to 24 months. Females enter lagoons to deliver 3-16 live (viviparous) pups. Lifespan is 40-50 years, but they have a high bycatch mortality rate.
- Humans catch them for their meat, fins, skin for leather, and liver for vitamins.
- Young are eaten by bull sharks.

# Frogfish

Kingdom: Animalia
Phylum: Chordata
Class: Actinopterygii
Order: Lophiiformes
Family: Antennariidae
Two sub families and 14 Genera

## Wow Facts

- Found in tropical and subtropical oceans and seas except for the Mediterranean ocean.
- In Australia, they are called anglerfish which is rather descriptive of how they fish or hunt prey. The front dorsal fin is called the illicium "rod" and the tip has an esca "lure" that resembles a tiny fish, shrimp, or worm. Like a true fisherman they move the rod back and forth to dangle the lure and entice a small fish to come closer to investigate. When the prey is close enough, they strike within six milliseconds. They can increase the volume of their mouth by 12 times the normal size and their stomach can increase twice their own body size. This all takes place so fast, there is no time to escape.
- They use aggressive mimicry and can look like stones, corals, sponges, or sea squirts by changing the texture of their skin or their color over as little as a few weeks. They also camouflage themselves with algae or hydrozoa. In some species, females may be ten times the size of males.
- They can walk or gallop using their pectoral fins or swim using their tail. They can also move by jet propulsion by expelling water out through their gills.
- The greatest concentration or diversity of frogfish is in Lembeh Strait which separates Lembeh Island from the north end of Sulawesi Island in Indonesia and where certain muck diving sites are known to be home to particular species of frogfish depending on the season.
- Young are known to mimic or look like poisonous sea slugs or flatworms to avoid predation.

# Great White Shark

Kingdom: Animalia
Phylum: Chordata
Class: Chondrichthyes
Order: Lamniformes
Family: Lamnidae
Genus: *Carcharodon*
Species: *carcharias*

Binomial Name:
*Carcharodon carcharias*

## Wow Facts

- *Carcharodon* comes from Greek for *karcharos* "jagged" and *odous* "tooth". First appeared 16-18 million years ago.
- They are not related to C. megalodon, but from the mako shark family of Lamnidae.
- Because of their counter shading of grey on top and white on the bottom they are hard to see while looking down through the water at their dorsal side (back), as they are when below them and looking up towards the surface at their ventral side (belly).
- Great whites use their Ampullae of Lorenzini to detect electromagnetic signals and this also draws them towards boats. The can detect one billionth of a volt which is equivalent to a heartbeat.
- Their *rete mirabile* blood system helps keep blood warm in their system. Their muscles and stomach can stay warmer than the surrounding water by this method.
- Females can weigh 1,950kg (4,300lb) and 6.1m (20ft) long. Males are smaller; 3.35-4m (11ft-13ft) long.
- Males are sexually mature at 26 years old and females at 33 years old.
- They are born 1.2m (3.9ft) long and grow some 25cm (9.8 inches) per year until fully grown.
- Males mature at 25 years and females at 33 years of age.

- The liver is high in fat and oils, which is used for long distance migrations and for buoyancy to reduce sinking and save energy.
- They are known to migrate from Mexico and California to Hawaii and from Africa to Australia; a 20,00km (12,000 mile) distance.
- They made feed on penguins or seals near the surface, or dive down some 1,200m (3,900ft) deep to hunt for squids.
- They are most likely to hunt within two hours of sunrise. They are looking for prey with the highest fat content. They die from the wound before will do a test bite on different One inanimate objects, items or animals in order to calculate fat content.
- In one bite, they can eat 14kg (31 lb) of flesh.
- As with many potential targets, they will do an initial test bite and let the prey become weak from loss of blood before returning to feed on the prey; especially if the prey has large claws or teeth.
- Most recreational scuba dive attacks are not detrimental, as recreational divers typically have a buddy to get the victim back to the boat or shore for help. Lone swimmers, surfers, or commercial abalone divers from Australia are more vulnerable to the initial test bite and the following blood loss unless potential help is located quickly.
- 30kg (66 lb.) of whale blubber can feed a 4.5m (14.8ft) great white shark for 1.5 months. They will gorge themselves on a whale carcass to the point of regurgitation, and then feed all over again if they find a section of blubber higher in fat content.
- Life span is 70 years. In captivity, they usually die within a year. Their only predator other than man is Orcas and they eat the liver.
- Their jaws are worth a single one-time price of £20,000, but tours to see Great Whites in just Africa alone generate £9,000-£27,000 each day charters go out to view them.

# Hammerhead Shark

Kingdom: <u>Animalia</u>
Phylum: <u>Chordata</u>
Class: <u>Chondrichthyes</u>
Order: <u>Carcharhiniformes</u>
Family: <u>Sphyrnidae</u>
Genus: *Sphyrna*
Species: *nine species*
Binomial Name:

## Wow Facts

- Hammerhead sharks are found in tropical and warmer oceans worldwide; near coastal regions and continental shelves. In the summer, they migrate to cooler waters.
- They have a hammer shaped cephalofoil which gives them a greater area of electro-receptors, Ampullae of Lorenzini which give them more range and ability to detect live sea creatures buried under the sand. Because their nostrils are larger, they have great smell detection ability and their eyes at the end of their stalks give them 360° vision for seeing better above and below at the same time. Plus, their head works as a large bow plane for swifter movements towards prey. Lastly, they can use their wide head to pin down prey until they are ready to eat.
- Hammerheads can get up to 6m (19.7ft) long and 580kg (1,279 lb). Of all species, only scallop, smooth, and great hammerheads are known to attack humans at least on 33 occasions, but with no fatalities. This is mostly due to their small mouth size which is perfect for eating fish, squid, small sharks, crustaceans, and rays.
- They swim in schools during the day and at night hunt alone. Scalloped and smooth hammerheads are known to swim in groups according to age and sex.
- The Bonnethead is unusual in that it can reproduce asexual through parthenogenesis.
- They give live birth "viviparous" to 2 to 42 pups.
- Their first fossilized teeth appear 20 million years ago in the Miocene Epoch.

# Harbor Porpoise

Kingdom: Animalia
Phylum: Chordata
Class: Mammalia
Order: Artiodactyla
Infraorder: Cetacea
Family: Phocoenidae
Genus: *Phocoena*
Species: *phocoena*

Binomial Name:
*Phocoena phocoena*

## Wow Facts

- They inhabit fjords, bays harbors, and estuaries in temperate and subarctic waters of the Northern Atlantic and Pacific oceans.
- They are one of six species of porpoise.
- They eat small fish such as capelin, pollock, sardines, and herring as well as squid and crustacean such as shrimp.
- They are found in pairs or groups of 6-19, but they may hunt in packs of 50-100 individuals to herd fish. They can eat 7-8% of their body weight per day.
- They are 67-85cm (26-33 inches) long. Females may weigh up to 76kg (168 lb.) males only 61kg (134 lb.).
- They dive down to 220 meters for 1-5 minutes at a time.
- When exhaling, they make a puffing noise that sounds like a sneeze.
- Predators include: great whites and orcas. They are harassed by bottlenose dolphins, and seals are known to take bites.
- In Greenland, they are sold for human consumption, but their meat may contain high concentrations of heavy metals, PCB's, and pesticides.
- They tend to get caught in gill nets and long lines too.

# Krill

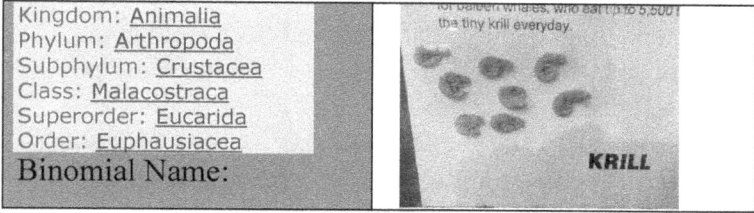

Kingdom: <u>Animalia</u>
Phylum: <u>Arthropoda</u>
Subphylum: <u>Crustacea</u>
Class: <u>Malacostraca</u>
Superorder: <u>Eucarida</u>
Order: <u>Euphausiacea</u>
Binomial Name:

for baleen whales, who eat up to 5,500
the tiny krill everyday.

KRILL

## Wow Facts

- They are found worldwide in every ocean.
- They are in the Superorder Eucarida along with the order Decopoda (shrimps, crabs, and lobsters). The order Euphausiacea has two families. One Family is Euphausiidae and is consists of 10 genera and 85 species. The other family is Bentheuphausia and contains only one species that lives in deep open bathypelagic waters 1,000m (3,300ft). They all have visible external gills that are easy to recognize. The two families split apart from each other over 130 million years ago during the early Cretaceous period.
- Krill is the Norwegian word to small fry or fish.
-  The Euphausiidae family species are all bioluminescent. Most of them are neritic (live near coasts) near the surface, but some can live down at depths of 4,000m (13,100ft).
- Many species come up near the surface to feed at night, then descend back down during the night. They feed on plankton and some even feed on zooplankton.  As they become full, they become inactive and start to sink downward. When they become hungry, they actively swim back upwards.
- When they are swarming and feeding, they can be so dense in numbers that they can be seen from space.
- Half of all krill are eaten by baleen whales, seals, penguins, and other fish and birds.
- They are fished commercially by Japan, Russia, and

the Ukraine. They are used in pharmaceuticals, aquarium food, aquaculture, and bait.

- The exoskeletons are removed because they are high in fluoride. The krill are eaten in Japan as "Okiami", in the Philippines they are called "alamang" and made into a paste called "bagoong".
- Krill feed on single cell plankton, and in turn are eaten by higher trophic level species. They are called the fuel that runs the engine of Earth's marine ecosystem.
- If they can't find enough diatoms to eat, the shearwater population falls and the salmon may not spawn, and the chain reaction continues.
- They have a brood sac that they carry eggs in until they hatch. After they hatch they go through several larval stages where they are part of the zooplankton.
- Their chitinous exoskeleton is similar to shrimp and prawns and they shed it in stages as they grow.
- Krill that live near the poles may live more than 6 years, those living in the mid-latitudes live for 2 years, and those in tropical waters may live for only 8 months.

# Lion Fish

Kingdom: Animalia
Phylum: Chordata
Class: Actinopterygii
Order: Scorpaeniformes
Family: Scorpaenidae
Genus: Pterois
Species: twelve
Binomial Name:

## Wow Facts

- These invasive species are originally native to the Indo-Pacific region, but now reside worldwide in warmer waters. The two most prolific species are *P. volitans* and *P. miles*.
- Lion fish are stripped similar to a zebra but the color and width of the lines varies between species and geographical regions; lionfish in the Flower Gardens Reef system in the Gulf of Mexico are darker than their cousins in the Caribbean or Guam.
- They also have venomous fin rays that protrude out from their body and warn other fish to stay away.
- They are 5-45cm (2-17.7) inches long.
- They have few natural predators besides moray eels, blue spotted coronet fish, some sharks, and large groupers.
- They have voracious appetites and can reduce the diversity of fish on a reef by 80%. Most juvenile fish are defenseless against lionfish, as they blow a jet of water towards their prey and their prey's natural response is to swim towards the emitted flow of water and that is when they are swallowed whole. They also eat small invertebrates; especially when reefs become depleted of young or small fish.
- They have highly developed muscles for buoyancy control that makes them a lethal hunter from just about any angle.
- Females may lay two clusters of eggs with up to 15,000 eggs each. They use currents to disperse their young.

- Juvenile larval forms can hitch a ride in the ballast tanks of ships to cover vast international distances.
- Pet owners may have originally released them into Florida waters prior to 1985, but hurricane Andrew released more in 1992 when it destroyed aquariums in Southern Florida.
- As for progression, lion fish migrated to the Bahamas in 2004, Barbados in 2013, and down to Brazil by 2014.
- They are found north as far as Delaware and they do not mind bays or fresh water rivers where the saline or salt level is quite low.
- It is reported that unless humans harvest 27% of them per month, then their population will keep on expanding.
- Typical ways to eat them include deep fry, ceviche, jerky, grilling, and raw sashimi.
- Special lion fish spear guns, gloves, and catch buckets are used to help avoid human contact with the spines.
- Contact with the spines can lead to headaches, nausea, fever, convulsions, numbness, vomiting, difficulty breathing, and paralysis, swelling of the tongue, reduced blood pressure, slurred speech, runny nose, heartburn, diarrhea, sweating, pain and other symptoms depending on the allergies of the victim.
- Fortunately, lionfish are not naturally aggressive, but if contact with the spines is made, leave the water immediately, inform others, and seek immediate medical attention.

# Mahi mahi

Kingdom: Animalia
Phylum: Chordata
Class: Actinopterygii
Order: Perciformes
Family: Coryphaenidae
Genus: *Coryphaena*
Species: *hippurus*

Binomial Name:
*Coryphaena hippurus*

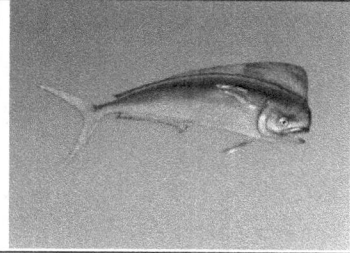

## Wow Facts

- In Hawaiian Mahi mahi means "very strong". They are also called dolphinfish, dorado, and by the misnomer *dolphin*, but they are a ray finned fish, not an ocean-going mammal.
- In 1978 (Spencer Wilkie Tinker) they still reached the size of 1.8m (6ft) long and 32kg (70 lb), but now they average 7-13kg (15-29lb), and a max of 18kg (40lb) before they are caught.
- They are found worldwide in warmer waters from the Caribbean, Costa Rica Gulf of Mexico, Florida, Africa, South China Sea, Asia, Tahiti, and Hawaii.
- They like to hang out under floating sargassum weeds in search of prey. Juveniles like to feed on plankton, shrimp, fish, and crabs, while adults like to feed on smaller fish such as mackerel.
- In turn, Mahi mahi are eaten by larger fish such as wahoo and swordfish, and by dolphins and toothed whales.
- They have gold colors on their sides, as well as bright blues and greens. Their pectoral fins are iridescent blue and they may have black diagonal stripes on their sides too. As they die they turn to a "dorado" golden color. Males are larger and have square faces.
- They mature in one year and can spawn 2-3 times a year.
- Lifespan is 5 years.
- Grilled Mahi mahi is a favorite worldwide.

# Mako Shark

Kingdom: <u>Animalia</u>
Phylum: <u>Chordata</u>
Class: <u>Chondrichthyes</u>
Order: <u>Lamniformes</u>
Family: <u>Lamnidae</u>
Genus: *Isurus*
Species: *oxyrinchus*
Binomial Name:
*Isurus oxyrinchus*

## Wow Facts

- There are actually two species of make shark. *Isurus oxyrinchus* is the short fin mako. *Oxy* means pointed and rhinchus means nose. The rare long fin mako is *Isurus paucus*. Mako means shark or shark tooth in the Maori language. Other species of mako died out between 100Mya to less than 1 million years ago. Mako are related to port beagle and great white sharks through the ancient species known as *Isurus hastalis.*
- Short fin mako sharks live in tropical to temperate waters worldwide. Long fin mako sharks live in warmer waters and the Gulf Stream.
- They can measure 2.5-4.5m (8.2-14.8ft) long and weigh 800kg (1,800 lb). Females are larger than males.
- Mako sharks are counter shaded with metallic blue on top and white on the underside and have a lunate tail.
- They are one of the fastest sharks and can swim 40km/h (25mph) with bursts up to 74km/h (46mph). They can travel 2,128km (1,322 miles) in 37 days. The Port of Limon in Costa Rica in the early 1970's was a great place to watch them leap in the water up to 9m (30ft).
- Smaller mako eat squid, mackerel, tuna, and bonito, while larger mako feed on other sharks, dolphins, porpoise, sea turtles, swordfish, and birds. They are smart and rely on vision, smell, and taste, and are known to scavenge long lives for already caught fish.
- Lifespan for females is 32 years, and 30 years for males. They never live more than five days in captivity.
- They are prized for their meat by humans.

# Manta Ray

| Kingdom: Animalia | |
|---|---|
| Phylum: Chordata | |
| Class: Chondrichthyes | 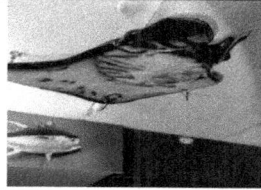 |
| Order: Myliobatiformes | |
| Family: Myliobatidae | |
| Genus: *Manta* | |
| Species: *alfredi & birostris* | |

## Wow Facts

- The word *manta* means cloak or blanket in Spanish and Portuguese. There are two species of manta.
- *Manta birostris* can grow up to 7m (23ft) wide and prefers temperate, tropical, and sub tropical open oceans worldwide. They dive 1,000m (3.300ft) deep and migrate great distances such as North Carolina to New Zealand. They have dark colored mouths and have large spots on their abdominal region.
- *Manta alfredi* can grow up to 5.5m (18ft) wide and are local residents of the indo-pacific and the eastern Atlantic. They dive to over 400m (1,312ft). They have white colored mouths and spots between their gill slits.
- Both species have wide mouths located in the front of their face, horned shaped cephalic fins, triangular pectoral fins, eyes on the sides of their heads, and are colored black or with shades of blue, gray, or brown on the top side and white on the bottom side with the skin covered by a protective layer of mucus. They have 18 ribbon like rows of teeth on the lower jaw only.
- These filter feeders eat shrimp, krill, and planktonic crabs at a rate of 13% of their body mass each week.
- In turn, they are eaten by large sharks and killer whales or nibbled on by cookie cutter sharks. Humans harvest their gillrakers to make traditional Chinese medicine. Dead mantas are worth $40-$500, but a single live one is worth millions in tourist dollars. **Indonesia** has the largest manta sanctuary in the world. In **Yap** you can scuba dive and view them hovering over cleaning stations. The **Andaman Sea** in Thailand is a great place to watch them filter feed.

# Megalodon

Kingdom: <u>Animalia</u>
Phylum: <u>Chordata</u>
Class: <u>Chondrichthyes</u>
Order: <u>Lamniformes</u>
Family: <u>Lamnidae</u>
Genus: *Carcharocles*
Species: *carcharias*

Binomial Name:
*Carcharocles*
*megalodon*

## Wow Facts

- From the Cenozoic era 23-2.6 million years ago (early Miocene to Pliocene).
- Greek (mega) means big and (odon) is tooth.
- Length 18m (59ft). Teeth up to 180mm (7.1 inch) long. 270 teeth sit in five rows of jaw. Jaw open 2m (6.6ft) wide with a posterior bite force of 108,514-182,201 Newtons. A great white bite force is only 18,216 Newtons.
- Megalodon is closely related to the broad tooth mako shark *Isurus hastalis*. They came into existence just as whales began to diversify.
- The largest Megalodons lived in the southern hemisphere.
- Megalodons ate cetaceans, dolphins, pinnipeds, squids, and turtles.
- Fossil evidence suggests that they took bites that crushed bones near hearts and lungs of whales; they rammed prey from below, bit off their fins and flippers to immobilize their prey. By the end of the Miocene tropical whales were few in number and far between as whales radiated out towards the Arctic and Antarctic oceans. Competition with orcas, delphinids, sperm whales, and great whites also depleted Megalodon's preferred tropical sources of prey.
- Their young were born at nursery sites similar in habit to great whites today. Newborns were 2-4m (6.6-13ft) long.

- During the late Pliocene to Pleistocene ice ages, the seas were lowered and cooled, reducing the warmer nursing locations around the world significantly.
- After they died out, the average size of whales increased dramatically.
- Movies and TV "Docufictions" are constantly repeating that Megalodons still exist. They do this without any proof, but the ratings are typically good because the thought of such a giant apex predator roaming the seas is right up there with the profound desire to encounter Godzilla and Bigfoot.

# Melon-headed Whale

Kingdom: Animalia
Phylum: Chordata
Class: Mammalia
Order: Artiodactyla
Infraorder: Cetacea
Family: Delphinidae
Genus: *Peponocephala*
Species: *electra*

Binomial Name:
*Peponocephala electra*

## Wow Facts

- Also called the electra dolphin. They are a close relative of the pygmy killer whale and pilot whale.
- They prefer oceanic deep water.
- Their body is dark gray and darker grey on their pointed face. Their flippers are long and pointed too.
- They can average 2.7m (9ft) long and weigh 210kg (460lb).
- They eat fish, squid, and crustaceans.
- They may congregate in groups of over 300 individuals off of the Philippines and over 800 members off of Hawaii.
- Their ear drums are quite sensitive to high power sonar equipment used by the Navy and industrial oil searching vessels and this will cause them to beach themselves (stranded) and other healthy individuals may join them in groups up to 150-200 members.
- Gestation is 12 months.
- Males live 22 years, and females 30 years.
- They are caught as bycatch by fisheries in some parts of the world such as Japan and other Pacific regions.

# Orca Whale

| | |
|---|---|
| Kingdom: <u>Animalia</u><br>Phylum: <u>Chordata</u><br>Class: <u>Mammalia</u><br>Order: <u>Artiodactyla</u><br>Infraorder: <u>Cetacea</u><br>Family: <u>Delphinidae</u><br>Genus: *Orcinus*<br>Species: *orca*<br>Binomial Name:<br>***Orcinus orcas*** |  |

## Wow Facts

- They are also known as Killer whales, but this is an incorrect translation of Spanish *asesina de ballenas* "whale killer".  Orcinus is Latin for "of the kingdom of the dead".
- Orca is the preferred name as they are not whales, but rather the largest species in the dolphin family. They branched off from some 35-other species of oceanic dolphins 11 million years ago.
- They are found in the Arctic, tropical, and Antarctic oceans.
- There are three basic groups: resident, transient, and offshore.
- Resident orcas eat fish and squid. The females are said to have more rounded dorsal fin tips. The live in matrilineal groups that may consist of four generations.
- Transient orcas eat fish, mammals, sharks, birds including penguins, and turtles. They will eat 32 species of cetaceans (whales, dolphins and porpoise including blue, gray, and beluga whales), and 20 species of seals, fur seals, sea lions, and walrus. They live in small pods of 2-6 members and have more triangular shaped dorsal fins.
- Offshore orcas feed on schools of fish and live in groups of 20-70 individuals and sometimes up to 200. They also have rounded dorsal fins.
- All three types have their own dialects and even seals can tell the difference. Residents may even swim

alongside seals and not see them as food, but seals in Seattle are known to jump right out of the water next to scuba divers and fishermen when they hear transient orcas even across the other side of the Hood Canal in the Puget Sound of Washington State. Both Transients and Residents give scuba divers a wide berth when they enter the water as orcas appear to not like the noise of the bubbles generated by diver's regulators. The transient orcas enter the Puget Sound every 2-4 years and reduce the harbor seal population quite effectively over a period of several months.

- The three types of orcas are said to have split from one another over two million years ago and have not interbred in 10 thousand years. The north pacific groups have been on their own for 700,000 years.
- Orcas are recognizable by their black colored back, white under belly, and the shape and size of their white patch behind the eye, and grey saddle patch behind their fin. The shape and size of their dorsal fin along with cuts, notches, and scars of there are unique to each individual as finger prints to humans; although sometimes they are born calico or white.
- Males are 6-8m (20-26ft) long and have dorsal fins 1.8m (5.9ft) tall. Females are smaller at 5-7m (16-23ft) long. The largest male on record was 9.8m (32ft) long. The largest female: 8.5m (28ft). Male dorsal fins are twice as high as a female's and more triangular in shape, where female dorsal fins are more curved.
- Calves are born 2.4m (7.9ft) long and 180kg (400 lb).
- Mother's mature at age 10 and are at their most reproductive stage at age 20 until age 40. They tend to have a calf once every five years and the gestation period is 15-18 months. The mortality rate for newborns in the first 7 months is 37-50%.
- They use their brain to solve problems and hunt more effectively. They catch herring using bubble nets, then slap their tails to stun and eat the fish. In New Zealand they pin stingrays to the ground and hold various sharks

upside down and put them in a tonic immobile state where they eventually suffocate and become easy to eat. In the Farallon islands of San Francisco, California they have used this technique to kill and eat the liver of a great white shark which can be high in fat and oils. They are known to suffocate gray whale calves by pushing them underwater with the weight of their bodies, just to eat the young calf's tongue. As for penguins, the will ride waves right up the sand and beach themselves temporarily to catch these elusive birds. For seals on ice flows, orcas have learned to spy hop, then generate waves and wash off the seal into the waiting circle of their peers or family members. They are also known to ram or head butt large prey such as seals and walrus. They have even learned how to take fish off fishermen's long lines.

- They can eat 227kg (500 lb) of food each day.
- Although they are not known to attack a human swimming in water, they are known to get aggressive with kayakers who have floated between a mother orca and its calf, and many people working at marine parks have been killed by captive orcas.
- In captivity, 60-90% of male dorsal fins have collapsed or fallen over to one side. In the wild, they can swim deep and/or cross 160km (100 miles) or ocean per day.
- Females may live 50-100 plus years in the wild. Males live 29-59 years in the wild. Captive Orcas average lifespan is just 25 years, but some may live up to 40 years.
- Although they are a top predator, noise and chemical pollution can harm orcas and navy sonar can cause brain and ear hemorrhages.

# Pilot Whale

Kingdom: <u>Animalia</u>
Phylum: <u>Chordata</u>
Class: <u>Mammalia</u>
Order: <u>Artiodactyla</u>
Infraorder: <u>Cetacea</u>
Family: <u>Delphinidae</u>
Genus: *Globicephala*
Species: *macrorhynchus and melas*
*Two Species*

## Wow Facts

- There are two living species. The short-finned pilot whale, *Globicephala macrorhynchus*, lives in warmer tropical and sub-tropical waters such as California and Hawaii year-round. The long-finned pilot whale, *Globicephala melas*, lives in colder waters off of Chile, Argentina, New Zealand, and Australia.
- Long fin males are up to 7.5m long and short fin males are 7.2m long, with females slightly shorter. The best way to tell them apart is to examine the skull and rostrum.
- Pilot whales are the second largest oceanic dolphin and the most often stranded on beaches.
- They eat squid, cuttlefish, octopus, herring, mackerel, cod, turbot, and spiny dogfish sharks. They hunt by echolocation
- They have sickle shaped fins, a light anchor patch under their chin, and a light saddle patch behind their dorsal fin.
- Females go through menopause, and then help nurse the young of other mothers. They calve once every 3-5 years, calves nurse for three years. Short fins females mature in 9 years and males in 13-16 years. Long fins; females 8 years and males 12 years.
- They live in matrilineal pods of 10-30 members, and sometimes up to 100, and both males and females stay with the pod for life. They do not last long in captivity.
- The lifespan for males is 45 years and 60 years for females.

- The Feroe Islands, Greenland, and Japan hunt them for their meat which has less fat and more protein than beef, but high amounts of DDT, PCB, cadmium, and mercury.

# Red-eared Slider

Kingdom: Animalia
Phylum: Chordata
Class: Reptilia
Order: Testudines
Family: Emydidae
Genus: *Trachemys*
Species: *scripta*
Binomial Name:
subspecies:
***T.s.elegans***

## Wow Facts

- They are a sub species of pond sliders and known to slide into the water as soon as they feel threatened.
- These **omnivores** are native to southern states along the Mississippi river and northern Mexico and because of their role as a popular pet; they are now one of the top ten invasive species worldwide.
- They are known for their red stripe behind their eye. Their head, legs, and tail have sketchy yellow lines.
- Maximum size is 40cm (16 inches) long and females are larger than males.
- Males have longer front claws for gripping, and a more rounded belly plate "plastron".
- They are poikilotherms and need to warm up by sun rays and this is why they are most commonly found in a pond resting on a log sunbathing.
- They are born leaf green but older individuals are brown to dark olive green.
- They usually "brumate" (become less active or motionless and don't eat or excrete) in October through March. Females lay 20-30 eggs in a clutch. Incubation is 59-112 days. Young enter the water 21days after hatching.
- Sex is determined by incubation temperature; above 22°C (72°F) they are born male, above 27°C (81°F) they are born females.
- They live 20-30 years on average and some up to 40 years.

# Round Stingray

| |
|---|
| Kingdom: Animalia |
| Phylum: Chordata |
| Class: Chondrichthyes |
| Order: Myliobatiformes |
| Family: Urotrygonidae |
| Genus: *Urobatis* |
| Species: *halleri* |
| Binomial Name: |
| *Urobatis halleri* |

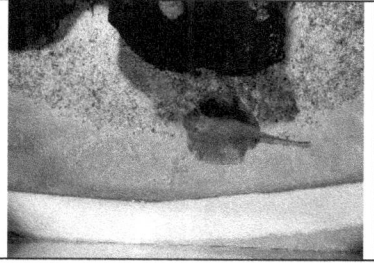

## Wow Facts

- They are found in the near coastal waters of the Pacific Ocean from Humboldt Bay in Northern California down to Panama. In the winter they descend to deeper ware or hang out near electrical generating plants where the outflow water is warmer than the surrounding coastal waters.
- Males, 25cm (9.9") wide, and juveniles remain in shallow waters, less than 15m (50ft), while the slightly larger females, 31cm (1ft) wide, may be found in deeper water; 91m (298ft) deep. The largest female recorded was 58cm (22.8") wide.
- They are almost completely round and brown or grayish brown on top and pale yellow underneath.
- They have a venomous spine on their tail that they use for defense, and unless you shuffle your feet through the sand, you might accidentally step on one buried in the sand and in turn become one of hundreds of people annually that get the serrated spine removed at a nearby hospital.
- Round stingrays eat worms, clams, mollusks, shrimp, and crustaceans such as crabs. The remove the sand substrate using their wings or pectoral disk, and mouth. Moving all this sand helps smaller fish find food before the sand settles.
- They are ovoviviparous and bear 1-6 live young; bigger females have more young.
- Lifespan is 10-12 years. They are preyed upon by elephant seals, sharks, and black sea bass.

297

# Sailfish

Kingdom: Animalia
Phylum: Chordata
Class: Actinopterygii
Order: Perciformes
Family: Istiophoridae
Genus: *Istiophorus*
Species: Two species

Binomial Name:
*Istiophorus albicans and*
*Istiophorus platypterus*

## Wow Facts

- The Sailfish is a bill fish that inhabits warmer waters worldwide. There are two species.
- They mainly hunt near the surface, but are known to dive down for squid. They hunt using their sail to herd fish, and they may swim at speeds up to 110km/h (68 mph). Their first dorsal fin of sail is almost as long as their body.
- Their upper jaw is twice as long as their lower jaw and they can use their bill to stun, injure, or cut small fish in half. Depending on what region they live in determines the type of prey they consume.
- Like squid, they can change colors instantaneously. They are blue on top with white on the bottom and they have blue dots dispersed across their body. They are light blue with yellow stripes when excited.
- Although their meat is tough and best when smoked. They are one of the most popular game fish from Bermuda, Puerto Rico, the Gulf of Mexico, Mediterranean Sea, Papua New Guinea, The Philippines, Tahiti, Marquesas, and Hawaii.
- Females are larger than males. And the largest live in the Pacific Ocean. They grow to 1.2-1.5m (3'11"- 4' 11") in a single year and max out at 3m (9.8ft) long.
- A large female may spawn 4,500,000 eggs.
- Predators include: birds and dorado (mahi mahi).

# Southern Stingray

Kingdom: <u>Animalia</u>
Phylum: <u>Chordata</u>
Class: <u>Chondrichthyes</u>
Order: <u>Myliobatiformes</u>
Family: <u>Dasyatidae</u>
Genus: *Dasyatis*
Species: *americana*

Binomial Name:
*Dasyatis Americana*

## Wow Facts

- They are found in the western Atlantic Ocean from New Jersey down to Brazil and throughout the Caribbean Ocean and the Gulf of Mexico.
- Adults are diamond shaped and may be olive-brown to green-gray colored on the dorsal or top side and cream to white colored on the ventral or underside. Females may be 150cm (5ft) and males 67cm (2.2ft) wide.
- They have a barb or spine on their tail that is covered in venomous mucus and they use this for defense only. The spine has 52-80 teeth on each side. The tail itself may be twice as long as the stingray's body.
- They are nocturnal and at night eat fish, crustaceans, worms, and mollusks such as clams, which they crush with their grinding plate. They tend to stay above 53m (180ft) deep. When not eating, they may cover themselves in the sand and pass water in through their dorsal spiracles, and out through their ventral gills.
- In Stingray City in Grand Cayman divers descend a mere 3.7m (12ft) and hand feed small fish or pieces of fish to stingrays passing by. The habituated stingrays have learned that if they nibble on loose long hair, the human might possibly drop the fish from their hand, whereby the stingray will swoop down and catch the falling feast. They may give a diver a bad hickey on the arm or leg if they feel teased or get too excited. This is partly due because they can't see their food, so they rely on taste, smell, and their electro-sensors, Ampullae of Lorenzini, to locate their food.

# Striped Marlin

Kingdom: <u>Animalia</u>
Phylum: <u>Chordata</u>
Class: <u>Actinopterygii</u>
Order: <u>Perciformes</u>
Family: <u>Istiophoridae</u>
Genus: *Kajikia*
Species: *audax*

Binomial Name:
*Kajikia audax*

## Wow Facts

- They are found in tropical to temperate waters, but they can with stand colder waters than blue marlins.
- They hunt near the surface and similar to sailfish, the herd sardines and bait fish into tight balls before attacking with their bills.
- The can weigh up to 190kg (420 lb) and are 4.2m (13.8 ft) long.
- They are prized game fish and the largest in the world are hooked off the coast of New Zealand.
- In Cabo San Lucus, Mexico, also called "Stripey central", they can be caught by the 100's in one day.
- They are also prized game fish in California, South America, Indian ocean, and Africa

# Tiger Shark

Kingdom: Animalia
Phylum: Chordata
Class: Chondrichthyes
Order: Carcharhiniformes
Family: Carcharhiniformidae
Genus: *Galeocerdo*
Species: *cuvier*
Binomial Name:
*Galeocerdo cuvier*

## Wow Facts

- They are a requiem shark and are found in tropical to temperate oceans worldwide usually near coastal regions, also in harbors, rivers, canals, and estuaries.
- They average 5m (16'5") but one in Australia was 5.5m (18ft) long; females are larger than males. The tiger stripes are more prominent in young tiger sharks.
- Tiger sharks eat just about anything. They usually are nocturnal hunters and will dive down to 900m (3,000ft) in search of squid, fish, small sharks, or crustaceans. They are known to attack ailing humpback whales, and dugongs off of Australia. Stomach contents may include pieces or horses, bats, goats, and manmade objects such as cans, chains, and car license plates.
- In Hawaii, they swim in 3m (10ft) deep water searching for turtles. Note: One swimmer died in Hawaii while wearing a swim suit that looked like a turtle shell, yet tiger sharks swim past scuba divers every day.
- Off shore in the Bahamas and in Fiji scuba divers watch as dive professionals feed tiger sharks on a regular basis and these tigers are worth millions in annual tourist dollars. However, feeding a tiger too close to a resort in the Red Sea turned tragic when the tiger shark began to equate any swimmer as a potential source of food.
- Tigers are ovoviparous and eggs hatch internally and the 10-80 pups are then born alive. They give birth September to November in Hawaii. Adults live 12-20 years. They are preyed on by killer whales and man for shark fin soup and trophies.

# Toothed Whales

Kingdom: Animalia
Phylum: Chordata
Class: Mammalia
Order: Artiodactyla
Infraorder: Cetacea
Parvorder: Odontoceti

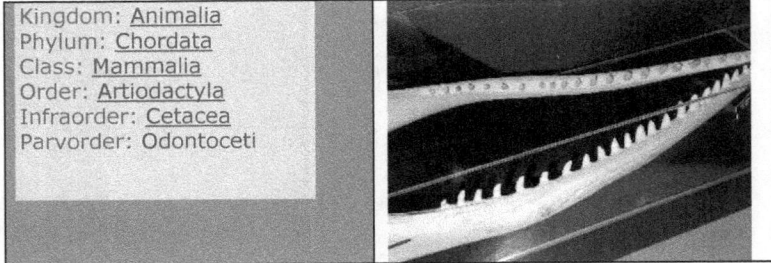

## Wow Facts

- They are found worldwide in the open ocean, coastal waters, and river dolphins are found in fresh water.
- The sperm whale may be 20m (67ft) in length, the vaquita porpoise is 1.4m long. Female toothed whales are typically larger than males.
- Their ancestors spit from dwelling even toed ungulates in the hippopotamus lineage some 54 Mya. They then split from a common ancestor with baleen whales 34 Mya. They have been dividing ever since and now there are some 70 species of toothed whales.
  Males are called bulls and Females are called cows. Females can produce milk so thick in fat for their young that the milk resembles toothpaste.
  Sperm whales on average dive down to 800m (2,620ft) deep, but sometimes descend to 2km (6,600ft) for an hour to hunt giant squid.
- Toothed whales, except for sperm whales, have torpedo shaped bodies and one blow hole on top of their head except for sperm whales that have it on the left side of their head.
- They exhale air before breathing in new air. When warm exhaled air is thrust out of the blow hole and meets cold air, it forms a spout that is unique to that particular species.
- Most toothed whales have pointed conical teeth with cementum cells over laying dentine cells.
- Those species that eat fish have more teeth than those that eat squid; a dolphin may have forty sets of teeth

while a beak whale has one single set of teeth. Adult male Narwhals may have an upper left tooth grow out 3m (10ft) long.

- Toothed whales feed on fish, crustaceans, squids, and octopus, and Orcas in particular, feed on penguins, seals, sea lions, sharks, rays, and even minke and gray whales. They have a two chambered (fundic and pyloric) stomach.
- Most toothed whales have fused neck vertebra except for river dolphins, belugas, and narwhals.
- Most of them have a thick layer of blubber to keep them warm except river dolphins.
- They have two flippers with four digits that they use for steering like a rudder. Back legs are typically vestigial or may have remnants hidden internally.
- They move their tail or fluke up or down to create forward motion with speeds up to 35 km/h (22mph) as seen in the sperm whale.
- Most of them have dorsal fins.
- The common names are not always precise as Orca whales, pilot whales, and melon headed whales are all part of the dolphin family.
- Most toothed whales have small slightly flattened eyes which give them two 10.7m (35ft) long fields of view.
- Olfactory lobes are absent and they have no sense of smell. Most have poor or few taste buds except for river dolphins that tend to prefer one type of fish over another.
- Toothed whales use echolocation to find food, evade predators, and to navigate. They have a melon or fluid filled space in their forehead that they use to transmit sounds made from their nasal air sacs just below the blowhole. The sounds reflect off of nearby objects and return to the sender via their jawbone, and then the sounds pass through their throat, and into their inner ear. From the received sounds, they can determine a nearby object's size, speed, shape, and surface conditions; including sensing prey under sand.

- The bigger the specie's melon, the more they depend on echolocation.
- Toothed whales make burst pulse sounds, whistles, and clicks. The rain of clicks will increase the closer a dolphin gets to an object of interest. Dolphins learn how to make sounds from their mother and a male's signature sounds will sound similar to his mother. They can even remember the whistle of another individual 20 years after they last heard that signature sound.
- Sperm whales make creaks, codas and slow clicks, but the slow clicks appear to be reserved for mating rituals.
- As far as intelligence goes, sperm whales have the largest brain mass on this planet; 8000cm$^3$ (490in$^3$) and 7.8kg (19lb). A human brain is a mere1, 450cm$^3$ (88in$^3$) and 1.5kg (3.4lb).
- It's been discovered that dolphins have elongated spindle neurons previously found only in humans and are associated with emotions, judgment, and theory of mind.
- Dolphins can teach, learn, cooperate, scheme, and grieve. They make bubble rings to hunt and corral fish, they put sponges on their nose to protect from stingray barbs, and display self-awareness using a mirror test.
- Life span for sperm whales is 70 years and 100plus years for orcas in the wild, but 9-25 years in captivity.
- Sperm whales utilize a waxy liquid called spermaceti that is used in candles, cosmetics, lubricants, soaps, and leather waterproofing. The blubber is reduced for lamp oil and other products. Ambergris, a solid flammable substance found in the stomach, is used to make perfume.
- Dolphin drive hunting is performed in the Solomon Islands Faroe Island, Peru, and Japan. The herding and killing of dolphins in Japan was capture in the documentary "*The Cove*", the Japanese now kill dolphins in tents and out of sight of the general public and foreigners. The story of captive Orcas such as *TiliKum* is exposed in the documentary "*Black Fish.*"

# Whitespotted Bamboo Shark

Kingdom: Animalia
Phylum: Chordata
Class: Chondrichthyes
Order: Orectolobiformes
Family: Hemiscylliidae
Genus: *Chiloscyllium*
Species: *plagiosum*

Binomial Name:
*Chiloscyllium plagiosum*

## Wow Facts

- They are found in the coral reef of the Pacific Ocean from Japan to India. They tend to rest during the day under coral heads and other places where they are not easily spotted.
- Because of their small size, they do not have to keep continuously swimming to get enough oxygen to pass through their gills and into their body.
- They are about 1m (37 inches) long and have white and dark spots covering their body.
- They typically feed at night, nocturnal, on small fish and invertebrates such as crabs, fish, clams, squid, scallops, and ghost shrimp.
- They use their electroreceptors (Ampullae of Lorenzini) to locate prey hidden under the sand.
- They use their teeth to grasp and crush their catch.
- The teeth are angled backwards to help in the crushing process.
- They have 26-35 teeth in the upper jaw, and 27-32 teeth in the lower jaw.
- They lay eggs; oviparous. The eggs hatch in 14-15 weeks and the young are 12.7 cm (5 inches) long.
- Sometimes females lay eggs and they hatch without being fertilized; a process known as parthenogenesis.
- Eggs at Sea World hatched and were albino. White bamboo sharks hatching in the open sea could easily be spotted and eaten by predators.

# Yellowfin Tuna

Kingdom: <u>Animalia</u>
Phylum: <u>Chordata</u>
Class: <u>Actinopterygii</u>
Order: <u>Perciformes</u>
Family: <u>Scombridae</u>
Genus: *Thunnus*
Species: *albacares*

Binomial Name:
*Thunnus albacares*

## Wow Facts

- In Hawaiian they are called "ahi". Albacores means "white meat" and they are a different species than albacore; *Thunnus alalunga.*
- They are found worldwide in tropical and subtropical oceans.
- Their large second dorsal fin and second ventral fin, as well as they are bright yellow.
- They weigh up to 180kg (400 lb).
- They typically swim and feed above 75m (246ft), but sometimes dive below 1,160m (3,810ft).
- They eat squid, pelagic crustaceans, anchovies, sardines, flying fish, flying fish, lantern fish, and skipjack tuna.
- Predators include: wahoo, sailfish, marlins, sharks, false killer whales, and sea birds.
- Industrial tuna fisheries catch the majority of yellowfin tuna. Deeper waters are where they catch the 25kg (55lb) or greater sashimi grade tuna on long lines.
- Sports fishermen like to catch them because they put up more of a fight than blue tuna twice their size.
- During the alternating El Niño years when the waters warm off the California coastline, yellowfin tuna can be caught off of Catalina Island or off the normally colder waters of South Africa, Australia, and New Zealand.

# Nevada Room

# Ants

| | |
|---|---|
| Kingdom: Animalia<br>Phylum: Arthropoda<br>Class: Insecta<br>Order: Hymenoptera<br>Family: Formicidae<br>Genus: *Formica*<br>Species: *.*<br>**Binomial name: *Formica *.*** | |

## Wow Facts

- Ants evolved some 100-130 million years ago from wasp-like ancestors. This was during the mid-cretaceous when dinosaurs ruled the world.
- There are more than 22,000 species of ants and only some 12,500 have been classified.
- They live in small colonies or in colonies consisting of millions of ants and there are over a million ants for every human on the planet.
- They have a cast system with one queen, and many workers and soldiers, and they have many different relationships with other forms of life.
- They are worldwide except for "Antarctica" which is ironic because the word ant is already in the name.
- They fill many ecological niches and most are **omnivores**.
- Some queen ants can live up to 30 years, while workers may live 1-3 years. They are said to live 100 times longer than other insects of similar size.
- Fire ants use a poison with piperridine alkaloids that make their bite painful and may cause an allergic reaction in some people.
- Fire ants use their poison to catch snakes, lizards, and other relatively small creatures.
- In turn, ants provide a readily available food source, for spiders, amphibians, lizards, birds, and some mammals. In some countries they are roasted or roasted and eaten by humans. In Mexico the eggs are made into caviar called escamoles.

# Badger

| |
|---|
| Kingdom: Animalia |
| Phylum: Chordata |
| Class: Mammalia |
| Order: Carnivora |
| Family: Mustelidae |
| Genus: *Taxidea* |
| Species: *taxus* |
| **Binomial name:** |
| ***Taxidea taxus*** |

## Wow Facts

- American badgers are found primarily in the Great Plains region of North America, but they are also found north into Canada and south throughout the mountainous regions of Mexico. They prefer to live in dry, open grasslands, fields, and pastures.

- They are easy to identify by their short powerful legs and narrow head with a white stripe running from the top of their nose to the back of their head and one white stripe on each side of their face.

- These **omnivores** literally eat everything, from grubs, eggs reptiles, amphibians, small mammals, fruits, and roots. They may become alcohol intoxicated after consuming fermenting rotten fruit.

- Badgers are excellent digging machines. Their powerfully built forelimbs allow them to tunnel rapidly through the soil, and they catch most of their food by digging and tunneling after ground dwelling rodents.

- The way their jaws interlock in the cavities of their head makes it almost impossible for them to dislocate their jaw, enabling them to hold on to almost anything, but in return this limits jaw movement to up and down motions with some side-to-side movement.

- They are active at night, nocturnal, and in winter can go thru states of torpor of up to 29 hours.

- Males are called **boars**, females are **sows**, and young are **cubs**, with colonies called **clans** or cete.

Their home is underground and called a sett.

- For short distances, they can run or gallop at speeds up to 31km/h (19mph).
- They are known to have cooperative "commensal" relationship with coyotes, and they will help each other dig up prey and rest next to each other with a coyote resting its head on the badger or licking the badger's face.
- Badgers have been the focus of folk tales, TV shows like Pokémon and in movies such as Walt Disney's 1973 film, *Robin Hood*, as Friar Tuck.

# Bighorn Sheep

| | |
|---|---|
| Kingdom: Animalia<br>Phylum: Chordata<br>Class: Mammalia<br>Order: Artiodactyla<br>Family: Bovidae<br>Genus: *Ovis*<br>Species: *canadensis*<br>Sub-Species: *O. c. nelsoni*<br>Trinomial name: ***Ovis Canadensis nelsoni*** |  |

## Wow Facts

- They inhabit alpine meadows, grassy mountain slopes and foothill country in proximity to rugged, rocky cliffs and bluffs.
- *Ovis canadensis* is found in the Rocky Mountains from southern Canada to Colorado, and as a desert subspecies (O. c. nelsoni) from Nevada and California to west Texas and south into Mexico.
- These **herbivores** eat a variety of desert plants and get most of their moisture from the vegetation or water from temporary rock pools.
- They can dehydrate and lose up to 30 percent of their body weight and quickly recover after drinking water. Few predators if any can stand or survive such conditions and environments.
- They can use ledges only 5cm (2 inches) wide for footholds, and bounce from ledge to ledge over spans as wide as 6m (20ft) using strong muscles and concave elastic hooves.
- They can move over level ground at 48km/h (30mph) and scramble up mountain slopes at 24km/h (15mph). They also swim freely, despite their massive bulk and the weight of their horns.
- Male **rams** have large set of curling horns while female **ewes** have straighter, smaller, and lighter horns. The horns of rams not only reveal their age by annual growth rings, but also their health, and fighting history.

- The desert subspecies, *Ovis canadensis nelsoni*, is somewhat smaller and has flatter, wider-spreading horns. An eight-year-old ram may have horns three feet wide and the horns may weigh over 14kg (30lb).
- Both rams and ewes use their horns to break open cacti, but prefer to eat grasses if available.
- Rams have double-layered skulls shored with struts of bone for battle protection. They also have a broad, massive tendon-linking skull and spine to help the head pivot and recoil from blows.
- The pelage of *Ovis canadensis* is smooth and composed of an outer coat of brittle guard hairs and short, gray, crimped fleece under fur. The summer coat is a rich, glossy brown, but it becomes quite faded by late winter.
- In the wild they live 10-20 years.
- Bighorn sheep are gregarious, sometimes gathering in **herds** of over 100 individuals, although small groups of 8 to 10 are more common.
- Tourists seasonally stop at Hemenway Valley Park near Boulder Dam in the morning to view and take pictures of a herd consisting of more than 65 members. Many of them wear collars for scientific study; the bighorn sheep that is. They may walk right by you as they have become accustomed to the presence of humans in close proximity, but it is best to keep a safe distance from them as they are wild animals and may act unpredictable if they perceive that they are being threatened or harassed by paparazzi, especially the males; the big horn sheep that is.

# Bobcat

Kingdom: Animalia
Phylum: Chordata
Class: Mammalia
Order: Carnivora
Family: Felidae
Genus: *Lynx*
Species: *rufus*
**Binomial name: *Lynx rufus***

## Wow Facts

- Bobcats are found throughout North America from southern Canada to southern Mexico. Bobcats can be found in a variety of habitats, including forest edges, semi-deserts, mountains, urban edges, swamplands, and brush land.
- They have short ear tufts, and ruffs of hair on the side of the head, giving the appearance of sideburns. They look like a cat with a bobbed tail, but they are twice the size of a housecat.
- They have smaller feet than the lynx and cannot compete with the lynx in deep snowy places.
- Bobcats are **carnivores.** Their food of choice is rabbits, but they will also eat birds, lizards, rodents, snakes, and carrion.
- Bobcats may ambush their prey by waiting motionless and then pouncing on them; the same hunting technique used by the mountain lions, or they may use stealth and stalk their prey, then pounce on it, depending on the size and type of prey in their home territory. They will sometimes attack livestock such as goats and sheep, but they are also known to scavenge livestock kills of other animals.
- They use urine, feces, and claw marks to mark their territory as well as their main den and shelters.
- 13 subspecies are recognized, including *Linx furus mohavensis* from the Mojave Desert.
- The bobcat appears to have evolved from the Eurasian lynx that came across the Bering Land

Bridge in the Pleistocene some 2.6 million years ago and modern bobcats first evolved around 20,000 years ago.

- The largest bobcats are found in Canada and the smallest from Florida.
- Mothers raise one to six kittens. They are born in April or May. The young can hunt by themselves by fall.
- They usually live six to eight years, but the longest to live in the wild is 16 years and 32 years in captivity.

# Burrowing Owl

Kingdom: Animalia
Phylum: Chordata
Class: Aves
Order: Strigiformes
Family: Strigidae
Genus: *Athene*
Species: *cunicularia*
**Binomial name: *Athene cunicularia***

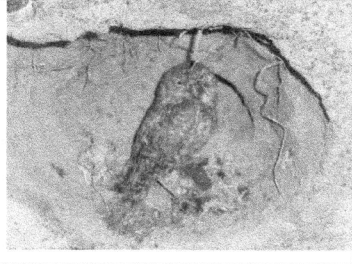

## Wow Facts

- They live in the desert regions and grasslands of western North America, and also in the drier areas of Central and South America and in airport grasslands and golf courses.
- They usually reside in a burrow dug out by small ground squirrels, prairie dogs, or a desert tortoise; half buried pipes and other manmade objects also work.
- They like to put cattle dung around their nests to help with the microclimate and attract insects to eat.
- They are **carnivores** and eat insects, small frogs, lizards, and rodents. Their longer legs help them sprint while hunting.
- Unlike other owl species, the female burrowing owl is similar in size to the male. Males may look lighter in color due to sun bleaching as they are outside the burrow more than females.
- The owl is also unique in that its entire head revolves in order to see its surroundings because its round yellow eyes are not capable of moving in the eye sockets.
- The burrowing owl is diurnal, and not nocturnal like most other species of owls.
- Although the burrowing owl may hover above the ground in search for prey. The owl spends most of its time on the ground and it will live together in loose colonies with other burrowing owls.

- As rattlesnakes also like the dens of prairie dogs, when threatened, a burrowing owl will retreat inside the den and make hissing and rattling sounds like a rattlesnake; a form of acoustic Batesian mimicry.
- They mate in early spring and 28 days later 3-12 eggs may hatch, but only 4-5 chicks survive. At 6 weeks, old the chicks can fly.
- They live up to 9 years in the wild and 10 in captivity.
- In the movie *Rango* a group of burrowing owls were a band of Mariachi players.

# Carole's Fritillary Butterfly

| |
|---|
| Kingdom: Animalia |
| Phylum: Arthropoda |
| Class: Insecta |
| Order: Lepidoptera |
| Family: Nymphalidae |
| Genus: *Speyeria* |
| Species: *carolae* |
| **Binomial name:** |
| ***Speyeria carolae*** |

## Wow Facts

- Their range area is limited to Mt. Charleston mountain range of Clark County, Nevada.
- Habitat: Mountain slopes, foothills, forest openings.
- On top they are bright orange with black markings. Silver marginal spots on underside.
- Life History: Males search open areas to find females. Females may delay egg laying until late summer. Eggs are laid singly on litter near violets. First-stage caterpillars over winter unfed; in the spring they feed on violet leaves.
- Caterpillar Hosts: Charleston Mountain violet (Viola charlestonensis).
- Adults feed on flower nectar.
- It was named after the actress Carole Lombard who died in a plane crash in the Spring Mountains (Potosi Mountain, NV) January 16, 1942. She was married at the time to Clark Gable.

# Chukar

| |
|---|
| Kingdom: Animalia |
| Phylum: Chordata |
| Subphylum: Vertebrata |
| Class: Aves |
| Order: Galliformes |
| Family: Phasianidae |
| Subfamily: Perdicinae |
| Genus: *Alectoris* |
| Species: *chukar* |
| **Binomial name:** |
| *Alectoris chukar* |

## Wow Facts

- This medium-sized partridge lives in arid, rocky terrain across the western United States and southern Canada.
- They make a chuck-chuck-chukar-chukar sound.
- Chukars are generally opportunistic **herbivores** and forage on vegetation throughout the morning and afternoon.
- The Chukar takes advantage of all water sources, from rivers and creeks, to springs and nearly stagnant seeps that hardly moisten the ground. They have been found getting water in mine shafts over 3m (10 feet) below ground level, and sometimes they have been observed well back in mine tunnels where only faint light revealed the water.
- Flight is generally restricted to short distances downhill, usually when flushed. They hop when crossing rough terrain and prefer running to flight.
- The primary social group is a **covey**, consisting of varying numbers of adults and their offspring, and the largest groups are found at water sources.
- During nesting season they may lay 7-14 eggs or an egg a day if collected.
- Prior to the late 1970's Kah-Nee-Ta Resort in Warm Springs, Oregon offered Chukar baked in clay as part of their native traditional meal choices on Thanksgiving Day.

# Coyote

| | |
|---|---|
| Kingdom: <u>Animalia</u><br>Phylum: <u>Chordata</u><br>Class: <u>Mammalia</u><br>Order: <u>Carnivora</u><br>Family: <u>Canidae</u><br>Genus: <u>Canis</u><br>Species: <u>*latrans*</u><br>Binomial name: ***Canis latrans*** | |

## Wow Facts

- Coyotes are extremely adaptable and use a wide range of habitats including forests, grasslands, deserts, and swamps. They are found throughout North and Central America and even in Alaska and up to northern Canada.
- The tail, which is half the body length, is bottle shaped with a black tip.
- They are **carnivores**; 90% of their diet is mammalian. Fruits and vegetables are a significant part of the diet of coyotes in the fall and winter months.
- Although coyotes are capable of digging their own burrows, they often enlarge the burrows of <u>woodchucks</u> or <u>badgers</u> and use these as their dens. Dens are used year after year. There are several entrances to a single den.
- They do not mind living next to humans and these nocturnal hunters are known to hunt stray cats and small neighborhood dogs.
- In Las Vegas, you may see them in the daytime usually on rare occasions when they have been flushed out of the storm drains by heavy rains.
- Their earliest ancestors are from the group of Eocene Miacids 38-56 million years ago.
- They diverged from gray wolves 1-2 million years ago and are a more primitive line and are evolutionary placed somewhere between the golden jackal and gray wolf. They were once larger, but

they became smaller as giant megafaunal game became extinct and the gray wolf filled the void left by the dire wolf becoming extinct.

- Coyotes are less likely to form packs than wolves; hunting is done individually, in pairs, or in family units depending on prey availability.
- They are still expanding into new territories: Costa Rice in the 1970's and Panama in the early 1980's and they are expected to reach into South America soon if not already. Currently there are 19 subspecies.
- Hybrids of coyotes with wolves and dogs are becoming more common and the white coyotes of Newfoundland get their color from genes inherited from golden retrievers.
- Eastern wolves and red wolves show heavy influence of coyote genes.
- They are known to live ten years in the wild, and 18 in captivity.

# Desert Tortoise

| |
|---|
| Kingdom: Animalia |
| Phylum: Chordata |
| Class: Reptilia |
| Order: Testudines |
| Family: Testudinidae |
| Genus: *Gopherus* |
| Species: *agassizii* |
| **Binomial name:** |
| ***Gopherus agassizii*** |

## Wow Facts

- The desert tortoise can be found in the Mojave and Sonoran Deserts of southern California, Nevada and Utah. They inhabit semi-arid grasslands, desert washes and sandy canyon bottoms below 1km (3,500ft).

- Desert tortoises are **herbivores**, surviving on low-growing plants and freshly fallen leaves as well as bark, stems, fruits, and/or flowers of trees, shrubs, woody vines, succulents, perennial and annual grasses, herbaceous perennials, and annuals.

- They are the kings of underground homemakers. 95 percent of their life is spent underground and every time they dig a new burrow, their old subterranean environment becomes a starter home for other reptiles, mammals, birds, and invertebrates.

- Desert tortoises are active spring to fall, hibernating during the winter months of November to March, though the timing of activity varies by habitat. Tortoises in the Mohave Desert concentrate their activity in the spring, aestivating during the hot, dry summers.

- When it rains, a tortoise can gain 40 percent of its weight by drinking water. If they are handled and they empty their bladder, they must drink again soon or they will be left vulnerable to dehydration.

- In June or July fertilized females lay 4-8 ping-pong ball sized eggs. The eggs hatch in August or

September. Only 2-5 percent of hatchlings reach maturity due to predators, drought, flood, fire, and human related activities.

- It takes them 16 years to reach a length of 8 inches.
- Males have to be 15-20 years old and females at least 10 years old before they are ready to reproduce.
- Because of their slow speed and low profile they are accidentally, and in many instances unknowingly, killed or injured by off road vehicles and dirt motorbikes.
- The desert tortoise can live 50-80 years.

# Elk

| | |
|---|---|
| Kingdom: Animalia<br>Phylum: Chordata<br>Class: Mammalia<br>Order: Artiodactyla<br>Family: Cervidae<br>Genus: *Cervus*<br>Species: *canadensis*<br>**Binomial name:**<br>***Cervus canadensis*** | |

## Wow Facts

- Roosevelt elk, *C. Canadensis roosevelti*, demographic range is the Western United States, through the Rocky Mountains down to New Mexico and the lower peninsula of Michigan. Elk can be found in coniferous swamps, clear cuts, aspen-hardwood forests, and coniferous-hardwood forests. Roosevelt elk do not have to migrate as much as other elk as their seasonal locations are relatively mild.

- Elk are **herbivores** that feed all day on grasses, sedges, and forbs in the summer months. They feed on woodland growth in the winter months.

- An elk's stomach has four chambers: the first stores food and the other three digest it.

- They are usually dark brown in the winter and tan in the summer. Calves are born with spots like deer.

- They are twice as heavy as a mule deer.

- Bulls may grow new sets of antlers with one new additional point for each year of growth, but this number may vary greatly. Cows (females) do not grow antlers. The antlers are shed in winter when their testosterone levels fall.

- Elk are social animals; they live in summer herds with as many as 400 individuals. In the winter, they live in smaller **harems** of some 20 cows.

- Bulls go in rut from August to early winter and the most successful bulls at defending their harem are around 8 years old.          Bulls less than 4 years old and over 11 years old generally do not have harems. A bull fighting to keep his harem can lose 20 percent of his body weight.

- Males make a loud bugling noise and are heard for miles. Females prefer buglers that are loud and bugle often.
- The areas just outside of town near Reedsport, Oregon, Cannon Beach, Oregon, and Sequim, Washington, Jackson Hole, Wyoming, and Yellowstone National park are some of the best places to photograph big herds of elk.
- They browse in the early morning and late evening. They are inactive during the day and the middle of the night, when they spend most of their time chewing their cud.
- They first appeared in the Oligocene in Eurasia 25 million years ago.
- They can live up to 15 years in the wild and 20 years or so in captivity.

# Gambel's Quail

| Kingdom: Animalia |
| --- |
| Phylum: Chordata |
| Class: Aves |
| Order: Galliformes |
| Family: Odontophoridae |
| Genus: *Callipepla* |
| Species: *gambelii* |
| **Binomial name:** |
| ***Callipepla gambelii*** |

## Wow Facts

- Gambel's quail are found almost exclusively in the southwestern United States and live in warm deserts with brushy and thorny vegetation.

- Gambel's quail are fast runners and only fly to escape danger, cross obstacles like roads, or fly to a roost at night. They flap their wings a few good strong beats, then glide the rest of the way.

- They are **herbivores** and various types of seeds and leaves are eaten throughout the year. Ninety percent of an adult Gambel's Quail diet comes from plants.

- The birds are not territorial and they tend not to migrate, so population density depends on brood productivity, which is dependent on the local yearly climate.

- A typical **covey** usually consists of an adult pair and up to sixteen young.

- Females lay 10-12 eggs and incubation is from 21-23 days. The chicks are born rather mature and ready to move in a few hours. However, the chicks are mainly insectivores.

# Gila Monster

| |
|---|
| Kingdom: Animalia |
| Phylum: Chordata |
| Class: Reptilia |
| Order: Squamata |
| Family: Helodermatidae |
| Genus: *Heloderma* |
| Species: *suspectum* |
| Binomial name: |
| ***Heloderma suspectum*** |

## Wow Facts

- The Gila monster ranges from the extreme southwestern Utah, southern Nevada, Arizona and southwestern New Mexico. The Gila monster can be found in arid areas.

- The Gila monster's **carnivore** diet consists of a variety of objects: small mammals (young rabbits, mice and squirrels), birds, lizards, and eggs (of birds, lizards, snakes, turtles, and tortoises). They can store fat in their tail.

- This is one of only two venomous lizard species in the North America (the other is the Mexican beaded lizard, *Heloderma horridum*).

- The Gila monster is a diurnal forager. It is referred to as being a "docile reptile." They may rise upwards and grunt to ward off threats before actually resorting to biting.

- The Gila monster has the capability to consume large amounts of food at one time (young can consume 50 percent of their body weight at a single feeding, adults can consume 35 percent). They may only feed 5 to 10 times a year.

- Prey is rarely envenomated, which indicates that venom is used mainly for defense. Unlike rattlesnake venom coming from the upper jaw, the Gila monster's venom comes from a salivary gland in the lower jaw and it is pumped into the victim continuously by making a chewing motion.

- Although the venom is a neurotoxin as toxic as a

coral snake, their bite is not fatal to healthy adults. If bitten on the hand, it is recommended to submerge the Gila monster underwater to make it let go.

- Helodermin, one of the components of the venom has been shown to inhibit growth of lung cancer. Exenatide a synthetic protein derived from the saliva is used to manage type-2 diabetes.
- Eggs can be detected by olfaction (the sense of smell) 6 inches underground. The Gila monster, like most snakes, uses its tongue for olfaction.
- The banded Gila monster is found in the Mojave Desert and the reticulated Gila monster is found in more southern regions.
- They are regarded as living fossils as they have changed relatively little since the Cretaceous times.
- They live 90 percent of their time below ground and hibernate until January or February. They mate in June or July. In July or August females lay 2 to 12 eggs 15cm (6 inches) under the sand. Hatchlings appear 9 months later in April to June and can already inject venom. They can live 20 years in the wild or 30 in captivity.

# Gopher Snake

| | |
|---|---|
| Kingdom: Animalia<br>Phylum: Chordata<br>Class: Reptilia<br>Order: Squamata<br>Family: Colubridae<br>Genus: *Pituophis*<br>Species: *catenifer*<br>**Binomial name:**<br>***Pituophis catenifer*** |  |

## Wow Facts

- Found from southwestern Canada south to northern New Mexico. Gopher snakes are found in a wide variety of habitats, including woodlands, deserts, agricultural areas (such as cultivated fields), prairies, chaparral, and shrublands. There are six subspecies.
- Gopher snakes can spend up to 90% of their time in underground burrows
- Gopher snakes constrict to kill prey which includes mammals, birds, lizards, snakes, insects, and eggs. They can also climb or swim to catch frogs.
- Like other snakes, gopher snakes go through periods of dormancy when resting or during periods of little food.
- They pass themselves off as rattlesnakes by flattening and spreading out their head, coiling up, hissing using the glottis organ in their mouth, rattling their tail under leaves, and striking with a closed mouth to scare off predators. Unlike rattlesnakes, they don't have black and white banding on the tail.
- Males will fight with other males in a territory combat dance.
- They make good pets if you provide a 30-gallon terrarium and a box or cave to hide in.
- Females can lay 2-24 eggs six weeks after mating and the young hatch in 10 weeks.
- Life span is 12-15 years in the wild and 33 years in captivity.

# Golden Eagle

| |
|---|
| Kingdom: Animalia |
| Phylum: Chordata |
| Class: Aves |
| Order: Falconiformes |
| Family: Accipitridae |
| Genus: *Aquila* |
| Species: *chrysaetos* |
| **Binomial name: *Aquila chrysaetos*** |

## Wow Facts

- In North America, golden eagles are found mainly in the western half of the continent and they inhabit the tundra, shrublands, grasslands, woodland-brushlands, and coniferous forests from Alaska to Mexico. They are also found in Eurasia and northern Africa.

- They are North America's largest predatory bird. Paleo subspecies were larger, heavier, and had broader skulls.

- They are **carnivores** and the diet of golden eagles is consists of small mammals such as rabbits, hares, ground squirrels, prairie dogs, and marmots. They also eat birds, reptiles and fish in smaller numbers. Golden eagles occasionally capture large prey, including seals (Phocoidea), ungulates, coyotes and badgers.

- Golden eagles can carry up to 3.6kg (8 lb) during flight. They can fly up to 129km (80 mph), though the average speed is 45-51km/h (28-32 mph), and may reach speeds up to 322km/h (200 mph) in a dive.

- In Las Vegas, you can sometimes see them flying around the edges of golf courses in search of rabbits. Their home range can be up to 124 square kilometers (77 square miles).

- They prefer to build large nests up in cliffs and females lay up to four eggs. One of two chicks survives and fledges in 3 months, by fall they usually fly off on their own, but half of them may not survive to 2 years of age.

- Some golden eagles migrate almost 3,000 miles to their winter ranges while others are non-migratory.

- Life span is over 32 years and 46 years in captivity.

# Jackrabbit (Black-Tailed)

Kingdom: Animalia
Phylum: Chordata
Class: Mammalia
Order: Lagomorpha
Family: Leporidae
Genus: *Lepus*
Species: *californicus*
**Binomial name:**
*Lepus californicus*

## Wow Facts

- Found throughout the southwestern United States and in to Mexico. They inhabit desert scrubland, prairies, farmlands, and dunes from sea level up to 3km (10,000ft).

- They are **herbivores** that prefer grasses and herbaceous matter, but they will eat twigs and young bark of woody plants when times are tough.

- Black-tails rely on speed and camouflage (along with the characteristic "freeze" behavior) for their defense.

- They are inactive during the hot afternoon hours and are mainly nocturnal, resting under large sagebrush or other suitable bushes by day. Black-tailed jackrabbits do not generally occupy burrows: rather, they dig shallow depressions in the earth in which to rest.

- When flushed from cover, they can spring 6m (20ft) at a bound and reach top speeds of 9-11km/h (30-35mph) over a zigzag course.

- Females are larger and breeding times are dependent on the local environment. Breeding peaks in winter.

- Young are born with open eyes and mobile within minutes. Young are nursed for 8 weeks.

- While many predators depend on them, humans tend to stay away because they are hosts to fleas, ticks, lice, mites and many endoparasites as well as many diseases; especially tularemia from ticks.

- Most hunters wear gloves when handling carcasses and cook the meat thoroughly.

# Kestrel

| |
|---|
| Kingdom: <u>Animalia</u><br>Phylum: <u>Chordata</u><br>Class: <u>Aves</u><br>Order: <u>Falconiformes</u><br>Family: <u>Falconidae</u><br>Genus: *Falco*<br>Species: *sparverius*<br>**Binomial name: *Falco sparverius*** |

## Wow Facts

- American Kestrels are found throughout most of North, Central, and South America. They inhabit tropical lowlands, deserts, urban areas, and open-altered lands, such as agricultural fields and open grounds with conspicuous places to perch.
- Kestrels feed mainly on crickets, grasshoppers, mice, voles, small birds, sandpiper chicks, amphibians, lizards, and snakes. When hovering, they swoop down from heights of 11-20m (35-65ft). They can even hover in barns.
- The American Kestrel is the smallest and most numerous of the North American falcons.
- The American kestrel nests in tree cavities, woodpecker holes, and crevices of buildings, holes in banks, nest boxes, or old nests of other birds. Basically they don't build their own nests.
- Most of the time they live alone, but form pair bonds during nesting season when the male is needed to help rear offspring. Males are more brightly colored than females.
- They diverged from other *Falco* 7-3.5 million years ago.
- They evolved in Africa, but by 1 million years ago reached all the way to Australia.
- Kestrels are ultraviolet sensitive and can detect small rodent trails such as vole trails that are scented with urine and feces and reflect UV light.

# Kit Fox

Kingdom: <u>Animalia</u>
Phylum: <u>Chordata</u>
Class: <u>Mammalia</u>
Order: <u>Carnivora</u>
Family: <u>Canidae</u>
Genus: *Vulpes*
Species: *macrotis*
**Binomial name: *Vulpes macrotis***

## Wow Facts

- Kit foxes are primarily found in the southwestern part of the United States and northern and central Mexico in arid regions, such as desert scrub, chaparral, and grasslands.
- They are found at 121m-1.89km (400- 6,200) feet above sea level.
- They mate in December to February. One to seven pups are born from March to April. After four weeks old pups may leave the den, they become independent at five to six months old.
- Pups have a 74 percent mortality rate the first year.
- Kit foxes are **carnivores** that primarily eat rodents like kangaroo rats, prairie dogs, voles, black-tailed jackrabbits, and cottontail rabbits. It also eats insects, snakes, lizard, fish, and ground dwelling birds as well as scavenge carrion.
- The Kit fox is classified as the smallest member of the family Canidae in North America.
- Kit foxes remain relatively inactive in their dens in pairs or small family groups during hot desert days, and are primarily lone nocturnal hunters.
- Life span averages of 5.5 years in the wild and up to 12 years in captivity.

# Mojave
# Sidewinder Rattlesnake

| |
|---|
| Kingdom: Animalia |
| Phylum: Chordata |
| Subphylum: Vertebrata |
| Class: Reptilia |
| Order: Squamata |
| Suborder: Serpentes |
| Family: Viperidae |
| Genus: *Crotalus* |
| Species: *cerastes* |
| **Binomial name: *Crotalus cerastes*** |

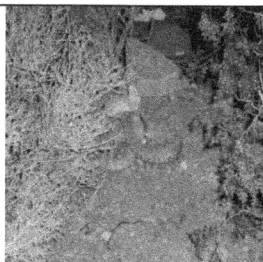

## Wow Facts

- The sidewinder ranges from the Mojave and Sonoran deserts of southeastern California, western Arizona, southern Nevada, and southwestern Utah. Sidewinders are often found in arid deserts, flatlands, loose, sandy washes, hard pan flats, and rocky areas below 1.5km (5,000ft) in elevation.

- Moving in a side winding fashion and leaving a repeated "J" pattern in the sand gives them extreme stability in the shifting sand dunes and also constantly transfers their point of contact with the substrate to minimize heat transfer to the skin. Humans can burn their heels and toes walking barefoot across the same patch of sand: not to mention slipping and sliding even up a small sandy incline.

- The sidewinder is a **carnivore**. The pit viper species eat lizards, small mammals like Kangaroo rats and pocket mice, other rodents that burrow, and sometimes birds. They hunt by smell and they have heat-sensing pits on their faces that detect heat radiation.

- They eat their prey headfirst.

- Most rattlesnakes bite and inject a hemotoxic venom that destroys tissue, causes swelling, internal bleeding, and severe pain. The sidewinder and a few other species have an additional neurotoxin that causes paralysis among other nervous system disorders.

- They rely on the sun for body heat and shade like burrows or cool platforms like rocks. If a sidewinder cannot find shade they can overheat and die.
- The pit organs are used to help find warm-blooded animals to prey on.
- Sidewinders are more nocturnal than other rattlesnakes. They are nocturnal in the hot months and in the cooler months become diurnal.
- Females are larger than males. Females produce up to 18 live 15-20cm (6-8 inch) long young. Juveniles use their tails to attract lizards.
- Females live about 5 years, and males live up to 13 years in the wild. In captivity, even females can live up to 20 years if childbirth is minimal.
- There are 32 different species of rattlesnakes and six types live in Nevada.

# Mountain Bluebird

| |
|---|
| Kingdom: Animalia<br>Phylum: Chordata<br>Class: Aves<br>Order: Passeriformes<br>Family: Turdidae<br>Genus: *Sialia*<br>Species: *currucoides*<br>**Binomial name:**<br>***Sialia currucoides*** |

## Wow Facts

- Found in agricultural areas and prairie-forest edges with groves of trees, short grass, and few shrubs. Live primarily on the western coast of North America.
- While males are blue, females are grayish green with hints of blue.
- This **omnivore** eats insects and small fruits.
- Hunts from perches or hovers like a miniaturized kestrel then dives down to catch prey. They also do some fly catching and gleaning.
- Only the female builds the nest. The male sometimes acts as if he is helping, but he either brings no nest material or he drops it on the way.
- They are known to nest in a house nests built by humans.
- In the winter they may join in large flocks in search of berries. Some migrate and others stay year round in Nevada.

# Mountain Lion

| |
|---|
| Kingdom: Animalia |
| Phylum: Chordata |
| Class: Mammalia |
| Order: Carnivora |
| Family: Felidae |
| Genus: *Puma* |
| Species: *concolor* |
| Binomial name: |
| ***Puma concolor*** |

## Wow Facts

- In North America, they can be found from British Columbia and southern Alberta to California and Texas, but they also extend down to Central and South America to the Andes Mountains.
- In these regions, only the jaguar is larger. Mountain lions are related more to felines such as house cats than they are to other subspecies of lions.
- Mountain lions are **carnivores** that eat large mammals including: moose, elk, white-tailed deer, mule deer, and caribou in North America. They will also eat smaller creatures like squirrels, muskrat, porcupine, beaver, raccoon, striped skunk, coyote, bobcats, other mountain lions, rabbits, opossums, birds, and even snails and fish.
- They may also prey on domestic livestock, including poultry, calves, sheep, goats, and pigs.
- Mountain lions have a distinctive ambush manner of hunting larger prey. The mountain lion quietly stalks the prey animals, if the prey is small. They will then leap at close range onto their back and break the animal's neck with a powerful bite below the base of the skull. If the prey is large, they go for a suffocating neck bite.
- The mountain lion (*Puma concolor*) is also known as the cougar, puma, panther, and catamount. It actually has over 40 names just in English and holds the Guiness record for total number of names.

- Populations in eastern North America were entirely exterminated, except for a small population of Florida panthers (*Puma concolor coryi*).
- In recent years, populations have begun to expand into areas of human habitation, especially in the western United States. Mountain lions are now fairly common in suburban areas of California and have recently been sighted as far east as urban Kansas City, Missouri, where several have been hit by cars.
- Mountain lions use a wide variety of habitats including mountain coniferous forests, lowland tropical forests, grassland, dry brush country, swamps, and any areas with adequate cover and prey. Dense vegetation caves and rocky crevices provide shelter.
- Mountain lions are solitary animals, with the exception of 1 to 8 days of associations during mating.
- Females may have 1 to 6 cubs and they alone defend and nurture the cubs.
- Cubs are born blind, covered with spots, and rings on their tails. When the eyes first open, they are blue.
- Pumas can't roar, but hiss growl, purr, chirp, and whistle like a house cat.
- They are believed to first appear in Asia 11 million years ago and came into North America 8-8.5 million years ago and South America 3 million years ago.
- Mountain lions may live 18 years in the wild. They can live slightly longer in captivity.

# Mule Deer

| |
|---|
| Kingdom: Animalia |
| Phylum: Chordata |
| Class: Mammalia |
| Order: Artiodactyla |
| Family: Cervidae |
| Genus: *Odocoileus* |
| Species: *hemionus* |
| Binomial name: |
| ***Odocoileus hemionus*** |

## Wow Facts

- Are named for their big mule-like ears and are usually found west of the Rocky Mountains, but also introduced to Argentina and Kauai, Hawaii.
- Mule deer are **herbivores** and in one study they were observed eating more than 788 species of plants. Although shrubs and trees make up the majority of their food during the fall and winter and almost half their diet the rest of the year.
- Mule deer antlers fork "bifurcate" as they grow. White tail deer antlers branch from a single main stem.
- By mid-February bucks shed their old antlers and new ones start growing.
- Males are larger than females and bucks typically weigh from 55kg-150kg (121-331 lb). Does weigh between 43-90kg (95-198 lb). One trophy buck weighed 208kg (460 lb).
- The rut or mating season is usually in the fall.
- Females typically have one fawn their first time then twins each additional birth season.
- It is thought that mule deer evolved from black tail deer, but generally lumped together as the same species, "conspecific", but can be grouped into 10 valid subspecies.
- Hybrids of mule deer and white tail deer are found in western Texas.
- A good place to see them is at Zion National Park.

12

# Northern Flicker

| Kingdom: Animalia |
| --- |
| Phylum: Chordata |
| Subphylum: Vertebrata |
| Class: Aves |
| Order: Piciformes |
| Family: Picidae |
| Genus: *Colaptes* |
| Species: *auratus* |
| **Binomial name:** |
| ***Colaptes auratus*** |

## Wow Facts

- Northern flickers are native to North America, Central America, Cuba, and the Cayman Islands. There are two living subspecies of the northern flicker. The red-shafted one in the west is called *Colaptes auratus cafer* and has a red belly and male have a red malar (mustache). The east subspecies is yellow underneath and males have a black mustache.

- The Guadalupe subspecies, *Colaptes auratus/cafer rufipileus,* went extinct by 1910 due to deforestation and the negative impact goats brought by early whalers had on the local Guadalupe ecosystem.

- The largest specimens of Northern flickers are found in Alaska during the summer months only. When winter comes, they migrate south. The smallest flickers are found in Grand Cayman Island.

- They eat berries, fruit, and seeds, but they are primarily insectivores and eat beetles, butterflies, and snails. Ants may make up 45% of their diet and they use acid from the ants to preen their feathers and ward off parasites.

- Unlike other woodpeckers, they prefer to eat on the ground or hammer into the ground in search of ant larvae; they have a 5cm (2in) long tongue to help lick up the ants.

- They tend to nest in tree holes, but also in tree houses.

- They communicate with a "Ki, ki, ki, ki" call, or by hammering on wood or metal for a louder sound.

- Life span is less than 9 years old.

# Raven

| | |
|---|---|
| Kingdom: Animalia<br>Phylum: Chordata<br>Subphylum: Vertebrata<br>Class: Aves<br>Order: Passeriformes<br>Family: Corvidae<br>Genus: *Corvus*<br>Species: *corax*<br>**Binomial name:**<br>***Corvus corax*** | |

## Wow Facts

- Ravens are a common sight in countries around the globe, and can survive in many different climates. They range from islands in the northern Arctic to deserts of North Africa, from the Pacific to the Atlantic Coasts of North America. They can be found in England, in Mexico, in Turkey, and Central America as far south as Nicaragua. Common ravens prefer open landscapes, such as treeless tundra, seacoasts, open riverbanks, rocky cliffs, mountain forests, plains, deserts, and scrubby woodlands. It is said that Ravens can be found in most types of habitats except for rainforests, and are guaranteed to be anywhere humans enjoy camping, leaving out food, or setting out garbage where they may forage in large groups.
- Common ravens are mainly scavengers. They eat a wide array of animal foods, including arthropods, amphibians, small mammals, birds, reptiles, and carrion. Vegetable foods include grains, acorns, fruits, and buds.
- Common ravens are known for their intelligence and complex social dynamics. They seem capable of learning innovative solutions to newly encountered problems.
- They are usually found alone or in pairs.

# Roadrunner

| |
|---|
| Kingdom: Animalia |
| Phylum: Chordata |
| Subphylum: Vertebrata |
| Class: Aves |
| Order: Cuculiformes |
| Family: Cuculidae |
| Genus: *Geococcyx* |
| Species: *californianus* |
| **Binomial name:** |
| ***Geococcyx californianus*** |

## Wow Facts

- The greater roadrunner is the largest member in the cuckoo family.
- They live in desert regions of the southern states as well as many states in Mexico.
- They are **carnivores** that prefer small snakes, insects, spiders, tarantulas, scorpions, mice, small birds, and lizards.
- They kill their prey by holding them in their bill and repeatedly slamming them down on the ground.
- With their long legs, they can run at speeds of up to 32km/h (20mph) and some are reported up to 42km/h (26mph), which is the fastest speed recorded for a flying bird, but way slower than a flightless ostrich. They are slower than a coyote; up to 72km/h (45mph), but roadrunners can easily escape most predators by simply flying away short distances.
- They have four toes on each foot with two facing forwards and two facing backwards, "zygodactyl".
- They lay 3-6 eggs in a stick nest and they hatch 20 days later. Chicks fledge, are ready for flight, in 18 days.
- They don't mind humans and have been seen at dusk in the employee parking lot of McCarran International Airport in Las Vegas, as well as new housing developments, roadsides, and state parks.

# Swallowtail Butterfly

Kingdom: Animalia
Phylum: Arthropoda
Class: Insecta
Order: Lepidoptera
Family: Papilionidea
Genus: *Papilio*
Species: *cresphontes*
**Binomial name:**
***Papilio cresphontes***

## Wow Facts

- Worldwide there are approximately 600 species of swallowtail butterflies.
- On all swallowtails, the back edge of their hind wings forms what looks like the tail feathers of a swallow bird.
- *Papilio cresphontes* is the giant swallowtail butterfly and many generations in one year can be found in the warmer southern United States.
- A good book called *Butterflies of the Southwest* by Jim Brock show many species indigenous to Nevada and the surrounding areas.

# Rainforest Section

# African Forest Buffalo

Kingdom: Animalia
Phylum: Chordata
Class: Mammalia
Order: Artiodactyla
Family: Bovidae
Genus: *Syncerus*
Species: *caffer*

**Trinomial name:**
*Syncerus caffer nanus*

## Wow Facts

- The dwarf forest buffalo mainly lives in rainforest areas of central and western Africa.
- From March until August they can be found in forest clearings where they feed on grass. From September to August they can be found on savannahs and in marshes where they wallow in mud to keep insects at bay.
- During the wet season, they like to rest on sand, and in the dry season they prefer to rest on dirt and leaves.
- They are **herbivores** and particularly partial to the tender shoots of grass, reeds, and leaves.
- The African forest buffalo has a dark face and long red-brown hair and 76cm (30 inch) long backward curving horns that rarely fuse together.
- At 1.1m (3.5ft) tall, they are smaller than typical short haired savannah buffalo.
- African forest buffalo live in small groups of 3- 20 individuals and on rare occasions up to 30 individuals, while Cape Buffalos form herds that number in the thousands.
- A herd may consist of one or two bulls and a harem of adult females, and their offspring. Bulls remain with the herd year-round. Larger groups allow individuals to spend more time grazing and less time remaining alert for danger.
- Their main predator is the African leopard.

# African Palm Civet

Kingdom: Animalia
Phylum: Chordata
Class: Mammalia
Order: Carnivora
Family: Nandiniidae
Genus: *Nandinia*
Species: *capensis*
**Binomial name:**
*Nandinia binotata*

## Wow Facts

- Also known as the two-spotted palm civet and found in the tropical jungles and forested areas of eastern and central Africa.
- Rodents, insects, eggs, carrion, pineapples, fallen fruit, birds, and even fruit bats are part of their omnivorous diet.
- The African palm civet is a solitary nocturnal animal that only comes out from dusk for about four hours, and then for a few hours before dawn.
- The Palm Civet is a very inconspicuous animal. The coarse, cryptically colored coat is blotched and mottled and blends with the rough bark of trees and the shadows cast by leaves.
- The eyes are yellow-green and the pupils close to a vertical hairline.
- The well muscled and sturdy tail, which is usually as long as the body, is employed as a brace when the forepaws are being used for prey.
- The only time civets accompany each other is when the female has young.
- They have short legs, small ears, and look like a cat.
- Research suggests that the genetically distinct palm civet diverged from other species of civets long before cats did, and that is why they are in their own family **Nandiniidae**.

# African Rock Python

| Kingdom: Animalia |
| Phylum: Chordata |
| Class: Reptilia |
| Order: Squamata |
| Family: Boidae |
| Genus: *Python* |
| Species: *sebae* |
| **Binomial name:** |
| ***Python sebae*** |

## Wow Facts

- African rock pythons are found throughout sub-Saharan Africa and prefer evergreen forests or moist, open savannahs.

- African rock pythons are **carnivores** and feed primarily on terrestrial vertebrates.

- Like many other snake species, African rock pythons are fairly solitary snakes except for breeding season.

- They have a relatively small, triangular head that is covered in irregular scales that are typically blackish to brownish-gray in color. The head also has two light-colored bands that form a spearhead shape from the snout to the back of the head just above the eyes, as well as a yellow, inverted V under each eye.

- Besides being preyed upon by humans, they are occasionally vulnerable to hyenas and wild dogs during periods of long digestion.

- You may have seen a complete skeleton of an African rock python if you ever visited a *Ripley's Believe it or not*, exhibit.

- Rock Python is a fictional Marvel Comics character that first appeared in Captain America #341, May 1988.

# Black-and-White Casqued Hornbill

Kingdom: Animalia
Phylum: Chordata
Class: Aves
Order: Bucerotiformes
Family: Bucerotidae
Genus: *Bycanistes*
Species: *subcylindricus*

**Binomial name:**
*Bycanistes subcylindricus*

## Wow Facts

- Black-and-white-casqued hornbills are found in forests, wooded areas, and savannas throughout West and Central Africa.
- Mainly **frugivorous**, figs make up 90% of their diet, they also eat 10% insects, and small animals in trees.
- They forage by hopping from branch to branch in the rainforest canopy and reaching for fruit with the tip of the bill. They then toss back the food and swallow it whole.
- The weight of a hornbill's casque and bill are so heavy that the first two vertebrae in their necks are fused to support the weight. Casque is French for helmet.
- They are large with males being larger than females.
- They are mostly black with white lower backs, rumps, and upper and under tail-coverts, thighs, bellies, and vents.
- They are active during the day. They are nomadic during the dry, non-breeding season and actively defend their nesting area, usually in tree cavities, when breeding.
- Carnivores such as apes, monkeys, snakes, raptors, and humans, all prey on hornbills.
- They first appear in the fossil record in the Late Miocene more than 5.6 million years ago from Morocco to Bulgaria.

# Black-and-White Colobus Monkey

Kingdom: Animalia
Phylum: Chordata
Class: Mammalia
Order: Primates
Family: Mustelidae
Genus: *Colobus*
Species: *guereza*

**Binomial name:**
*Colobus guereza*

## Wow Facts

- This species, also known as the mantled guereza, is found in the lowland tropical rainforest to the upper reaches of the mountain forests in equatorial Africa.
- They are **herbivores** that feed off the Hackeberry tree: primarily young unripe leaves 58%, 13.5% fruit, 12.5% mature leaves, 4% leaf buds, 2% flower blossoms, of.
- Their ruminant (four chambered stomach) like digestive system enables them to live in niches inaccessible to other primates, but it also makes them want to rest for long periods of time as they digest food and off gas methane and carbon dioxide.
- They are diurnal and prefer to live in trees (arboreal) but will feed and travel on the ground if necessary.
- Colobus derives from a Greek word meaning "docked" and unlike other monkeys, they have short stump thumbs.
- They live in groups of about nine individuals: one male, females, and offspring.
- Their sloppy eating habits make them important contributors for seed dispersal.
- There are five species of Colobus monkeys and eight subspecies.
- Predators include: crowned hawk eagles, leopards, chimpanzees and humans as "bush meat".

# Bongo

Kingdom: Animalia
Phylum: Chordata
Class: Mammalia
Order: Artiodactyla
Family: Bovidae
Genus: *Tragelaphus*
Species: *eurycerus*
**Binomial name:**
*Tragelaphus eurycerus*

## Wow Facts

- Bongos predominantly inhabit the lowland forests of West Africa and Zaire to southern Sudan, but small populations are also found in the mountain forest regions of East Africa where they reside in the thick forest and bamboo zone.
- Bongos are **herbivores** that typically eat leaves, flowers, twigs, thistles, garden produce, and cereals.
- Bongos are the largest forest antelope. They have a prehensile tongue that they use to grasp grass with like an okapi or giraffe. They stay within the bushes and shrubs of the forest during the day and only come out to the salt licks during the night.
- Females and young are chestnut red, with darker legs. The larger males start out this chestnut color and proceed to darken with age, eventually becoming a dark brownish black. Both sexes have horns that slightly spiral once.
- Bongos have shorter legs than other African antelopes and a body shape characteristic of forest ruminants that help such a large animal move quickly in dense forest habitats.
- Bongos are the only forest antelope to form herds; 6-20 female individuals and young. Bulls are solitary.
- They bleat like a goat, but can also grunt, snort, and females do weak mooing to call for young.
- They are known to live up to 19 years.
- Predators include leopards, spotted hyenas, and poachers for bush meat.

# Cape Genet

Kingdom: Animalia
Phylum: Chordata
Class: Mammalia
Order: Carnivora
Family: Viverridae
Genus: *Genetta*
Species: *tigrina*

**Binomial name:**
*Genetta tigrina*

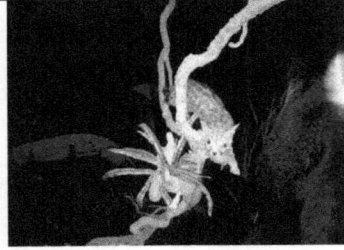

## Wow Facts

- Also known as the blotched genet, large spotted genet, and muskeljaattkat.
- Thick cover is an essential element of their habitat; although they are seen hunting in grassland, they are much more commonly found in woodlands.
- Genets are **omnivores** and their diet depends on where they live. They may eat small rodents, birds, reptiles, fruit, and invertebrates such as spiders and scorpions.
- A genet arches its back and grooms itself in much the same way as a cat. It also purrs, hisses, spits and meows, but makes an un-catlike "churring" sound when distressed.
- Genetta tigrina is short-legged, long-bodied, has a black and white ringed tail with a black tip, and a dorsal stripe that runs from the shoulders to the base of the tail.
- Their yellowish gray fur is lighter in dry regions and darker when living in moist areas. Some are "melanistic" all black.
- Genets are nocturnal, arboreal, and solitary. They are nimble climbers and often rest in clumps of foliage high in the tops of trees during the day.
- Strong musky scent glands are used to mark territory.
- Life span in the jungle is 8 years and 34 years in captivity.
- They play a role in rodent and insect control and therefore, disease control.

# Greater Honeyguide

| |
|---|
| Kingdom: Animalia |
| Phylum: Chordata |
| Class: Aves |
| Order: Piciformes |
| Family: Indicatoridae |
| Genus: *Indicator* |
| Species: *indicator* |
| **Binomial name:** |
| ***Indicator indicator*** |

## Wow Facts

- Greater honeyguides favor large open areas including savanna, shrub land, forest edge, riverside or orchard habitats.

- *Indicator indicator* mainly eats the products of bees, such as eggs, larvae and wax, as well as other insects.

- The greater honeyguide as well as *Indicator variegates* guide stronger animals like the honey badger, to locations of beehives to help gain access, which they are not strong enough to do by themselves.

- Greater honeyguides are the largest bird of the Indicatoridae family and are called brood parasites as they lay on egg in the brood nest of another species of bird such as woodpeckers or barbets. Within seven days they may lay up to five parasite eggs.

- Honey guide eggs are internally incubated an extra day before laying their parasite eggs to make sure they hatch first to eject the host's eggs or kill the other offspring in the host's nest.

- Greater honeyguides have a unique, highly wax-based diet and require enzymes in the digestive system to breakdown this normally indigestible food. They also feed on grubs and larvae found in Hymenoptera hives, and insect wings of flying swarming colonies.

# Honey Badger

| | |
|---|---|
| Kingdom: <u>Animalia</u><br>Phylum: <u>Chordata</u><br>Class: <u>Mammalia</u><br>Order: <u>Carnivora</u><br>Family: <u>Mustelidae</u><br>Genus: *Mellivora*<br>Species: *capensis*<br>**Binomial name:**<br>*Mellivora capensis* |  |

## Wow Facts

- The Ratel or Honey badger is **omnivorous**. It is most often observed consuming small reptiles, rodents, birds, insects and even carrion but it also eats fruits, berries, roots, plants, and eggs.
- They frequently attack beehives, to eat the stored honey and larval bees. This habit has resulted in the evolution of a mutual relationship between them and the greater honey guide bird, which eats honey, larvae, and wax from beehives.
- They are found all across Africa, the Middle East, and India. They prefer temperate climates, over deserts and jungles.
- Ratels are nomadic and have a large home range. They are very secretive and usually nocturnal, hunting at night.
- They are listed as the "most fearless animal in the world" in the Guinness Book of Records.
- They have extra thick skin and powerful sharp teeth and jaws. They will take on a lion if protecting their kill and usually win by wounding and/or wearing the lion out.
- They are black, with a shoulder's wide white stripe that originates just above the eyes and terminates at the tip of the tail.
- Anatomically they are similar to weasels and polecats.
- They arose in the middle Pliocene in Asia and evolved from a now extinct genus of *Eomellivora*.

# Leopard

| |
|---|
| Kingdom: <u>Animalia</u><br>Phylum: <u>Chordata</u><br>Class: <u>Mammalia</u><br>Order: <u>Carnivora</u><br>Family: <u>Felidae</u><br>Genus: <u>*Panthera*</u><br>Species: <u>*pardus*</u><br>**Binomial name:**<br>***Panthera pardus*** |

## Wow Facts

- They thrive in mesic (moist) woodlands, grassland savannas, and forests from Sub-Saharan Africa, Asia, and the Middle East to Siberia.
- Leopards are Carnivorous and eat birds, mammals, reptiles, and fish. They are ambush predators, pouncing on their prey before it chance to react.
- Its tawny or light yellow coat in warm dry habitats to a reddish-orange coat in dense forests is covered with dark, irregular small circles called "rosettes."
- The elegant, powerfully built leopard has a long body, relatively short legs, and a broad head with large powerful jaw muscles.
- Their scapula have specialized attachment sites for climbing muscles. They can run up to 58 km/h (36 mph).
- They have small round ears, long whiskers extending from dark spots on the upper lip, and long whiskers in their eyebrows that protect their eyes while moving through dense vegetation.
- Leopards are solitary, nocturnal **carnivores**. Although they sometimes hunt during overcast days, they are less diurnal in areas close to humans in comparison to uninhabited areas.
- They mark their territory with urine, feces, and claw marks and communicate with one another by growling, roaring, and spitting when aggravated, and purring when content.
- There are eight subspecies of *Panthera pardus*;

*Panthera pardus pardus* is found in Africa, *Panthera pardus nimr*, Arabia, *Panthera pardus saxicolor*, Central Asia, *Panthera pardus melas*, Java, *Panthera pardus kotiya*, Sri Lanka, *Panthera pardus fusca*, the Indian sub-continent, *Panthera pardus delacourii*, southeast Asia into southern China, *Panthera pardus japonensis*, northern China, and *Panthera pardus orientalis*, far east Russia, on the Korean peninsula and in north-eastern China. In Sri Lanka where there are no lions or tigers, leopards are the largest in the world.

- Early extinct leopard species fossils from the Pleistocene are 2-3.5 million years old. Modern leopards evolved in Africa 470,000-825,000 years ago
- They have been eliminated or exterminated from Hong Kong, Singapore, Kuwait, Syria, Libya, Tunisia, and perhaps Morocco.
- Leopards may have emerged from the *Panthera* genus after snow leopards and tigers, but before lions and jaguars. Leopards are one of the five big cats in the genus Panthera.
- Males are 30% larger than females. Body size and color patterns of leopards vary geographically; this probably reflects adaptations to particular habitats.
- Leopards look like a smaller version of the Jaguar and both Jaguars and Leopards may give birth to "melanistic", all black offspring, that are erroneously, but colloquially termed Black Panthers. Melanism is a selective advantage for nocturnal ambush predators.
- A rare genetic condition can overproduce red pigment or under produce dark pigment leaving the leopard strawberry colored or looking like a Pink Panther.
- DNA studies reveal that leopards are closely related to lions, but mitochondrial DNA studies show that they are closely related to snow leopards.
- Leopards can live 21 to 23 years in captivity and 12-17 years in the wild.
- Because of their stealth, people are often unaware how close these big cats may live near human communities.

# Potto

| Kingdom: <u>Animalia</u><br>Phylum: <u>Chordata</u><br>Class: <u>Mammalia</u><br>Order: <u>Primates</u><br>Family: <u>Lorisidae</u><br>Genus: *Perodicticus*<br>Species: *potto*<br>**Binomial name:**<br>*Perodicticus potto* | |

## Wow Facts

- Also known as Bosman's potto and "Softly-softly".
- Kinkajous and olingos look similar in appearance and behavior, but they are part of the raccoon family.
- Pottos live in the rain forest canopy and are seldom seen.
- They move slowly and deliberately, always holding on to a branch by at least two limbs.
- Their index finger is vestigial or stump like. In their hands fingers three and four are slightly joined together by a skin fold and on their feet, toes three through four have a slight skin web at their bases.
- Mothers make a high pitched "tsic" sound to contact offspring that may have been hidden by leaves while she was off hunting.
- They are **omnivores** with strong jaws, and 65% of their diet consisting of fruit, 21% hard tree gums, and 10% insects. They are known on occasion to catch birds and bats.
- They have large scent glands used to mark their territory and they are said to smell like curry.
- Because they live so high from ground and are nocturnal, they have no natural predators other than humans, occasional palm civets, and chimpanzees snatching them from their daytime sleeping places.
- They are known to live up to 25years.

# Yellow Backed Duiker

Kingdom: <u>Animalia</u>
Phylum: <u>Chordata</u>
Class: <u>Mammalia</u>
Order: <u>Artiodactyla</u>
Family: <u>Bovidae</u>
Genus: *Cephalophus*
Species: *silvicultor*

**Binomial name:**
***Cephalophus silvicultor***

## Wow Facts

- Yellow-backed duikers prefer forested habitats with dense undergrowth, although they can be found in a variety of forested habitats, including savannah and farmland.
- Yellow-backed duikers are primarily **frugivores** (feeding mainly on fruit); however, they will eat a variety of other foods in small quantities, including flowers, roots, rotting wood, bark, fungi, and some insects (particularly ants), as well as (eats, shoots, and leaves).
- Yellow-backed duikers are the largest of the 15 known duiker species and known for their yellow triangle patch near their tail.
- Duiker is the Dutch word for "diver". When frightened, they dive into the thick brush. Most Duikers rest in "forms", regularly used resting sites, during the day and forage at night, but the Yellow Backed Duiker can be active day and/or night.
- They are known to follow monkeys and birds to eat fallen fruit and they are prominent seed dispersers for some plants.
- Predators include: African hunting dogs, leopards, and lions. Humans hunt them for fur, meat, and horns.

# Outside
# The Rainforest

# Cape Buffalo

Kingdom: <u>Animalia</u>
Phylum: <u>Chordata</u>
Class: <u>Mammalia</u>
Order: <u>Artiodactyla</u>
Family: <u>Bovidae</u>
Genus: <u>*Syncerus*</u>
Species: <u>*caffer*</u>
**Binomial name:**
*Syncerus caffer*

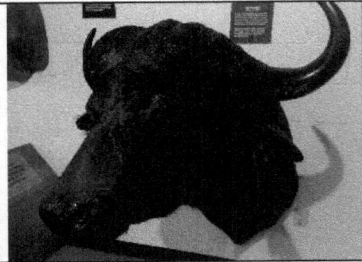

## Wow Facts

- Cape buffalo live in open savannas and grasslands near a permanent source of water including areas with rivers, lakes, and swamps and flood plains.
- They like to take mud baths to cool down and remove ticks.
- They are herbivores and eat tall, coarse grasses.
- Cape buffalos are extremely social and live in large, mixed non-territorial herds of up to 2000 members. The herds are composed of related cows, which are arranged in a linear dominance hierarchy.
- Their ears are large and droopy. The horns either spread out and downward, upward, or out and back.
- The color of buffalo hair ranges from brown to black.
- Their front hooves are wider than the back hooves.
- Old bulls have whitish circles under their eyes.
- Adult (5-6 years old) bull's horns are fused at the base forming a bone shield.
- Bulls may weigh up to 907kg (2,000 lb).
- They will respond as a herd and mob a lion and use bellows, grunts, honks and croaks like cattle to move or change direction.
- They gore or kill over 200 people each year. They are known to ambush and attack hunters.
- Main predators include: lions, spotted hyenas, crocodiles, and humans.

# Eland

| | |
|---|---|
| Kingdom: <u>Animalia</u><br>Phylum: <u>Chordata</u><br>Class: <u>Mammalia</u><br>Order: <u>Artiodactyla</u><br>Family: <u>Bovidae</u><br>Genus: <u>*Taurotragus*</u><br>Species: <u>*oryx*</u><br>**Binomial name:**<br>***Taurotragus oryx*** | |

## Wow Facts

- Elands live in both steppe and sparse forests and are found from Ethiopia and southern Zaire down to South Africa.
- Elands are herbivores and their diets consist of grasses, herbs, tree leaves, bushes, and succulent fruits. They can get most of their water from food.
- The eland is the most predominant animal in the rock art of East Africa.
- Hides are a uniform fawn color with some vertical white striping on the upper parts.
- A dewlap, thought to be an adaptation for heat dissipation, hangs from the throat and neck.
- Heavy horns are twisted in a corkscrew fashion and grow up to 1.2m (4ft) long on males, 67cm (2.2 ft) long on females.
- Herds usually number up to 25 individuals, although larger temporary aggregations of some 500 females and calves occur during the wet season.
- They are the slowest antelope at 40km/h (25mph), but can jump 2.4m (8ft) when startled.
- They are domesticated in many areas and known for their rich butterfat content, and they live 25 years in captivity, but only 15-20 years in the wild.
- They evolved 20 million years ago in Africa and their fossils are found from Africa to France.

# Kudu

| |
|---|
| Kingdom: <u>Animalia</u> |
| Phylum: <u>Chordata</u> |
| Class: <u>Mammalia</u> |
| Order: <u>Artiodactyla</u> |
| Family: <u>Bovidae</u> |
| Genus: *Tragelaphus* |
| Species: *strepsiceros* |
| **Binomial name:** |
| ***Tragelaphus*** |
| ***strepsiceros*** |

## Wow Facts

- Lesser kudus are found in arid savannas; they rely on thickets for security and are rarely found in open or scattered bush. Greater kudus are found in woodlands and bush lands.
- Greater kudu are **herbivores**. They eat a wide variety of leaves, herbs, fruits, vines, flowers, some new grass, and they love oranges and tangerines.
- During the rainy seasons, greater kudu remain in the deciduous woodlands. During the dry season they can be found in along the banks of rivers where there is rich vegetation.
- They are capable of surviving in waterless areas.
- Their cryptic coloring and markings protect kudus by camouflaging them. If alarmed they usually stand still and are very difficult to spot.
- Adult males have horns averaging 120cm (4ft) in length are used to make Shofars a horn, for Rash Hashanah.
- The body color of the greater kudu varies from reddish brown to blue-gray, with the darkest individuals found in the southern populations.
- Females live in herds of 1-3 adults and their offspring. Female groups may combine to form larger groups, but these groups are temporary. Males live in bachelor herds, which range in number from 2 to 10 males.
- They can live 7-8 years or up to 23 years in captivity.

# Out of Africa Primates (Great Apes)

# Orangutan

Kingdom: <u>Animalia</u>
Phylum: <u>Chordata</u>
Class: <u>Mammalia</u>
Order: <u>Primates</u>
Family: <u>Hominidae</u>
Subfamily: <u>Ponginae</u>
Genus: *Pongo*
Species: *pygmaeus and abelii*
Binomial Name: **Two species**

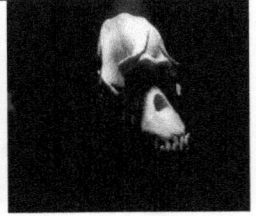

## Wow Facts

- Orangutans split from other great apes 14-19 Mya. In Malaysia and Indonesia, "Orang" means person and "hutan" means forest. Most of the time they are in trees, and walk bipedal on small branches to reach fruit.
- *P. abelii* lives in Sumatra, *P. pygmaeus* lives in Borneo; they diverged from each other 400,000 years ago.
- They eat mostly fruit, but also bark, honey, insects, and bird eggs and live in diptercarp (two-wing-fruit) forests and peat swamp forests where fruit is plentiful.
- They use tools, and use plant leafs to make hats, and construct well made day or night sleeping nests with pillows, blankets, roofs and even bunk beds. They also use plants for anti-inflammatory balm and eat clay for minerals or to absorb toxins.
- An extinct species, *Gigantopithecus*, is the largest primate ever discovered and lived in China, India, and Vietnam.
- Males 15-20 years old develop large cheek pads, throat pouches, and long fur.
- Orangutans measure reciprocity and keep track of giving and receiving gifts. One female learned 40 signs in sign language. They also use leaves to make sounds that deceive others. Except for mothers and offspring, they live mostly solitary lives.
- They can live 30 years.
- Predators include: tigers and wild dogs. Mothers are killed and infants stolen for illegal animal trade. They are also affected by fire, logging, and deforestation.

# Gorilla

Kingdom: Animalia
Phylum: Chordata
Class: Mammalia
Order: Primates
Family: Hominidae
Subfamily: Homininae
Genus: *Gorilla*
Species: *gorilla and beringei*
**Binomial Names:**
*G. gorilla, G. beringei*

## Wow Facts

- Gorillas split from other great apes 7Mya. *Gorilla gorilla* is the western lowland gorilla. *Gorilla beringei* (Eastern Gorilla) has three subspecies including the mountain gorilla. Eastern and western gorillas diverged some 261,000 years ago.
- Closest relative to chimpanzees and humans. 95-99% DNA similar to humans. Plus 15% of human DNA is closer to gorilla than chimp DNA.
- Construct (mainly ground) nests for day and night use.
- On rare occasions, males will fight leopards or other males to death. Live in troops with one lead male (silver back).
- Give birth after 10 years old, then in four year intervals. Although they mate year round. Gestation 8.5 months.
- Koko, a female, learned 800 signs in Gorilla sign language.
- Gorillas laugh, grieve, and have rich emotional lives and strong family bonds. Gorillas think about past and future. Have spiritual feelings and/or religious sentiments and are known to mate face to face like humans and bonobos.
- They use tools and although they mostly knuckle walk, they also walk bipedally to carry things or when in a defensive posture. They also have individual fingerprints.
- Lifespan 30-40 years. 58 years in captivity. They are subject to habitat destruction, and poaching.

# Chimpanzee

Kingdom: <u>Animalia</u>
Phylum: <u>Chordata</u>
Class: <u>Mammalia</u>
Order: <u>Primates</u>
Family: <u>Hominidae</u>
Subfamily: <u>Homininae</u>
Genus: *Pan*
Species: *troglodytes and paniscus*

**Binomial Names:**
***Pan troglodytes &***
***Pan paniscus***

Chimpanzee

## Wow Facts

- There are two extant (living) species. *Pan troglodytes* are chimpanzees from west and central Africa and *Pan paniscus* are bonobos from the Democratic Republic of Congo.
- Chimpanzees (chimps) are omnivores (they eat both meat and plants) while bonobos are mostly frugivores (fruits).
- Chimps are the closest living relative to humans and had a common ancestor 4-6 million years ago. Depending on how you count it, 94-99% of our genes are identical.
- Male chimps average1.2m (3.9ft) tall, 70kg or 150lb, and their brain size is between 282-500cc; average 393cc. Females are smaller.
- The dominant community male is the most politically manipulative and dominant community females may remove him from his position if required.
- They may display altruistic behavior in groups.
- They knuckle walk or walk on all fours. They may walk bipedal if carrying food. Bonobos walk upright more often than chimpanzees and are known to mate face to face like gorillas and humans.
- They have a long narrow pelvis, long toes with opposable big toe, long curved fingers, and long arms for reaching branches in trees.

- Hunting strategies include cooperation, influence by rank, deception, and manipulation.
- They understand some parts of human language, concepts of numbers, and numerical sequence: they have an aptitude for photographic memories with numerical digits.
- The female chimp Washoe over time could understand 2000 human words and learned 800 signs in American Sign Language, but sentence syntax and grammar is missing.
- They can plan for the future or an event.
- They use tools such as stones as anvils and hammers. They sharpen spears with their teeth in order to hunt bush babies.
- They build nests complete with mattresses in trees to sleep in at night.
- They solve puzzles for fun, vocalize laughter, and are ticklish.
- Some unfortunate individuals have been used for science experiments for over 40 years.
- Males may be very territorial and aggressive and may kill other chimps. They will kill red colobus monkeys then share pieces with other community members according to rank, political lines, favors, or for impressing females.
- Only humans and bonobos are fertile year-round and show no signs of estrus.
- Puberty is at 8-10 years of age, and as captive pets grow, they are more likely to bite off an owner's fingers or cause severe facial damage; not a good pet.
- Females give birth at 11-14 years of age and then every 3-6 years. Gestation is 201-260 days; 6.7-8.6 months.
- Lifespan is 35 years in the jungle, but up to 62 years in captivity.

# *Australopithecus afarensis*

Kingdom: Animalia
Phylum: Chordata
Class: Mammalia
Order: Primates
Family: Hominidae
Subfamily: Homininae
Genus: *Australopithecus*
Species: *afarensis*

**Binomial Name:**
*Australopithecus afarensis*

## Wow Facts

- *Australopithecus afarensis* lived 4-2 Mya (million years ago) and were found in Hadar, Ethiopia, and Kenya.
- Foot prints at Laetoli left 3.6 million years ago by three individuals are similar to modern man. They first used stone tools 3.4 million years ago.
- Brains one third size of modern humans: 380-430cc. 1.2m-1.4m (3' 11" to 4'7") tall. Bipedalism is thought to develop 6-7 million years ago, so way before brains began to develop and enlarge.
- Females were much smaller than males.
- The 40% complete skeleton of Lucy is 3.2 million years old.
- Scapula and curvature of phalanges (toes and fingers) are ape like, but big toe is no longer able to hold on and climb limbs; also making it more difficult for young to hang on to mother if in a tree.
- Their wide pelvis is more human like than ape like, as well as their wide sacrum, so they must have walked bipedal most of the time.
- *A. afarensis* are phenotypically similar (look like) Bonobos and they are a direct ancestor to humans.

# *Australopithecus africanus*

Kingdom: Animalia
Phylum: Chordata
Class: Mammalia
Order: Primates
Family: Hominidae
Subfamily: Homininae
Genus: *Australopithecus*
Species: *africanus*

**Binomial Name:**
***Australopithecus africanus***

## Wow Facts

- Cheek teeth and jaw larger than A. afarensis.
- Found in South Africa.
- *Australopithecus africanus* lived 3.03-2.04 million years ago.
- Brain size 400- 500cc. Average size 485cc.
- Larger brain size and more human like facial features. Foramen magnum (hole in skull) for spine placement is at base or underside of skull for up right posture as opposed to back of skull spine placement for movement by four limbs.
- Pelvis slightly improved for bipedalism and metacarpals more human like for better tool use.
- *Paranthropus robustus* is thought to be a descendant of *A. africanus.*

# *Paranthropus boisei*

Kingdom: <u>Animalia</u>
Phylum: <u>Chordata</u>
Class: <u>Mammalia</u>
Order: <u>Primates</u>
Family: <u>Hominidae</u>
Subfamily: <u>Homininae</u>
Genus: *Paranthropus*
Species: *boisei*

**Binomial Name:**
***Paranthropus boisei***

## Wow Facts

- AKA *Australopithecus boisei.*
- They lived 2.3-1.2 million years ago.
- Found in Rift Valley sites, Kenya, and Ethiopia.
- Largest of Paranthropus species and nicknamed "nutcracker man".
- Brain size of modern chimp 500-550cc.
- Males 49kg (108lb) 1.37m (4'6") tall.
- Females 34kg (75lb) 1.24 (4' 1") tall.
- They were made for hard nut and tuber chewing like a gorilla with large heavy enameled back molars twice as large as in modern humans and they had a strong muscle anchoring sagittal crest (midline ridge) running along the top of the skull.
- They ate more plant matter than any other hominim.

# *Paranthropus robustus*

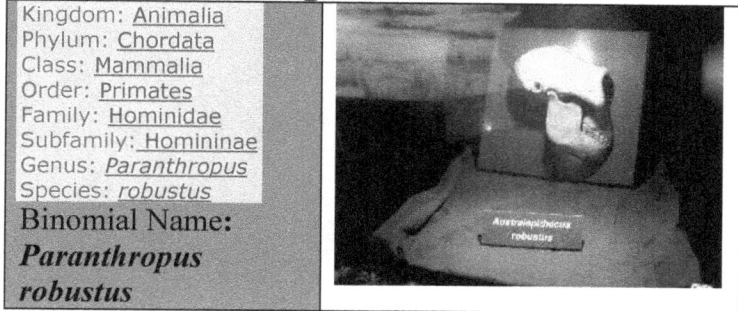

Kingdom: Animalia
Phylum: Chordata
Class: Mammalia
Order: Primates
Family: Hominidae
Subfamily: Homininae
Genus: *Paranthropus*
Species: *robustus*

**Binomial Name:**
***Paranthropus robustus***

## Wow Facts

- AKA *Australopithecus robustus*.
- Found in South Africa.
- *Paranthropus robustus* lived 2.0 to 1.2 million years ago.
- Heavy chewing like a gorilla with slightly smaller sagittal crest.
- They ate nuts and tubers in a woodland savannah.
- Rarely lived past 17 years old.
- Brain size 410cc to 530cc (same as a chimp).
- Males stood 1.2m (4ft) tall and 54kg (120lb). Females stood 1m (3'2") tall and 41kg (90lb).

# *Homo habilis*

Kingdom: Animalia
Phylum: Chordata
Class: Mammalia
Order: Primates
Family: Hominidae
Subfamily: Homininae
Genus: *Homo*
Species: *habilis*

**Binomial Name:**
***Homo habilis***

## Wow Facts

- "Handy man" short with long arms. They lived when forests were receding and savannas were expanding in the Olduvai Gorge, Tanzania, at Lake Turkana (Kenya) and South Africa. 2.1-1.5 million years ago.
- They are associated with primitive tool sets and flakes (lower paleolithic Oduman). They used tools to opportunistically scavenge meat from carrion.
- Brain size was 550cc to 687cc making their brain half the size of modern humans and about the same size as chimpanzees, but 50% larger than australopithecines.
- Their skull was larger, rounder, yet thinner so this suggests they did not rely as much on chewing muscles as more primitive *Homo* species.
- They existed during the ebbing life span of *Paranthropus boisei* and they coexisted with *Homo erectus* for some 500,000 years.
- 1.3m (4ft 3") tall

# *Homo erectus*

Kingdom: Animalia
Phylum: Chordata
Class: Mammalia
Order: Primates
Family: Hominidae
Subfamily: Homininae
Genus: *Homo*
Species: *erectus*
**Binomial Name:**
***Homo erectus***

## Wow Facts

- "Upright man" lived 1.9 million to 50,000 years ago. They died out at the same time as the Toba volcano exploded in Indonesia. So, they survived for over a million years.
- Originated in Africa and spread out through Asia to Java beginning 1,800,000 years ago.
- Brain size originally 850cc (125,000 more neurons and double the size of *Homo habilis*), but later averaged 1100cc; at least one individual up to 1300cc.
- Males were 25% larger than females. 180cm tall (5'11") and 60kg (130lb).
- They had thick brow ridges, wide cheek bones, and
- First hunter gatherer society, first to leave Africa, and first to use fire and complex tools.
- In Indonesia, may have given rise to *H. floresiensis*; the hobbit like dwarf.

# *Homo ergaster*

Kingdom: <u>Animalia</u>
Phylum: <u>Chordata</u>
Class: <u>Mammalia</u>
Order: <u>Primates</u>
Family: <u>Hominidae</u>
Subfamily: <u>Homininae</u>
Genus: *Homo*
Species: *ergaster*

**Binomial Name:**
*Homo ergaster*

## Wow Facts

- Lived 1.8 million to 600,000 years ago.
- Found in East Africa in Rift Valley, Uganda, Southern Africa, and Northwest Africa in Algeria, and Morocco.
- Brain size 600-910cc.
- They had a pronounced brow ridge, but higher domed skull. Shorter narrow face with smaller molars.
- They were tall and thin like modern day Masai of Kenya.
- Males 1.85m (6'1") tall and only slightly taller than females.

# *Homo heidelbergensis*

Kingdom: Animalia
Phylum: Chordata
Class: Mammalia
Order: Primates
Family: Hominidae
Subfamily: Homininae
Genus: *Homo*
Species: *heidelbergensis*

**Binomial Name:**
*Homo heidelbergensis*

## Wow Facts

- Lived 800,000 to 300,000 years ago.
- Found in Europe and Africa
- Most likely the common ancestor to both *H. neanderthalensis* and *H. sapiens*.
- Brain size 1,100-1,400cc.
- 180cm (5'11") tall and 90kg (200lb) in weight.
- Heavy limb bones, low flat forehead, and arched and separated eyebrows. Built like professional athletes, but with larger ankle and wrist muscles. They were powerful hunters.
- They had thick skull walls. Front teeth were larger than back teeth. Nose and cheeks were forward facing.

# *Homo neanderthalensis*

Kingdom: Animalia
Phylum: Chordata
Class: Mammalia
Order: Primates
Family: Hominidae
Subfamily: Homininae
Genus: *Homo*
Species: *neanderthalensis*

**Binomial Name:**
*Homo*
*neanderthalensis*

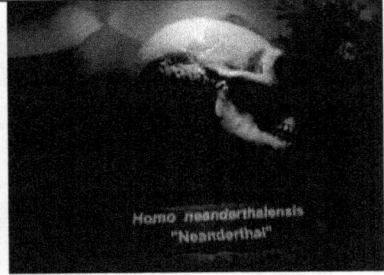

Homo neanderthalensis
"Neanderthal"

## Wow Facts

- Lived 400,000 to 30,000 years ago; in Asia Proto-Neanderthal 600,000 to 350,000 years ago. True Neanderthals emerged 250,000 to 200,000 years ago.
- Found in Europe and Southwest Asia.
- Cousins of modern man with 99.5% of genome identical.
- 1-4% Neanderthal genes in modern Europeans suggest interbreeding some 50-60,000 years ago, but no matriarchal Neanderthal mitochondrial DNA is found in modern humans.
- Their DNA suggests they had light skin and some had red or blonde hair. Through interbreeding, they may have given *Homo Sapiens* that entered their regions greater DNA immunity systems to resist local diseases.
- Brain size 1,200-1,900cc, so larger than modern humans. The skull was bun shaped towards the back and they had a forward-facing face and large nose.
- Died out in Europe 41,000 to 30,000 years ago.
- Sailed the Mediterranean 110,000 years ago. First to use a complex thermo and industrial process to make synthetic pitch material from birch bark to hold a spear blade firmly in place. Used feathers and colored material for decoration or for distinguishing one group from another.

- Cooked plant matter is found in teeth and in coprolites.
- They were built like professional football players, but because of their extreme muscular physic, they needed larger quantities of energy in the form of food to survive.
- Lived in small isolated populations. Modern humans entered their areas at a ratio of ten to one and most likely through interbreeding swallowed up their culture and genome completely, over a short geological period of time.
- Neanderthal genes are not found in modern humans residing in Africa.

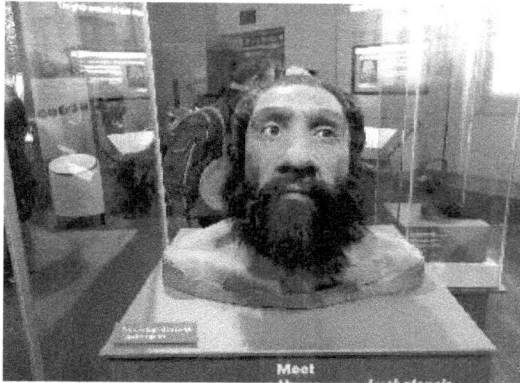

# *Homo sapiens*

Kingdom: <u>Animalia</u>
Phylum: <u>Chordata</u>
Class: <u>Mammalia</u>
Order: <u>Primates</u>
Family: <u>Hominidae</u>
Subfamily: <u>Homininae</u>
Genus: *Homo*
Species: *sapiens*

**Binomial Name:**
***Homo sapiens***

*Homo sapiens sapiens*

## Wow Facts

- The "wise man" first appeared in Africa in modern form 200,000 to 100,000 years ago. An archaic form of *Homo sapiens* dates back to 400,000 to 250,000 years ago.
- Some left Africa around 60,000 years ago.
- Khomani San people are one of 14 ancestral populations.
- Modern humans have 2-4% Neanderthal alleles, and Melanesians also have 4-6% Denisovan alleles.
- Some modern humans went out of Africa some 60,000 years ago and were in Australia by 45,000 years, and reached Argentina by 15,000 years ago.
- *Homo sapiens* have wide faces and small teeth, a high rounded cranium, and a smaller jaw with protruding chin.
- *Homo sapiens* have a short wide pelvis, short slender fingers, shorter arms, and big toe in line with the foot for walking. The skull is centered over "S" shaped spine for balance.
- *Homo sapiens* shared world with *Homo erectus*, *Homo neanderthalis*, and *homo floresiensis* until 30,000 years ago.
- Homo sapiens may directly kill or indirectly starve millions of their own kind over disputes of natural resources or political or religious differences.
- Males were genetically modified over 200,000 years to become strong strategic hunters and focus

singularly on hunting or running down a single wounded prey, while females became highly skilled multitasking gatherers.

- It should be noted that while most animals are faster than humans, no animal can out run modern man over long distances; an animal will eventually stop and lie down due to sheer exhaustion, and that is when man will catch them.

- Transition from hunter-gather society to farming was within last 10,000 years. The dawn of automobiles, airplanes, and the computer age occurred within the last 100 years. *Homo sapiens* are extremely adaptable; to be otherwise, is to risk extinction.

- *Homo sapiens* can live over 100 years in captivity.

THE END